Local and Global

Local and Global
The Management of Cities in the Information Age

Jordi Borja and Manuel Castells

in collaboration with

Mireia Belil and Chris Benner

United Nations Centre for Human Settlements (Habitat)

Earthscan Publications Ltd, London

Translated from Spanish

Based on a Habitat Report
first presented at the Istanbul Conference, June 1996

First published in the UK in 1997 by
Earthscan Publications Limited

A catalogue record for this book is available from the British Library

ISBN: 1 85383 441 6

The views expressed in this publication are those of the authors and do not
necessarily reflect the views of the United Nations Secretariat.

Typesetting and page design by PCS Mapping & DTP, Newcastle upon Tyne
Printed and bound by Biddles Ltd, Guildford and Kings Lynn
Cover design by Andrew Corbett

For a full list of publications please contact:

Earthscan Publications Limited
120 Pentonville Road
London N1 9JN
Tel: (0171) 278 0433
Fax: (0171) 278 1142
Email: earthinfo@earthscan.co.uk
World Wide Web: http://www.earthscan.co.uk

Earthscan is an editorially independent subsidiary of Kogan Page Limited and
publishes in association with WWF-UK and the International Institute for
Environment and Development.

Contents

List of Figures, Tables and Boxes

FIGURES

TABLES

BOXES

LIST OF ACRONYMS AND ABBREVIATIONS

AMCAL	World Assembly of Cities and Local Authorities
ATO	Arab Towns Organization
CDC	Community Development Corporation
CEPAL	Comisión Económica Para América Latina
CMRE	Council of Municipalities and Regions of Europe
ECE	Economic Commission for Europe
EPZ	Export Processing Zone
ESCAP	UN Economic and Social Commission for Asia and the Pacific
FMCU	Fédération Mondiale de Cités Unies
GATT	General Agreement on Tariffs and Trade
GDP	Gross Domestic Product
Hm	Hectometres
ILO	International Labour Office
IULA	International Union of Local Authorities
MIT	Massachusetts Institute of Technology
MOPTMA	Ministerio de Obras Públicas, Transporte y Medio Ambiente
NAFTA	North American Free Trade Agreement
NATO	North Atlantic Treaty Organization
NGO	Non-Governmental Organization
OECD	Organization for Economic Cooperation and Development
R&D	Research and Development
RIDC	Regional Industrial Development Corporation
SEADE	Fundaçao Sistema Estadual de Analise de Dados in São Paulo
SPEDD	Southwestern Pennsylvania Economic Development District
SVA	Steel Valley Authority
UAT	Union of African Towns
UCCI	Unión de Ciudades Capitales Iberoamericanas
UN	United Nations
UNCHS	United Nations Centre for Human Settlements (Habitat)
UNDP	United Nations Development Programme
UNESCO	United Nations Educational, Scientific and Cultural Organization
UNFPA	United Nations Population Fund
UNICEF	United Nations Children's Fund
UTDA	United Towns Development Agency
UTO	United Towns Organization

Introduction

Humanity is heading towards a world in which urbanization is the rule. Not just because the data suggest that most of the planet's inhabitants will be living in urban areas by the beginning of the twenty-first century, but also because rural areas will be part of the urban centre-inspired system of relations in economics, politics, culture and communication. If this is so, if urbanization is the usual form of spatial settlement for the human species, does it make any sense to continue to speak of cities? If the trend is for everything to be urban, should we not rather shift our mental categories and our management policies towards an approach that differentiates between the various forms of relationship between space and society? And all the more so given that another two of the phenomena that define our historical period point to the possibility that cities will disappear as a territorial form of social organization: the information technology revolution and the globalization of the economy and of communication. The new information technologies enable social processes to be articulated with no regard for distance, whether within metropolitan areas (teleworking, teleshopping, tele-information, tele-entertainment), between regions or between continents. The globalization of the economy makes the wealth of nations, companies and individuals dependent on capital movements, chains of production and distribution and management units that are interrelated throughout the planet as a whole, thereby undermining the specificity of any particular territory as a unit of production and consumption. Although, as we shall see in Chapters 1 and 2, things are more complicated than that, and although the articulation of technology, economics, society and space is an open, variable and interactive process, it seems clear nonetheless that, in the information society, the global moulds the local, and electronic flows shape the economy through relations between units that are far away from each other in terms of space. What is more, communication, which lies at the heart of society's forms of cultural expression and the individual's mindset, is becoming increasingly globalized through the emerging system of multimedia controlled financially and technologically by large international groups, even if their products are diversified for specific segments of the market. Territory-based cultures, while not disappearing, will have to seek forms of relating, usually in a subordinate way, with powerful, globalized media which, even if they do not actually determine consciousness, do form to a large extent a hypertext of communication and symbolic interaction.

In short, three interrelated macro-processes – namely globalization, informationalization and generalized urban spread – seem to be converging towards the disappearance of the city as a specific form of relating society to territories. After existing for millennia, cities would seem to be falling into an inevitable historical decline on the threshold of the new millennium. This does not mean that urban problems will go away. On the contrary, now more than ever before, widespread urbanization highlights, as matters of dramatic urgency, the issues of how to deal with housing and urban services and how to protect the environment, these problems having been aggravated by a form of territorial settlement that is more predatory than previous forms. Yet if urbanization reaches its historical climax, then cities on the other hand might disappear as forms of social organization, cultural expression and political management.

This book challenges that increasingly widespread vision, and broaches the possibility, or even the necessity, of renewing the specific role of cities in a world of generalized urbanization, proposing that a dynamic, creative relationship be built up between the local and the global.

For that purpose, we start out by drawing a distinction between urbanization and the city. Without launching into academic disquisitions that would be out of place here, by urbanization is meant the spatial articulation, whether continuous or discontinuous, of inhabitants and activities. The city, on the other hand, both in the tradition of urban sociology and in the consciousness of citizens the world over, implies a specific system of social relations, of culture, and in particular of political institutions for self-government. We will not withdraw into some nostalgic vision of the city as it was of old, or into some ethnocentric espousal of cities with strong local personalities. We do not take the view that the future of cities is restricted to reproducing Siena or Barcelona. We do, however, address the possibility of citizens controlling their own lives, as was shown almost everywhere in the nineties by citizens in significant local elections, from Tokyo to Bogotá, and from Curitiba to St Petersburg. Nevertheless, relaunching cities as dynamic life and management forms is just one possibility. We could indeed evolve towards a world without cities, at least for much of the planet and most of its inhabitants. A world organized around great diffuse agglomerations with economic functions and human settlements spread out along transport arteries, with semi-rural areas in between, uncontrolled peri-urban areas and services unequally shared out in a discontinuous infrastructure. The global could be organized around managerial, technological and residential centres of elites, connected together by long-distance communications and electronic networks. For their part the inhabitants could individualize their habitat within the diffuse urban area described above, or group themselves into defensive communities with quasi-tribal ideologies to ensure their survival in a world that is structured globally at its centre and destructured locally in a multiplicity of peripheries. The hues of science fiction in our argument are merely an attempt to draw the reader's attention to a process that is under way, part and parcel of the logic of the powerful techno-economic system that is emerging, though not one we are irremediably condemned to. For indeed our present-day technological revolution and the economic dynamism it brings with it, with potential increases in productivity that are just beginning to materialize after two decades in which the new information technologies were spreading, hold out promises of material prosperity and cultural creativity for mankind. But control by society of economic development, with public institutions directing that development to society's benefit without stifling the economic zest of private enterprise, is an old dilemma that lies at the heart of all development processes. From the standpoint we seek to set out in this book, the articulation of society and economics, technology and culture in the new system can be arranged with greater efficacy and fairness on the basis of reinforcing local society and its political institutions. The global and the local complement each other, jointly creating social and economic synergy, as they did back at the beginnings of the world economy in the fourteenth to the sixteenth centuries, a time when the city states became centres for innovation and commerce on a worldwide scale.

The strategic importance of the local as a managerial centre for the global in the new techno-economic system can be seen in three main fields: economic productivity and competitiveness, socio-cultural integration and political representation and management.

From the economic point of view, the territorial context is, however paradoxical it might seem, a decisive element in generating competitiveness in economic units in a globalized economy. If this is so it is because, for one thing, companies depend to a large extent on their operative environment to be competitive and, for another, the liberalization of the terms of international trade – particularly in the wake of the Uruguay Round of the General Agreement on Tariffs and Trade (GATT) and the setting up of the World Trade Organization – considerably limits the actions that can be taken by nation states in favour of companies located in their territory. It is now local governments (municipal or regional) that, without falling into protectionism, can most effectively contribute to improving productive and competitive conditions for the companies on which, in the last analysis, the welfare of the local society depends. For indeed the competitiveness of companies in the new economy depends not so much on tariff barriers or political favours as on the generation of positive conditions for productivity in the territorial area in which they operate. This includes, as we shall discuss in Chapter 6, the existence of adequate technological infrastructure, a communications system ensuring that the territory is connected up to global flows of people, information and goods, and above all the existence of human resources capable of production and management in the new techno-economic system. Those human resource provisions include an education system able to supply a skilled work force at all levels including university level. But they also require the existence of satisfactory living conditions in terms of housing, urban services, health and culture, to make that educated work force a group of individuals and families that are balanced, productive and even happy within reason. The point is that producing and managing the habitat and the collective facilities that form the social base for economic productivity in the new informational economy is fundamentally the responsibility of local and regional governments. The link between private companies and local governments, in the framework of global relations regulated by negotiations between nation states, is the fundamental institutional and organizational foundation for wealth-creating processes.

The second sphere that is significant for local institutions is the cultural integration of ever more diverse societies. In a world in which communication is becoming globalized, it is essential to maintain distinct cultural identities in order to stimulate the sense of belonging in a day-to-day manner to a specific society. As against the hegemony of universalist values, the defence and construction of distinctive identities on a historical and territorial basis is a basic element of the meaning of society for individuals. Without some common cultural denominator to hold each society together, societies would break up into individuals and family units competing among themselves and taking up fragmented stances with respect to the global flows of power and wealth. The disintegrating potential of that situation is heightened in societies that are increasingly plural in their culture and in their ethnic composition. The great urban conglomeration, which will be the main form of settlement in the near future, brings individuals and groups with widely varying cultural bearings and behaviour patterns together. Without a system for social and cultural integration that respects differences while also establishing codes for communication between the various cultures, local tribalism will be the other side of the coin of global universalism. And that cultural fragmentation, by making the outsider a foreigner and the foreigner a potential enemy in the competition for survival, tends to destroy bonds of solidarity and tolerant attitudes, and can even threaten social harmony itself. What might seem like a moralizing warning is already, unfortunately, a description of daily life in many urbanized territories all over the planet.

National states are still forces for social cohesion and cultural integration in many countries. However, in many cases national states were forged in historical terms by repressing regional or national cultures that are still the main identity factor for most of the population in certain territories. This is the case in Catalonia or the Basque Country in Spain, or in Scotland, Wales and Northern Ireland in the United Kingdom, or in other plurinational and plurilingual European societies such as Belgium or Switzerland, or in others still that have been there in the past, such as France. Yet there are numerous and still more important examples to be found in that majority of the planet's societies that have at one time or another in their history suffered the mark of colonization. Many African states were formed on the basis of arbitrary colonial frontiers, which have split historically common ethnic groups, tribes and cultures into nations. In so far as challenging the frontiers would be a threat to peace, it is essential that national and/or local societies develop mechanisms to integrate differing ethnic groups and cultures. Similar problems, though with varying intensity, are also found in Asia, in America and in the republics that have arisen in the territory of the former Soviet Union. Furthermore, population shifts associated with globalization have generated multicultural societies and, in particular, multicultural urban areas, as we shall discuss in Chapter 4. Managing the socio-cultural differences of the various population groups cohabiting an area, and integrating them in a shared culture that does not deny their specific historical, cultural and religious features, is one of the main challenges for societies and governments in our time. And in this context, nation states, through having to maintain a balance between very diverse social groups and through having to emphasize instrumental aspects of politics over and above the integrating dimension of their institutions, face greater difficulties than local governments in managing the integration of cultural differences, particularly when, as is usually the case, those cultural differences manifest themselves in specific territories. Thus representation in local or regional institutions also acts as representation for cultural identities which, once recognized, can be integrated into a second institutional level within the framework of the nation state. Hence the territorial articulation of the state enables distinctive identities to be recognized and to express themselves in local and regional spheres, while also integrating them and rendering them compatible in the national sphere.

In short, local governments acquire a revitalized political role through the structural crisis of areas of authority and power that is affecting nation states in the new global system. Simplifying somewhat, it could be said that nation states are too small to control and direct the global flows of power, wealth and technology of the new system, and too big to represent the plurality of social interests and cultural identities of society, thus losing legitimacy both as representative institutions and as efficient organizations. In this sense the globalization of capital markets, markets for goods and production facilities makes it ever more difficult for nation states to exercise any effective economic policy. As a reaction against this, the states have begun to build supranational political or para-political institutions that are intended to correspond to the global sphere of operation of financial flows and multinational companies. The development of the European Union is the most important process in this line, but the new world panorama is also being affected by the Free Trade Association in North America (with extension in the future to the rest of Latin America), the setting up of an economic cooperation zone in the Pacific, the world economic coordination entrusted by the G–7 club (with Russia as an observer) to the International Monetary Fund and the World Bank, and other initiatives currently in the making. Similarly, in the political sphere, the United Nations, North Atlantic Treaty Organization (NATO) and other organizations for international political cooperation are taking on an increasing number of functions designed to regulate international relations, with joint military intervention when required. Yet this explicit recognition by nation states of their incapacity to solve single-handedly the essential problems of the economy and of international political relations is increasingly draining away the content of national institutions, turning them into intermediate mechanisms of a more complex machine with a wider reach, and thus weakening their functions as directly representing the citizens in their territories. Moreover, societies, and particularly local societies, are tending to reinforce their identify and to defend their autonomy in the face of the increasingly uncontrollable whirlwinds of global change. For the purposes of this function of socio-cultural integration, nation states often seem too distant from the interests and cultures of specific population groups, largely because they must give equal satisfaction to differing cultures, regions and nationalities as well as bearing in mind the requisites of negotiations with the agents of the world system of economic and political relations. Furthermore, in some cases nation states represent cultures and interest groups that are not in line with the interests of specific population groups, thus increasing their distance from citizens who organize their lives in the local sphere.

Local and regional governments depend for their part, in administrative and financial terms, on the nation states, and have even less power and fewer resources than them for controlling global economic and political agents. However, in a situation of scant control over those global flows in the hands of nation states, the difference is one of degree, not of kind: being even more impotent than a well nigh impotent institution is not particularly significant in the specific world of managing the global. On the other hand, however, local governments have two important advantages over their national guardians. For one thing, they enjoy greater representativeness and legitimacy with regard to those they represent: they are institutional agents for social and cultural integration in territorial communities. For another, they have much more flexibility, adaptability and room for manoeuvre in a world of cross-linked flows, changing demand and supply and decentralized, interactive technological systems. It is true that ill-conceived localism may lead to excessive, destructive competition between various places and regions. Yet it is also to be hoped (and recent experience confirms this) that cities and regions will be able to build networks in cooperation and solidarity with each other in order to negotiate constructively with companies with a view to reaching agreements of mutual interest. Of course the type of local and regional institutions we are referring to has nothing to do with certain municipal situations found around the world, situations still dominated at best by disinformation and bureaucracy and at worst by local bigwigs and corruption. But the potential of local governments to be agile forms for managing the global, with the cooperation of their guardian institutions at the national and international level, can be developed through enhancing the skills of their staff, modernizing their management technology, and increasing their financial resources and their areas of authority. That is the object, and the objective, of our analysis: how to respond to the globalization of the system through the localization of the managing and representing institutions, bringing together participatory democracy and informational development, administrative decentralization and cultural integration. The challenge is not easy: the difficulty of the issues addressed sets the obstacle-ridden agenda of this book, a book which is the result of its authors' research, reflections and professional experience on the subject of cities and their administration. Yet more difficult still is attempting to solve the problems of the new economy and the new society with obsolete formulae handed down from bygone times that still weigh heavily on – and paralyse – the institutions of cities struggling to cope with the new period of history. How to turn cities, their citizens and their governments into the actors of this new history is the subject of this book.

Chapter 1
Globalization, Informationalization and Management of Cities

INTRODUCTION

Cities and societies all over the world are experiencing now, as the twentieth century draws to a close, a far-reaching historical transformation in their structure. At the heart of this transformation lies a technological revolution that is organized around information technologies. Based on the new technological infrastructure, the process of globalizing the economy and communication has changed the way we produce, consume, manage, inform and think. Not every economic or cultural activity in the world is global. In fact, by far the greater part of that activity, in terms of the proportion of participants, is local or regional in its sphere. However, the strategically dominant activities, at all levels, are organized in global decision-making and exchange networks, from financial markets to audiovisual messages. The planet is asymmetrically interdependent, and this interdependence is articulated every day in real time through the new information and communication technologies, a phenomenon that is new in historical terms and one that is in fact opening up a new era in the history of humanity: the information era.

Urbanization processes, cities and citizens are caught up in these structural changes. We are in fact witnessing the fastest and most wide-ranging urbanization process in history (Figure 1.1). In just a few years most of the world's population will be urban, and the vast majority of that urban population will be living in cities, located in countries that are now developing countries. The era of telecommunications is not diluting urban centres, as technological determinists prophesied – on the contrary, by enabling distant urban and rural systems to be managed and to communicate together, they tend to concentrate the population in territorial agglomerations, partially discontinuous ones of huge size and of historically new socio-spatial characteristics, as we shall seek to set out in this book. In a sense, the destiny of humanity is being played out in urban areas and, in particular, in the great metropolises.

Managing those cities and building new life-models capable of respond-

Figure 1.1 Metropolitan agglomerations, 1995

ing to the new productive and cultural forms poses enormous challenges. Not just on account of the accumulation of functional, social and environmental problems in the new type of human settlement, but also because we are facing processes of transformation that are little understood. Urban policies pursued to date seem behind the times with regard to the globalization of the economy and of technology as against the localization of society and culture. Municipal governments are often overtaken by events occurring in spheres that are beyond their control. Hence the essential step for redefining the instruments for urban management is analysing the technological, economic, cultural and institutional processes that underpin the transformation of cities. That is the issue, in outline, which this chapter will seek to address.

STRUCTURAL TRANSFORMATION PROCESSES: THE INFORMATION SOCIETY AND THE GLOBAL ECONOMY

Over the last two decades, a new technological paradigm has come into being, one that we call informational and one which amounts to a historical watershed as important as the industrial revolution was in the past. The present-day technological revolution is centred on information technologies, which include microelectronics, computer science, telecommunications, and also, though with marked specificity, genetic engineering (Castells et al, 1986; Castells, 1996a). Although the scientific foundations of this revolution go back a long way, and although some of its industrial elements have been around since the 1940s, the time when it became a technological system that spread and found applications was in fact in the 1970s, starting to a large extent in the American techno-industrial centres of California and New England. It spread initially to military technology and international finance. It moved on to industrial factories at the beginning of the 1980s, spread to offices at the end of the 1980s, and is now reaching our homes through the so-called information superhighways (Sullivan-Trainor, 1996). The effects of this change of paradigm vary depending on the countries, cultures, institutions, levels and forms of development concerned, but some common features can be noted that affect all societies with varying intensity and under varying modes. We will outline here some of these fundamental traits arising from the reciprocal interaction between technological revolution and social structure. It is important to stress that while the new information technologies are not the cause of the phenomena that will be reviewed here, they are the infrastructure that is a prerequisite for their existence: if there were no computers and no global telecommunications, for example, there would be no global economy and no world-scale communication.

First and foremost among the elements associated with the informational paradigm is the formation of a global economy as the operative economic unit of today (Chesnais, 1994). Let us pin down the exact meaning of the term. We are not dealing with a world economy, which has existed in fact since the sixteenth century, or even with an economy whose activities are subjected to internationalization. By the global economy we mean an economy in which the strategically dominant activities function as a unit at the planetary level in real or potentially real time. This is the case with capital markets, which are integrated world-wide via instantaneous electronic connections processed by information systems with large memories and high processing speed. However, the technology, information and management of the leading companies, and of their auxiliary branches, are also globally articulated, as are, increasingly, industrial production, advanced services, and markets, whether through multinational companies, networks of companies or exchange mechanisms. Highly skilled labour is also taking the form of a global market, though the masses of unskilled emigrants act more as a reserve army than as a form of globalization. In general, capital is global, but most labour is local (Campbell, 1994). What characterizes the new global economy is its extraordinarily – and simultaneously – inclusive and exclusive nature. It includes anything that creates value and is valued, anywhere in the world. It excludes what is devalued or undervalued. It is at once a dynamic, expansive system and a system that segregates and excludes social sectors, territories and countries. It is a system in which the creation of value and intensive consumption are concentrated in segments that are connected throughout the world, while for other broad sectors of the population, whose size varies from country to country, a transition is setting in moving from the previous situation of exploitation to a new form of structural irrelevance, from the point of view of the system's logic (Carnoy, Castells, Cohen and Cardoso, 1993). These tendencies are not inexorable. Yet to counter them, by using the creative potential of the new technologies to benefit the majority of the population, policies acting as correctives to the present imbalances are needed.

The global economy is also an informational economy – ie an economy in which increases in productivity do not depend on a quantitative increase in the factors of production (capital, labour and natural resources) but rather on the application of knowledge and information to management, production and distribution, both in processes and in products (Foray and Freeman,

1992). The generation and strategic processing of information has become one of the essential factors for productivity and competitiveness in the new economy (Dosi et al, 1988). This has far-reaching consequences for regional economic development policies, which must henceforth be based on policies for communication, informationalization and human capital (see Chapter 4).

The informational economy is also characterized by a flexible model of production, built around the ever more widespread pattern of the network company. By this we do not mean a network of companies, but rather a new form of organization. What we are seeing in the economy (and to a large extent in society as a whole) is the decentralization of large companies and the creation of semi-autonomous business units; the proliferation of small and medium-sized companies; the formation of networks for cooperation involving small and medium-sized companies, or just small companies, or just large companies, eventually making up networks of networks (Ihmai, 1990). Since strategic alliances involving large companies vary by product, by technology, by market or by country, it can be held that the new structure of the economic system is made up of specific, ever changing networks, in a variable-geometry system. Hence at any given time and place, the real economic agent is not a company in the traditional sense of the term but rather a segment made up of a network of company segments. It is this absolutely flexible and dynamic – but also unstable – form of economic activity that characterizes the new processes of organization, management and production (Piore and Sabel, 1984; Harrison, 1994). And if it succeeded in emerging fully only at this point in history, it is thanks to the flexibility allowed by the new information technologies.

On the basis of the technological and organizational transformation of the new informational/global economy, we are witnessing far-reaching change in labour relations and in the structure of employment in all societies (Freeman and Soete, 1994; Carnoy and Castells, 1996; Castaño, 1994). However, contrary to an opinion as widely held as it is uninformed, the new technological paradigm does not cause unemployment. The results of empirical research over the last ten years (OECD, 1994) show that historical experience, the theory of economics, available data and the most reliable projections all enable the simplistic hypothesis of jobs being destroyed by present-day technological development to be rejected. Thus among Organization for Economic Cooperation and Development (OECD) members, the most technologically advanced societies are the ones that create the most jobs: in the United States in the period 1992–95, six million new jobs were created, and Japan's unemployment has never risen above 3.2 per cent. Furthermore, in both countries the growth rate for more skilled employment is very much higher than that recorded for non-skilled employment (Carnoy and Castells, 1996). The problem of structural employment is a problem for European countries, due principally to macroeconomic policies that are excessively obsessed with European convergence indicators and to institutional rigidities in the labour market and in the mechanisms of the Welfare State. A globally interdependent economy cannot do without a global social chapter. Moreover, on a world-wide level, the new development processes in Asia and Latin America are creating an unprecedented wave of industrialization, with the result that the number of industrial jobs planet-wide, despite the de-industrialization of OECD countries, is higher than ever before in history: the number of industrial jobs in the world grew from 102.9 million in 1963 to 176.9 million in 1989 (the latest data available), ie a growth of 72 per cent in just 26 years (Wieczorek, 1995), though the geographical distribution of employment did change radically, shifting away from OECD countries to the newly industrialized countries, particularly Asian ones.

Yet if the new technological paradigm does not in itself destroy jobs, it does profoundly affect employment conditions and the way in which work is organized. On the one hand, bearing in mind the global interdependence of networks of companies, sectors that are open to world-wide competition tend to converge (though not fully to coincide) in their employment conditions, with the result that companies tend to relocate in areas with lower costs and less stringent regulations or, alternatively, to take supplies of products generated in those areas. On the other hand, in all societies, the new technological system clears the way for and accentuates the historical process of work dispersal on the basis of a new flexible model for labour relations. Indeed, while the industrial revolution consisted in aggregating the work potential of peasants driven away from their lands and craftsmen stripped of their means of production to form the social system of the factory, the present-day technological revolution is on the contrary leading to the individualization of tasks and the fragmentation of the work process, the unity of that process being reinstated through communication networks. Thus the phenomena of subcontracting, the decentralization of production, outworking, job sharing, part-time work, self-employment and consultancy are all growing apace, and already account for between a quarter and a third of the work force in the main developed societies (Carnoy and Castells, 1996). Societies resisting this dispersal, such as the societies of Spain and France, pay the price for it in high unemployment. Thus company decentralization and work dispersal result in, for one thing, an extraordinarily flexible, dynamic process, enabling companies to achieve cost savings and competitive gains, though there may be negative consequences for productivity in the long-term through undermining the accumulation of technological knowhow within the company itself. At the same time, however, this flexible model for labour relations makes employment precarious, undermines the Welfare State, hangs a question mark over the role of trade unions, and consequently induces a structural crisis in the institutions upon which social harmony in companies and in society are currently based (Navarro, 1994).

In developing countries, the transformation of work comes about through two distinct mechanisms. On the one hand, the formation of industrial production and advanced services networks without the stability and social control of the previous model: the new industrialization already functions in accordance with the patterns of the flexible model from the very outset. On the other hand, the expansion of casual, informal work in the urban nuclei of a world in the throes of transformation. The new technologies enable archaic forms of local over-exploitation to be articulated together with modern productive networks geared to global competition (Portes, Castells and Benton, 1989). The informal economy, at once ancient and new, is the extreme form of flexibility characterizing the new relations of production in an informational, globalized and polarized economy.

THE DIGITALIZATION OF COMMUNICATION, MEDIA-BASED POLITICS AND THE CRISIS OF THE NATION STATE

The historical transformations under way are not restricted to the technological and economic spheres: they also are affecting culture, communication and political institutions, in an interdependent system of social relations. Since this is the realm in which cities and their governing bodies work, the major trends in those spheres of society must be noted.

Communication, and consequently culture, in the information society have been organized for some time now around the audiovisual system. Yet over the last few years a more far-reaching phenomena has appeared: the increasing digitalization of all messages – audiovisual, printed or interpersonal – to form a globalized, interactive hypertext. This is enabling the present-day mass media to turn into media that are individualized, segmented and geared to specific audiences, though production and technological and financial control still display global characteristics. We live not so much in a global village as in individual little chalets that are joined together to a greater or lesser extent, and globally produced and distributed (Negroponte, 1995; Doyle, 1992). Along with this, the extraordinary development of the Internet is multiplying sources of information and horizontal exchange, though it is still limited to a world élite of some thirty million people (Anderson et al, 1996). The most significant point, for the time being, is that the breadth and flexibility of the new communication system has increased its capacity to absorb all kinds of cultural, social and political expression, in a digital universe that is electronically communicated and transmitted.

As a consequence of this, given that culture is a system of communication and that our society is increasingly organized around the production, distribution and manipulation of symbols, the political arena has essentially been engulfed in the arena of the media. It is not so much that politics only functions in the media but rather that, in democratic societies at least, the political process is essentially decided in the media (Castells, 1995a). This means that the symbolic level of politics is more important than ever, and that consequently messages are obliged, first and foremost, to generate symbols capable of winning support, and associated with credible, reliable and if possible charismatic personalities. However hard it may be for intellectuals to accept this fact, politics is not decided by political programmes. And however unfair it may be for administrators, good administration does not guarantee public support. Politics in the information society is symbolic communication, conflictually expressed in the arena of the media.

To guide our exploration of the new urban world that is in gestation, we shall put forward the hypothesis that, through all the transformations described as a whole, we have entered a new type of society that could be called 'the flow society' (Castells, 1996a) – a society in which the material basis for all processes is made up of flows, and in which power and wealth are organized in global networks carrying information flows. These flows are asymmetric and they express power relationships. Yet more important still than flows of power is the power of flows: financial flows, technological flows, image creation flows, information flows. The logic of the flow society often escapes its controllers, as is well known to governments struggling to regulate financial markets, and political or economic leaders tossed about by the conflicting and contradictory campaigns and conspiracies conducted through the media.

However, to understand the new political game, it must be added that flows are not the only thing in current societies. There is another history, another dynamic, that is developing not in parallel with, but rather in reaction to, and contradiction with, the global flow system: the assertion of identity, whether historical or reconstructed (Calhoun, 1994; Rubert de Ventós, 1994; Castells, Yazawa and Kiselyova, 1996). The creation and development in our societies of systems of meaning increasingly arises around identities expressed in fundamental terms. Identities that are national, territorial, regional, ethnic, religious, sex-based, and finally personal identities – the self as the irreducible identity. In opposition to the extraordinarily excluding nature of the system of the global economy and the flow society is the exclusion of all that excludes: concrete fundamentalism as against abstract globalization. In a society in which power and function are organized in flows, the meaning of experience is organized on the basis of potentially irreducible identities. The emergence of fundamentalisms of all kinds in our society is simply the symmetrical mirror of the gradual emptying of content, of experience, of social control, in the arena of flows in which global power networks express themselves.

The result of these contradictory processes between techno-economic globalization and the growing specificity of identities is the systemic crisis of nation states. On the one hand, their areas of authority are insufficient to enable them to control the global flows, and their organization is usually too rigid to adapt to the constant changes in the world system. On the other, the plurality of territorial and cultural identities aspiring to be represented by nation states generates increasingly conflictive processes and, in the last instance, tends to delegitimize the idea of national representation. Moreover, the more centralized a state is the more difficult it is for it to build bridges between the global system and the various cultures and territories that make up the nation. Under these circumstances, local and regional governments are emerging, all over the world, as more flexible bodies, keeping close to the bedrock of their identities, and potentially capable of negotiating continuous adaptation to the variable geometry of the power flows. The difficulty for local governments is, however, partly their dependent status in administrative terms and their scant capacity in terms of economic resources, and partly the risk of drifting towards political localism and cultural tribalism if the defence of identity turns into fundamentalism. The reconstruction of a flexible, dynamic state, articulated throughout its different levels, would seem to be the only historical possibility for overcoming the information society's dissolving tendencies, stemming from the dichotomy between power flows and the individual nature of experience, thus introducing a new outlook for the management of cities.

THE MANAGEMENT OF CITIES IN THE NEW GLOBAL ECONOMY

The new global economy is articulated in territorial terms around networks of cities (Sassen, 1994). Cities, for their part, increasingly depend on the forms of their articulation with the global economy as regards their standards and modes of living. That is why the new frontier for urban management consists in getting each city ready to face global competition, since the welfare of its citizens depends on that. There is however a simplistic view, and one which is ultimately self-destructive, of the mechanisms and objectives of competitiveness in the case of cities: that investors must be attracted at any price, by reducing taxes and controls and accepting lower salaries and a lower level of social protection. When that policy becomes the norm, it generates downward-spiralling living conditions, and it ends up depressing and impoverishing all urban communities, thus proving detrimental for companies. Competitiveness properly understood in the new informational global economy does not primarily involve cutting costs, but rather increasing productivity. And that productivity depends essentially on three factors: connectivity, innovation and institutional flexibility (Brotchie et al, 1995).

By connectivity we mean linking cities into the circuits for communication, telecommunication and information systems in the regional, national and global spheres.

By innovation we mean the capacity that any given city possesses for generating new knowledge, as applied to economic activities, based on its capacity for obtaining and processing strategic information. This involves having adequate human resources available, provided by a high quality education system at all educational levels. But it also involves both offering a quality of life that is likely to attract or to keep the most highly educated professional groups, and also setting up applied research institutions, linked to economic life, with flexibility and a business oriented outlook, for the purpose of incorporating global technological innovations into the city's productive system.

By institutional flexibility we mean the internal capacity and the external autonomy of local institutions when it comes to negotiating the articulation of the city with companies and institutions that operate in supralocal spheres.

These three conditions are to be understood in relative terms, in keeping with the level of development and the institutional context in which any given city finds itself. Not every metropolitan area can be, or indeed should be, Silicon Valley or Yokohama. But each one does require that combination of technological infrastructure, human resources and flexible local management systems, for without it they will be subjected to the wild and increasingly destabilizing ups and downs of the global flows of the economy and communication.

So cities, while taking up positions in the global economy, must also integrate and structure their local societies. Without a solid base in the citizens, city governments will not have the strength that is needed to navigate those global circuits. In this sense the local and the global are complementary rather than antagonistic. This social integration requires democratized political mechanisms, based on administrative decentralization and the participation of the citizens in municipal management (Borja, 1988). Yet it also requires a local economic policy – eg maintaining an employment sector related to public and para-public services – that is independent of the global sphere of authority. Local fiscal policy must be brought into line with this aim, imposing taxes on economic activity in the local territory that are neither excessive nor insufficient for the purpose of ensuring the social integration of the local population and the existence of generic conditions for productivity in the urban system, which benefits companies. The economic, social and environmental controls that local governments must exercise cannot be developed in isolation in a context of global economic interdependence. Municipal authorities must act in concert at national and international levels. This requires certain technological, institutional and political conditions to be met. From the technological point of view, information systems must be set up based on intermunicipal databases, with permanent on-line access and real-time intellective capacity. In institutional terms, associations of cities and municipal governments must abandon their languid existence devoted only to formal, official relations and become dynamic, active networks, with permanent, nimble administrative machinery, a business oriented outlook, and capable of taking initiatives in the name of the municipal governments they represent. In political terms, municipal governments must come to terms with their own power and be capable of asserting their community of interests over and above any internal party or ideological differences. They must be capable of defending their specific interests with regard to their respective national governments, without slipping into destructive separatism though accepting the need for negotiated conflict as the usual form of political existence in a plural institutional system. At the same time, the networks of cities, represented by their governments, could set about becoming powerful, dynamic collective actors on the global economic scene, capable of negotiating constructively with multinational corporations and supranational institutions. However, their collective action will depend on how they work together, reaching any compromises necessary regarding the interests of the various members.

Chapter 2

The Impact of Globalization on the Spatial and Social Structure of Cities

INTRODUCTION

The process of globalization, and the informationalization of the processes of production, distribution and management, are profoundly altering the spatial and social structure of societies all over the planet. This is the most direct meaning of the articulation between the global and the local. The socio-spatial effects of this articulation vary according to the levels of development of the countries, their urban history, their culture and their institutions. Yet it is in this articulation that the sources of new urban transformation processes lie – and hence the points of intervention for urban, local and global policies capable of reversing the process by which the quality of life in cities deteriorates.

Our analysis is organized around a sequence of three issues that synthesize and seek to make sense of a mass of apparently disparate information: the articulation of the local and the global in the new, strategically dominant productive processes – advanced services and high-tech industry; the emergence of new patterns of spatial settlement, both in developed and in developing countries, special attention being given to the emergence of megacities, 'dispersed city' models, and the articulation between old and new forms of urbanization; and establishing an urban quality on the basis of intrametropolitan space-polarization processes, in a historically new sense, as we shall attempt to show in our analysis.

LOCAL MANAGEMENT OF THE GLOBAL ECONOMY: GLOBAL CITIES OR GLOBAL NETWORKS OF URBAN NODES?

The global informational economy is organized on the basis of managerial centres capable of coordinating, managing and innovating the activities of companies structured in networks for interurban, and often transnational, exchange (Hall, 1995). At the heart of the new economic processes are activities concerned with finance, insurance, property, consultancy, legal services, advertising, design, marketing, public relations, security, information provision and computer system management (Daniels, 1993). Research and Development (R&D) activities are likewise of decisive importance in industry, agriculture and services. All these activities have something in common: they are flows of information and knowledge (Norman, 1993). Consequently, on the basis of a highly developed telecommunications system, they could be located anywhere on the planet. However, numerous empirical studies have concluded that the new pattern for the spatial location of advanced services is characterized by its being at once concentrated and dispersed: the important feature is its inter-relation through a flow network (Graham, 1994; Moss, 1987). What is being observed is, on the one hand, that advanced services (characterized by activities such as those mentioned in the preceding paragraph) are the sectors of activity with the fastest growth in terms of number of jobs and in terms of the proportion of gross domestic product (GDP) that they account for in most countries, they having become the most dynamic and most heavily investing sectors in the main metropolitan areas (Enderwick, 1989). On the other hand, while these activities are present in all large cities and in nearly all countries, the higher levels of the advanced services networks are concentrated in certain nodes in some countries (Harasim, 1993; Daniels, 1993). This concentration follows a hierarchical model among urban centres, with the most important functions, in terms of skills, power and capital, being concentrated in the chief metropolitan areas of the world (Thrift, 1986; Thrift and Leyshon, 1991). The classic study by Saskia Sassen on the global city has shown the joint dominance of New York, London and Tokyo in international finance, and in consultancy in business services for companies of international reach (Sassen, 1991). However, other metropolitan centres are important too, even dominant in some segments of specific markets. For example, Chicago and Singapore in the options and futures markets, which were actually invented in Chicago in 1972. Other world cities make up the links in the dominant chain of global management, such as Hong Kong, Osaka, Frankfurt, Paris, Zurich, Los Angeles, San Francisco, Amsterdam and Milan (Sassen, 1994). And new 'regional centres' emerge as the network of interactions on which the global economy is based grows outwards: among others, Madrid, São Paulo, Buenos Aires, Mexico, Taipei and Moscow. Moreover, as soon as a region in the world becomes articulated into the global economy, thereby dynamizing its local economy and society, the setting up of an urban node for advanced services becomes a prerequisite, and it is invariably organized around an international airport, a satellite-telecommunications system, luxury hotels with appropriate security systems, English-language secretarial support, financial and consultancy firms familiar with the region, local and regional government offices capable of providing information and infrastructure to back up international investors and a local labour market having personnel skilled in advanced services and technological infrastructure. Thus for example when the Russian Pacific – a region with vast future potential – began to integrate itself into the global economy in the 1990s, the first step towards integration was the establishment of a local management node for global networks in the region's economic capital, Khabarovsk (Minakir, 1994) (Box 2.1).

Box 2.1 Khabarovsk: A Global Node in the Russian Pacific

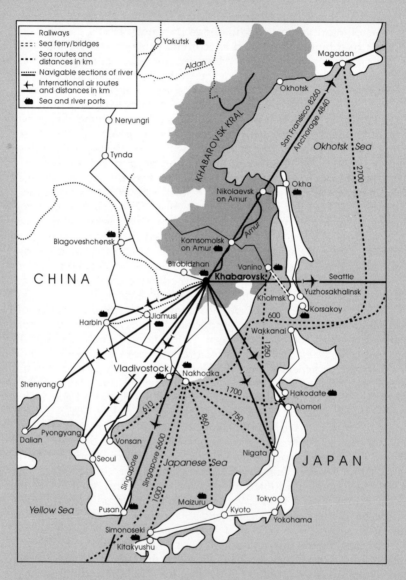

Railways
Sea ferry/bridges
Sea routes and distances in km
Navigable sections of river
International air routes and distances in km
Sea and river ports

The new Russia's connection to the global market economy is taking place through a growing diversity of connection points. The Russian Pacific, a region traditionally remote from world circuits and until recently closed to foreigners for reasons of military strategy, is perhaps one of the regions with the greatest potential for development in the early years of the next century. However, though the Asian Pacific looks set to become the main industrial centre in the world economy as well as one of its financial centres and probably the largest market of the future, it has a weak point: its extreme dependence on outside supplies of energy and natural resources. That dependence, which is already evident in the case of Japan, will become more marked as the development of China begins to call for a level of resources that is way above what is available in China itself, and even in excess of the productive capacities of its main present-day suppliers, particularly Indonesia. The Russian Pacific, and Siberia beyond, would appear to be the privileged region capable of supplying resources (scarcely explored as yet, though certainly vast) in the form of natural gas, oil, coal, rare minerals of strategic and industrial importance, wood, fish and a wide range of raw materials that are imperatively needed by Asian countries for their accelerated process of development. Consequently, during the 1990s, as soon as the Russian Pacific opened up to foreign investment and to international contacts, a great many companies from Japan, South Korea, the United States and China put out feelers in the region, with the enthusiastic support of the local governments who competed among themselves to attract much-needed foreign investment. Khabarovsk, a city of some 600,000 inhabitants and a historical river port on the Amur, became the principal connection node to the outside world because at that time it had the only international airport in the area, with regular air links being established with Anchorage, Niigata, Seoul and Harbin (see map).

In 1992 the provincial government began to organize infrastructure for welcoming foreign investors, based on hotels of international standard, multilingual services for companies, satellite telecommunications, business centres equipped with computer systems and secretarial services, tourism and guide services for foreign visitors, and a network of banking and financial services. The first foreign investments were in fact made in joint ventures for services companies, with the provincial government and public enterprises taking part to supply the operational infrastructure needed by foreign companies. By 1995 some 300 companies with foreign capital participation were trading in Khabarovsk, including a major television set factory owned by the Korean company Gold Star. In 1994, the value of the region's exports to other Asian countries amounted to 150 million dollars. However, the main interest of foreign investors in Khabarovsk is to establish a presence and a management structure with a view to commencing productive activity, in the near future, in a vast territory lying beyond Khabarovsk itself, including oil and gas in the ocean in the vicinity of Sakhalin, the great forests of eastern Russia and the extraordinary mineral and precious metal resources of Western Siberia, particularly in Yakutia. Even though some of the regions that are potential producers of these raw materials are a long way from Khabarovsk, the articulation of this region of the world as a whole to the global economy requires a connection and management centre through which the productive complex now forming can be controlled and supplied with information and capital, and decision-making arranged.

Though other centres, such as Vladivostok or Nahodka, are also trying to take on that role, Khabarovsk rapidly became the node connected to the global network since, with its airport, it was the obvious entry point in the region. It was also the first to set up a services and communications network to assist with handling foreign investment and the flows of capital, information technology and raw materials through which the material base for the future global dominance of the Asian Pacific in the world economy is being laid.

Source: Kiselyova et al (1996)

Similarly, when Mexico became fully integrated with the North American economy through the Free Trade Agreement, and thereby integrated with the global economy, the Federal District reinforced its management and international coordination functions, deeply transforming its spatial structure in line with those functions (Gamboa de Buen, 1994). Thus 8 of the 15 banks that operate in Mexico, and 16 of the 22 firms of brokers, are located in the financial district established around the Paseo de la Reforma, to the west of the Zocalo (the historical centre). New property development projects out west, such as the Santa Fe complex, provided an exclusive area of 650 hectares for the headquarters of companies such as Hewlett Packard, the Cifra Group and Televisa, plus dozens of luxury shops, and high-status hotels and residences. In the Federal District as a whole, several new international hotels were built, along with hundreds of thousands of square metres of high-class office space and a new building for the Stock Exchange (Araneta, 1995). The modernization of Mexican telecommunications, particularly international, satellite-based ones, together with the spread of computer systems, increased the instantaneous management capacity of the new Mexican economy in world circuits (Skezely, 1993). Ironically, it was precisely this far-reaching technological and financial integration that sparked off the country's bankruptcy in 1994, when information on the real state of its economy, and on the depth of its governmental crisis, began to circulate around international financial markets.

In the case of Europe, the study by Cappelin (1991) on service networks in European cities shows the increasing interdependence and the complementary nature of medium-sized urban centres. Thus, according to that study:

'the relative importance of relations between city and region seems to diminish with respect to the relations which link the cities of various regions or countries to each other ... New activities become concentrated on specific poles, which leads to a growing disparity between the urban poles and their respective hinterlands.'

Some notion of the new architecture of inter-urban economic relations can be gleaned from the study by Michelson and Wheeler (1994) on business mail traffic, using data from Federal Express, an American company that is international in scope. The analysis points on the one hand to the preeminence in the US of New York and Los Angeles, and on the other to the existence of privileged international connection circuits in business mail traffic. They conclude that:

'All the indicators point to a reinforcement of the structure of the control functions which determine exchange of information ... Locational concentration of information has its origin in high levels of uncertainty induced by technological change, lack of market capacity and deregulation and globalization of the market. But as the new [economic] era develops, the importance of flexibility as a basic management mechanism, and of the economies of agglomeration as a preeminent locational force, will continue. The importance of the city as a centre of gravity of economic transactions will not just fade away. But with the forthcoming regulation of international markets ... and less uncertainty about the rules of the economic game and about its players, concentration of the information industry will be slower, and elements of [information] production and distribution will move towards lower levels of the international urban hierarch.'

Indeed, what nobody can guarantee in the new economy is the permanence of that interurban hierarchy, it being subject to fierce competition in such volatile sectors as finance or property investment. Thus in one of the most exhaustive studies on the subject, Daniels (1993) explains the relative failure of the Canary Wharf urban development project in London's Docklands as resulting from the speculative strategy of the well-known Canadian company Olympia & York (now bankrupt), which proved unable to absorb the shock of lower employment levels in financial services in London and New York in the first half of the 1990s. Daniels concludes that:

'the expansion of services in the international market has brought to the global urban system a higher degree of flexibility and, in the last analysis, of competition than existed previously. As the experience of Canary Wharf shows, the results of large-scale city planning and development projects in the cities have become hostage to external international factors over which there is little control.'

For indeed in the first half of the 1990s, as urban centres exploded – fuelled by the expansion of their global business – in cities such as Bangkok, Taipei, Shanghai, Buenos Aires or Bogotá, at the same time the cities of Madrid – which experienced its golden age of globalization in the period 1986–90 – New York, London and Paris went through a severe depression in their property markets, as a result of the oversizing of their urban projects and the speculative nature of a good deal of the investments made in services and building. And when the Mexican economy crashed in 1994, the depression of financial and property markets in Mexico City led to negative repercussions in Buenos Aires, those two emerging financial markets being lumped together in the fears of international speculative investors. The fickleness of the development of urban centres illustrates the utter dependence today of cities on uncontrollable flows of global investment.

So if new information technologies enable managing centres to be dispersed in space, why does the world continue to be organized in the form of a network of managerial centres based on agglomerating services in the limited, saturated and over-priced space of business districts? Taking the research cited and existing data as a starting point, Sassen (1991) puts forward a convincing hypothesis:

'the combination of spatial dispersion and global integration has created a new strategic role for the large cities. Over and above their long record as international centres of trade and finance, these cities now operate in four new ways: firstly, as directional points of organization of the world economy; secondly, as key locations for finance and specialized services firms; thirdly, as places of production, including the production of innovation in these advanced [services] sectors; and fourthly, as markets for the products and innovations created.'

The business districts of large cities are high-value productive complexes focusing on the production and processing of information, ones in which the headquarters of companies and financial firms can find both the suppliers they need and the highly skilled employees they require. The flexibility of this productive system requires the formation of a medium providing a high spatial concentration of resources, including human resources, that are not permanently engaged by any one company but rather used as needed in accordance with demand and with company projects. The flexibility and adaptability of the new productive system are possible on the basis of the combination of agglomerating functions and personnel at the nodes of a global network and connecting a multitude of secondary functions to these nodes, dispersed around the region, the country and the planet, and linked up by rapid transport systems, telecommunications and computer systems (Graham, 1994). Once these activities have become concentrated in certain metropolitan nodes, various factors contribute to maintaining that concentration. For one thing, the substantial property investments made by large companies in those managerial centres would become devalued if large-scale relocation were to come about. Personal contacts are essential in high-level decision-making in the business world, bearing in mind not only the importance of personal confidence but also the legally ambiguous nature of some transactions. And then large cities offer the best opportunities for personal development, ranging from education for children to access to culture and entertainment, and taking in proximity to power centres and socially prestigious circles. All this combines to make them the places of work and residence of the social and professional élites, the managers of the global economy (Mollenkopf and Castells, eds, 1991; Mollenkopf, ed, 1989; Machimura, 1994).

Nevertheless, along with managerial concentration in the centres of large metropolises, a dispersed, articulated network for service management has become established, located in the peripheral districts of the metropolises and in lesser regional metropolitan centres. Secondary management centres have emerged in the United States (eg Atlanta or Omaha), in Europe (eg Barcelona, Nice, Stuttgart or Bristol) and in Asia (Bombay, Bangkok,

Shanghai). The peripheries of large metropolitan areas are buzzing with advanced service activity, as can be seen in the examples of Reading in the case of London, or Walnut Creek in the case of San Francisco. In some cases, new managerial centres have become established in the shadow of the city centre, La Defense in Paris being the most typical example. In general, however, most service activities decentralized to the periphery consist of routine office work connected with large-scale, automated processing of information, employing frequently underpaid female labour. What is significant in the spatial process described is not the concentration or the dispersal of activities, but the relationship between the two trends – ie the establishment of an interdependent, hierarchically organized network of service-producing complexes working with telecommunicated information flows.

In short, the globalization of the economy, and in particular of the advanced services that organize and manage the system as a whole, does not lead to the spatial dispersion of functions, and neither does it lead to the exclusive concentration of managerial functions in just a few metropolitan areas. The global city is not New York, London or Tokyo, even if they are the most important managerial centres of the system. The global city is a network of urban nodes, at differing levels and with differing functions, that spreads over the entire planet and functions as the nerve centre of the new economy, in an interactive system of variable geometry to which companies and cities must constantly and flexibly adapt. The global urban system is a network, not a pyramid. And the changing relationship with respect to that network determines, to a large extent, the fate of cities and citizens.

THE NEW INDUSTRIAL SPACE

While advanced services are the nerve centre of the informational economy, industry is still the most productive sector and the material base for the wealth of nations (Cohen and Zysman, 1987). The patterns of industrial location have a fundamental effect on the spatial structure and processes of cities and on their dynamism. These patterns have been deeply transformed by the new microelectronics-based technologies. Though information technology industries are the most dynamic industrial sector, and the one that expresses the new spatial logic most directly, it can be argued that industrial structure as a whole is characterized by the new pattern of location, in so far as the use of microelectronics is spreading to the machinery and the production processes of all branches of industry.

The logic of the new industrial space was made clear by, among other sources, a series of studies completed during the 1980s at the Institute of Urban and Regional Development of the University of California at Berkeley (Castells, 1989). The essential observation is the technological and organizational ability of companies to divide up the production process across different locations, while restoring the unity of the process through telecommunications and through microelectronic manufacturing technologies that enable precision to be achieved in component production together with flexibility in design and in output levels. The geographical specificity of each phase of the production process was seen to be determined by the particular features of the workforce required for each phase and by the social and environmental characteristics corresponding to the living conditions of each segment of the workforce. It should be borne in mind that high-technology industries display a pattern of occupations that differs greatly from that of traditional manufacturing: its employees are concentrated at the two extremes of the professional scale – engineers and highly qualified researchers on the one hand, and a mass of semi-skilled jobs on the other – with fewer administrative employees and skilled workers than in previous periods of history. Electronics companies, particular American ones, began their development, back in the 1960s, on the basis of an international division of labour in terms of spatial location across their various sites, taking advantage of the low weight of their products relative to their value and the expansion of the global communications network: the first semiconductor plant in Asia was that of Silicon Valley's pioneering company Fairchild, in Hong Kong in 1962 (though Hong Kong did not then go on to develop as an electronics centre, multinationals opting rather to locate in Singapore and Malaysia).

In general terms, in the cases of both microelectronics and the computer industry, the location pattern is organized in terms of four factors, each of which relates to one of the four operations of the production process:

1. R&D, innovation and prototype production activities are concentrated in high-level, technology innovation sites, in metropolitan centres of global industrial significance, such as Silicon Valley or Tokyo. There is, however, an internal hierarchy among such centres, secondary innovation sites being developed to foster an industrially deconcentrated technology industry system, examples being Southern Paris in France, Munich in Germany, or Campinas-São Paulo in Brazil.
2. Highly skilled manufacturing activities are often concentrated in areas of recent technological industrial development in central countries – in the case of the United States, in zones in the west and south-west, and in the case of France in new centres of activity such as Toulouse or Nice-Sophia Antipolis.
3. Large-scale electronics production, which for a long time needed abundant semi-skilled labour, was quickly decentralized to South East Asia.
4. For customer-related production and after-sales repair and service operations, companies need to be close to the main metropolitan markets, these units being dispersed throughout the entire area of the industrialized and rapidly industrializing world.

European and Japanese companies long maintained a location pattern based on their protected home territories. In the 1980s, however, in the face of global competition and needing to step up the rhythm of technological innovation, they adopted a similar location pattern, relocating premises to South East Asia (for example, Thomson-SGS in Singapore, or heavy Japanese investment in Thailand and Malaysia), subcontracting activities out to Indian companies in Bangalore and Bombay, establishing a presence in the chief technological sites, such as Silicon Valley, and spreading their adaptation-to-customers antennae in the main markets, particularly the fastest growing one, the Asian Pacific (Aoyama, 1996).

A key element in the new pattern for industrial location is the decisive importance of the means of technological innovation, not just for electronics but for the whole industrial structure of regions and cities. The forming of those centres and their spatial distribution is a key factor in the new urban economic geography. Castells and Hall (1994) have studied the formation and location of the main sites for technological innovation across the world, seeking to ascertain, on an empirical basis, the conditions for their development and the location factors behind what they call the 'the world's technopolises'. The results of their research can be summarized as follows:

Firstly, technopolises display different urban formats. It is important to stress that, with the highly significant exception of the United States, the world leader in technology, and with Germany as a special case, the main technopolises have taken root in the great metropolitan areas of each country: Tokyo-Yokohama, Southern Paris, the M4 corridor in London, Milan, Seoul-Inchon, Moscow-Zelenograd and, following at a considerable distance, Singapore, Taipei-Hsinchu, Nice-Sophia Antipolis, Stuttgart, Shanghai, São Paulo, Madrid, Barcelona, etc. The partial exception of Germany, where Munich, and Bavaria in general, form the chief centre for technological innovation in electronics, can be explained in terms of political history: the destruction of Berlin's industry, which was the main centre for European technology in the early twentieth century, and the hurried relocation of Siemens from Berlin to Munich (the zone to be occupied by the Americans) in the final months of the Second World War. Thus in contrast with the image of technopolises as innovation centres springing up outside the traditional spatial structure of metropolitan domination, there is in fact historical continuity, in most cases, in the location of innovation clustering around the economic, scientific and political power of large cities, though within those cities the centres for technological innovation in industry tend to be developed out in the suburban periphery, usually centring on the areas of greatest quality and social prestige, such as the south-west quadrant of the Paris region, focusing on the historical tradition of Versailles, or the northern axis of the Madrid region, where the Tres Cantos Technology Park is located.

Nevertheless, the world's leading sites for technological innovation, along with Tokyo, are to be found in newly industrialized regions of the United States (Silicon Valley near San Francisco, the technopolis of southern California around Los Angeles, Austin-Texas, the Research Triangle in North Carolina, and Seattle), or in reindustrialized regions on the basis of a new business framework (Highway 128 in Boston). The formation of these technological industrial complexes stemmed from the spatial articulation of specific factors of production – capital, labour and raw materials – combined with an institutional agent and based on a particular form of territorial social organization. Specifically, the raw material was new scientific and technological knowledge, relating to major fields of industrial application, generated by research institutions such as Stanford University, the California Institute of Technology and the Massachusetts Institute of Technology. The work-force was the engineers and scientists provided by an excellent education system that is superior in those fields, including the universities named plus other nearby ones such as Berkeley, San José State or Santa Clara, in the case of Silicon Valley. The capital needed for those technology companies was also specific: it came originally from Defense Department financing, which was seeking technological excellence rather than profit, and later on venture capital – which is particularly plentiful in that part of the world – seeking a high return in exchange for taking on the risk implied in investing in technological innovation. The articulation of these factors of production initially came about through an institutional agent: Stanford University, which created the Stanford Industrial Park in 1951, in the case of Silicon Valley, and the group of businessmen, journalists and Air Force generals who clubbed together in Los Angeles to win the military contracts for the aeronautics and electronics companies on which the industrial development of southern California was based. Finally, in those areas, and particularly in Silicon Valley, media for social relations were formed bringing engineers, researchers and technology businessmen together, and this enabled ideas to circulate, the workforce to be exchanged and the development of a culture of business emulation on a territorial basis. Thus, if the general rule for the location of the sites for technological innovation is continuing metropolitan dominance, the experience of the United States points to the possibility of new industrial spaces springing up on the basis of the complex described, in which the factors of production and the social and institutional conditions capable of generating synergy are articulated in space (Saxenian, 1994).

Sites for technological innovation, once formed, tend to deepen their synergy and to accentuate their dominance, forming global networks of industrial connection between discontinuous territories. The research by Camagni and the European Group for Research on Innovative Environments (Camagni, 1991) shows the increasing interdependence of these innovation sites, both in Europe and in the rest of the world. For indeed, as Amin and Robbins (1991) argue in their study on the subject, the new industrial system is neither global nor local, but rather characterized by 'a new articulation of global and local dynamics'. In this context, a recent study by Gordon (1994) on Silicon Valley companies in the 1990s shows that the innovation sites do not turn in on themselves as industrial districts, but rather take the form of central nodes in a global network for production and innovation. He ends his study by asserting that:

> 'in this new global context, localized agglomeration does not constitute an alternative to spatial dispersion, but rather takes shape as the main basis of participation in the global network of regional economies ... Regions and networks in fact constitute interdependent poles in the new spatial mosaic of global innovation.'

Consequently, the new industrial space does not necessarily mean the decline of the old metropolitan areas that were the headquarters of traditional industry and the rise of the new regions organized around high technology. Neither can it be seen in terms of a simplistic divide between research being carried on at the centre of the system and manufacturing out on the periphery, in so far as the productive networks at their various levels are cross-linked throughout the planet's industrial geography. The industry of the information age is spatially organized in a changing hierarchy of innovation and manufacturing articulated in the form of global networks. The management and architecture of these networks are subject to constant movements of cooperation and competition between companies and

between territories, with varying results: sometimes industrial history is reproduced, and sometimes there is a break in location patterns on the basis of
new collective business initiatives. What characterizes the new logic of industrial location is its geographic discontinuity built up on the basis of far-flung
territorial production complexes. The new industrial space is organized
around information flows that simultaneously separate and reunite their
various territorial component parts, in accordance with cycles and companies. And this spatial logic of information technology industries spreads out
to industry as a whole in so far as production and management are
organized on the basis of those technologies. The result is the emergence of
a new industrial space characterized by a multiplicity of global industrial
networks whose intersections, inclusions and exclusions transform the very
notion of industrial location: we have moved on from manufacturing zones
to flows of manufactures.

THE TRANSFORMATION OF THE SPATIAL STRUCTURE OF CITIES

The set of informationalization and globalization characteristics of our historical period, and the transformation of industrial and service productive
structures that we have just outlined, lead to a deep-seated transformation
of the urban spatial structure. However, the technological and economic
processes that form the basis for this transformation intermesh with the
history, culture and institutions of each country, region and city, giving rise to
great diversity in spatial models. We nonetheless make bold to single out
some of those processes as being typical of the new informational society. In
particular, we believe that the formation of the so-called megacities,
especially in newly industrialized countries, amounts to the most significant
urban phenomenon for the twenty-first century. We shall accordingly present
the main features of that process, taking as an example the megacity now
being formed between Hong Kong and Canton, and then examine the
historico-geographic change shown in the new model for urbanization,
taking current trends in American and European cities into account.

Urbanization in the Third Millennium: Megacities

Megacities are rather more than gigantic territorial agglomerations of
human beings. We are indeed witnessing the process of formation of human
settlements of over ten million inhabitants (at least 13 of them by 1992), and
of over 20 million inhabitants in the near future (at least four) (see Table 2.1
and Figures 2.1–2.5). But size is not really the defining factor of megacities.
They are in fact the nodes of the global economy and of the most powerful
nations. Concentrated in their territory are the higher functions of planetary
management, production and administration, political power centres, control
of the media, and the symbolic capacity for creating and spreading the
dominant messages. They have names, ones that in nearly all cases are
different from the European-American matrix that is still dominant: Tokyo,
São Paulo, New York, Mexico City, Shanghai, Bombay, Los Angeles, Buenos
Aires, Seoul, Beijing, Rio de Janeiro, Calcutta, and Osaka, according to the

Table 2.1 World's Largest Urban Agglomerations in 1992

Rank	Agglomeration	Country	Population (thousands)
1	Tokyo	Japan	25,772
2	São Paulo	Brazil	19,235
3	New York	United States of America	16,158
4	Mexico City	Mexico	15,276
5	Shanghai	China	14,053
6	Bombay	India	13,322
7	Los Angeles	United States of America	11,853
8	Buenos Aires	Argentina	11,753
9	Seoul	Republic of Korea	11,589
10	Beijing	China	11,433
11	Rio de Janeiro	Brazil	11,257
12	Calcutta	India	11,106
13	Osaka	Japan	10,535

United Nations' classification for the year 1992. Yet to that club must be added, in the mid 1990s, Jakarta, Moscow, Cairo, New Delhi, London, Paris and, possibly, in connection with their subcontinental hinterland, Lagos, Dhaka, Karachi and Tianjin. Not all of them are dominant centres in the global economy – Lagos and Dhaka, for example, are not – yet in all cases they connect processes and functions affecting hundreds of millions of people into that global economy. Megacities must be defined in terms of their gravitational pull on broad regions of the world. The megacities articulate the global economy, connect up the informational networks and concentrate world power. Yet they are also at the same time the recipients of huge sectors of the population that are struggling for survival. Concentrated in the megacities is all that is best and all that is worst in our societies, taking in everything from the innovators and the powerful to the sectors that are of no significance to society from the point of view of the system's impeccable logic. The most significant thing about the megacities is that they are externally connected to the global networks yet also internally disconnected from those sectors of their local populations that are regarded as unnecessary or as forces for social disturbance: the 'rejectables' as they are known in Bogota. The thesis we put forward is that this is as true of New York as it is of Mexico DF or Jakarta. What makes megacities a new urban form is their being established around their connection to a global network, of which they are fundamental nodes, while being internally segmented and disconnected in social and spatial terms. Megacities are a spatial form characterized by functional links established over a broad territory while at the same time evincing great discontinuity in their land-use patterns. Their social and functional hierarchies are confused, organized in segregated territorial units and strewn with territorial fragments whose social customs are not recognized by the system. Megacities are discontinuous territorial constellations made up of spatial fragments, functional spheres and social segments. To illustrate this analytic perspective, Box 2.2 shows in some detail one of the

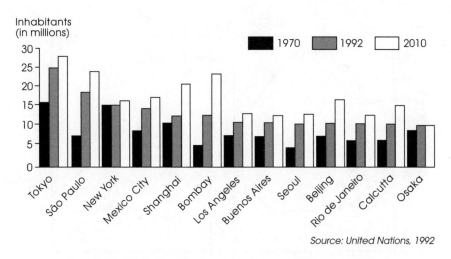

Source: United Nations, 1992

Figure 2.1 World's largest urban agglomerations

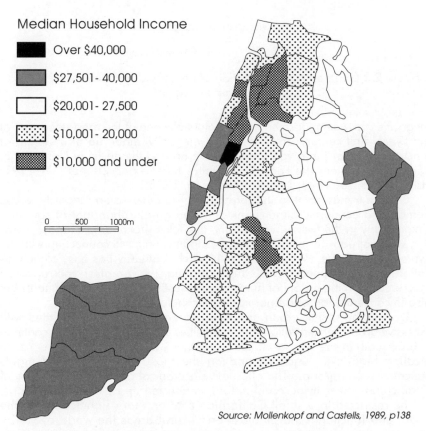

Source: Mollenkopf and Castells, 1989, p138

Figure 2.2 Urban segregation by income, New York City

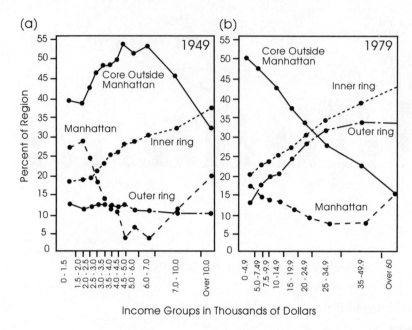

Income Groups in Thousands of Dollars

Source: Mollenkopf and Castells, 1989, p139

Figure 2.3 Geographical distribution of households by income, New York Metropolitan Region

megacities now being formed that is potentially one of the most important of the twenty-first century: the Pearl River megacity, made up of a system of functional relations in a vast territory lying around the nuclei of Hong Kong, Shenzhen, Canton, the Pearl River Delta, Macao and Zhuhai (Sit, 1991; Hsing, 1995; Lo, 1994; Leung, 1993; Ling, 1995).

Current trends point to the formation of another Asian megacity whose human and economic dimensions are even greater than that of southern China: early in the twenty-first century, the Tokyo–Yokohama–Nagoya corridor, which already forms a functional economic unit, will connect up with the Kyoto–Osaka–Kobe constellation, with which it already has easy communication by high-speed train, thus creating the greatest metropolitan macroregion in the history of humanity, not just in number of inhabitants but also in concentration of economic and technological potential.

Despite the social, urban and environmental problems associated with excessive urban concentration, the megacities are growing, and will continue to grow, both in size and in the attraction they exert both for the purposes of locating high-level functions and on the most well-heeled and highly educated social groups. The alternative ecological dream of a universe of small communities living amid nature, connected up by electronic means, will be restricted to a small Californian élite or, more significantly, to the social and functional marginalization of rural areas the world over. The information age is, and will be more and more, the age of megacities (Cole and Cole, 1993; Messmacher, 1987; Chapman and Baker, eds, 1992; Kresl and Grappert, eds, 1995). This is so chiefly for the following reasons:

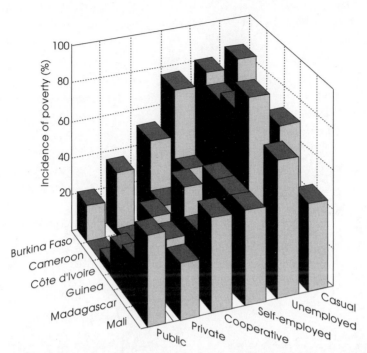

Figure 2.4 Percentage of poor people in selected African countries, by professional occupation

- Megacities are the centres of economic, technological and business dynamism in their countries and in the global system. They are in fact the motors of the development process. Their countries, beginning with the United States and China – two societies dominated by the ideology of the rural, communal paradise – depend essentially on what their megacities do (Kresl and Grappert, eds, 1995; Kwok and So, eds, 1995).
- They are centres of cultural innovation, symbol creation and scientific research, ie of the strategically decisive processes in the information age.
- They are the centres of political power, even in cases where the government resides in other cities, on account of the ideological and economic force they represent.
- They are the connection points for the world communication system. For example, the Internet, despite its electronic ubiquity and its flexible architecture, cannot bypass megacities and their systems, because it depends on telecommunications systems that are structured around large metropolises (for example teleports and fibre optics rings), and because it depends for its power on the information systems and the highly educated social groups concentrated in the megacities.

Of course some consideration must be given to certain factors that will slow down the demographic growth of the megacities of the future. Among others, birth-control policies are up and running, and reducing birth rates. Some

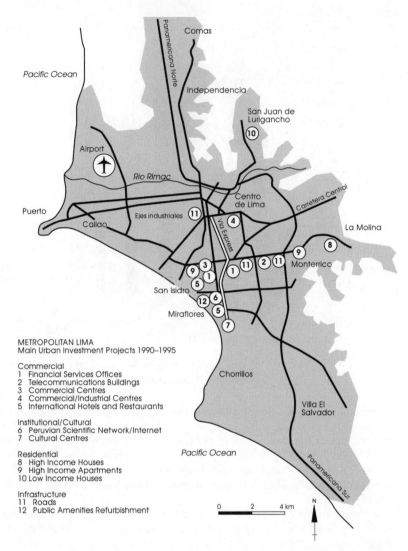

METROPOLITAN LIMA
Main Urban Investment Projects 1990–1995

Commercial
1 Financial Services Offices
2 Telecommunications Buildings
3 Commercial Centres
4 Commercial/Industrial Centres
5 International Hotels and Restaurants

Institutional/Cultural
6 Peruvian Scientific Network/Internet
7 Cultural Centres

Residential
8 High Income Houses
9 High Income Apartments
10 Low Income Houses

Infrastructure
11 Roads
12 Public Amenities Refurbishment

*Figure 2.5 Lima's transformation since its entry into the global economy,
1990–1995*

policies on regional development or promoting medium-sized cities may
divert part of the migration flows and decentralize economic activity on the
basis of better communications, as seems to be shown by initial observations
in the case of China during this decade (Hsing, 1995). It is also possible,
unfortunately, that the social disintegration, violence and even the epidemics
that will arise in the megacities, if the deterioration of their current living
conditions goes on, will make them less attractive as places for settlement.
However, despite all that, megacities will grow further still in functional
dominance, in social power and in their concentration of population and
activities, for they are self-nourishing, in an accumulative manner, taking in
all that is valuable in their societies and in the planet as a whole. Since they

are the connection and management nodes of the global system, the future of humanity is being played out in the megacities. Any attempt to reject the inevitable, instead of adapting it to social needs and managing its contradictions and conflicts, will lead to a growing distance between the realities of cities and urban theory. Our immediate future is one of generalized urbanization, with that urbanization being concentrated in strategic nodes of great human and territorial size to which we are beginning to refer by the still hazy term megacities.

However, since this new urban reality has generally been associated with urbanization processes in developing areas, we shall analyse the specific features of the new urbanization processes in the developed areas of the United States and Europe. In both cases we are witnessing similar processes, though each under its own patterns as determined by differing urban histories.

The Territorial Diffusion of the New American Suburbanization

America in the 1990s is experiencing a new wave of territorial expansion in its urban peripheries, and this is being imitated in a way in other countries. The journalist Joel Garreau (1991) dubbed the new spatial form 'Edge City' in his popular book on the subject, defining the new spatial form empirically as a combination of five criteria:

1. a territory in which at least five million square feet of office space are concentrated – the workplace of the information age;
2. it has at least 600,000 square feet devoted to shopping premises;
3. it has more jobs than homes;
4. people perceive this territory as a specific place;
5. there was nothing there that could be called a city 30 years ago.

He then goes on to record the impressive development of this type of territorial complex in the urban peripheries of Boston, New Jersey, Detroit, Atlanta, Phoenix, Texas, southern California, San Francisco and Washington DC. Each of these spatial units spreads over dozens of kilometres of office buildings, shopping facilities and increasingly dense residential areas, all newly built and connected by a superhighway network. It is an ex-urban civilization, in which life is organized around the two poles of computer working and individualized homes dominated by audio-visual culture.

The development of these ex-urban constellations highlights the functional interdependence of different units and processes of the urban system over long distances, minimizing the role of territorial proximity and maximizing the importance of communications networks – both telephone lines and overland transport.

This urbanization model comes in response to American historical and cultural experience, characterized by a continual attempt to overcome economic, social and urban problems through geographic mobility (Kunstler, 1993). Initially, through emigration to America to escape from conditions in the countries of origin, then through the westward march and the colonization of a vast continent. Later on, through the middle classes abandoning

BOX 2.2 THE HONG KONG–GUANGDONG MEGACITY

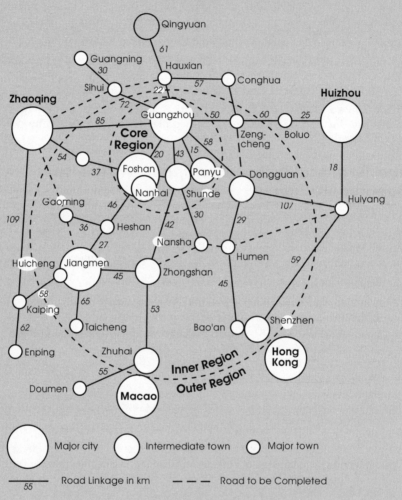

Source: Castells, 1996

In this last decade of the second millennium, one of the largest human settlements in history is being formed, though with territorial gaps, between Hong Kong, Shenzhen, Canton, the industrial centres of the Pearl River delta, Macao and Zhuhai (see map). In 1995, this de facto settlement – one with no name and no administrative definition (although it includes the main urban centres of the Guangdong province) – covered 50,000 square kilometres, with a population of some 50 million inhabitants. Its component parts are diverse, with some large cities with several million inhabitants, international centres such as Hong Kong or national centres such as Canton. Shenzhen is an agglomeration of services and manufacturing that grew up under the wing of its legislative status as a special economic zone: though non-existent in 1980, it now has a million and a half inhabitants. Zhuhai is a busy city geared to national and international trade. Macao is a centre for tourism, entertainment, gambling and miscellaneous businesses, and is preparing the way for its transition from being a Portuguese colony to coming under Chinese sovereignty. And all over the delta region, small villages have been transformed into industrial zones scattered among rural areas, with some six million workers from all over China. These factories work as subcontractors for the industrial companies of Hong Kong or for companies from all over Asia with their headquarters in Hong Kong. Rural areas and hills divide the various units of the megacity, though a dense communications network enables it to function day in and day out as a single unit. The railways have been electrified and the track grid doubled in size; a motorway network is being built; sea and river communications by hovercraft and ferry have grown significantly; and local flights between Hong Kong and Canton operate as a shuttle service. A fibre-optic circuit is being installed to increase the telecommunications provision linking the various centres, connected up to the rest of the world via satellites. Cellular systems, already up and running in Hong Kong, will cover the whole of this urban system by the year 2000. The multiple articulation of this megacity with the global economy is assured. In 1995, five new airports were being built: two of them – Lantau airport in Hong Kong and Canton airport – are large-capacity international airports and, together with the others at Shenzhen, Macao and Zhuhai, they have a combined traffic-handling capacity of 150 million a year. Similarly, new container seaports were also being built in North Lantau (Hong Kong), Yiantian (Shenzhen), Goalan (Zhuhai) and Huangpo (Canton), forming the largest port complex in the world in terms of goods handling capacity. Zhuhai was also planning to reinforce its connection with Hong Kong through the building of a 60 kilometre bridge over the ocean. Underpinning the formation of this megacity are two interrelated processes: the opening of China to the global economy, making use of its special connection with Hong Kong, and the competitive strategy of Hong Kong companies, using cheap labour and favourable institutional circumstances for investment in China, with a view to decentralizing most of their industrial production to the Pearl River Delta. By 1995, 10,000 joint ventures involving Hong Kong investors had set up in the delta, plus 20,000 industrial factories, generally medium-sized ones. The workers usually live in dormitories near the companies, and these are normally run by the municipal authorities. Raw materials, machinery and technology come from Hong Kong, while the industrial products, once processed, are returned to Hong Kong for export, though the new ports of Yiantian and Gaolan are intended to diversify the exporting centres. The engineers and managers are based in Hong Kong and Shenzhen, service infrastructure for production in Canton, and local supervision in the factories themselves. A large number of managers and engineers travel from one to three times a week between the various points in the production network. This megacity as a whole possesses extreme internal diversification, in terms of both the society and the natural setting, yet it does maintain a certain unity as a metropolitan economic system and as a communications system. Its multinuclearity also evinces a marked hierarchy, with Hong Kong being the cosmopolitan global centre and Canton taking up its role as the provincial political power base. Shenzhen uses its special connections with the central power to become the mechanism relating the rest of China to the export platform of Hong Kong. And Macao, lastly, is becoming increasingly specialized in being the Las Vegas of Southern China, as a many sided recreational centre for this gigantic dynamic pole in the new global map.

Source: Woo (1994)

city centres and setting up a new suburban civilization based on the car, the television and ownership of a detached house subsidized by the government. And now, through leaving behind the established suburbs, deserting rural areas and forming these 'edge cities' along superhighway arteries whose only reference points are the similarly dispersed workplaces, individual residences in dense lots, with no urban focus, and service centres at the superhighway junction nodes. It is not the end of the city, since New York, San Francisco and so many other urban centres in dozens of metropolitan areas continue to throb with social, cultural, commercial and managerial activity. Yet we are witnessing the detachment of a growing proportion of the American population (over half at the time being) from any urban experience in their daily lives. The new communication systems tend to concentrate activities and to disperse the population. The countryside is being left empty. And the cities exist and will continue to exist, but with fewer and fewer inhabitants. It is there in the regular sequence of suburban living quarters clinging to internodal telephone lines and superhighways where a new urban form is being established, the expression of an American urban tradition of a 'fuite en avant' in space, yet it is also a possible future for emerging megacities in other parts of the world.

The Articulation of Old and New Urban Forms in European Cities

The new urbanization processes, resulting from the deep-seated globalization trends of the economy and the informationalization of society, mesh into existing spatial forms to produce the new urban structure that characterizes our epoch. This articulation can be seen particularly clearly in Europe's old cities, currently undergoing a far-reaching functional, cultural and spatial reorganization (Hall, 1995; Martinotti, 1993; Borja et al, 1990; Siimo, 1994). A number of simultaneous processes characterize their transformation:

Managerial business centres constitute, as they do in other areas, the motor for development of the cities, connecting the city up to the global economic networks. The business centre is established around an infrastructure of communications, telecommunications, advanced services, office buildings, technology centres and educational institutions. To these is usually added a complex of catering and hotel activities aimed at tourism and people passing through the city. The managerial centre is also the central node for an inter- and intra-metropolitan system (Dunford and Kafkalas, 1992; Robson, 1992; Tarr and Dupuy, 1988).

The new managerial and technocratic élite at the summit of the new system creates exclusive spaces for itself, as the preceding bourgeois élite had done. But since the high-status professional classes are proportionally much more numerous, their presence in the urban space is more evident, and this accentuates the spaces of social segregation. In most European cities (Paris, Brussels, Rome, Madrid, Amsterdam), unlike American cities with the exception of New York, the higher classes live mostly in the city centre of the metropolitan area, in distinct neighbourhoods not always coinciding with the urban areas of the greatest historical or cultural value, though in all cases the best kept areas with the best amenities. English cities, however, display an intermediate case of social segregation in that large areas of the city centre, particularly in London, have become commercial areas, and some segments of the élite have chosen to withdraw to a pseudo rural life in historical villages near the large cities.

The suburban world of European cities shows sharp divisions. They include in particular working-class and service-worker peripheries centring on state-owned or subsidized housing estates built in the heyday of the Welfare State. They are also sites for industrial production, whether of the traditional kind or involving new technologies. And in several countries (France, Sweden, England) they have been structured around 'new cities' occupied generally by the professional middle classes and nuclei of activity in decentralized services, often public or para-public. On top of this social and functional diversity, a large number of state-owned housing units in the suburbs have gradually turned into ghettos for immigrant ethnic minorities (eg La Courneuve in Paris) as their original inhabitants opted for better alternatives in the private housing market.

The mixture of historical time periods and the superposition of functions and cultures in a single space also characterizes the city centres of the main European cities. Therein are still to be found traditional working-class districts, facing the twin assault of professional groups seeking proximity to the urban cultural centre and immigrant groups seeking to overpopulate deteriorated space that is strategically located in the informal urban economy (Belleville in Paris, Les Marolles in Brussels or the Barri Gotic in Barcelona are examples of this twin dynamic regarding the reappraisal or passing on of a traditional space). Yet young people belonging to the counter-culture have also made the urban centres – and particularly the ones that are least attractive to the élites – their area for socializing, as is shown by the urban dynamics of Berlin, Amsterdam or Copenhagen. And finally, the city centres of Europe have also formed ethnic ghettos, some in marginalized conditions, such as Tower Hamlets or Hackney in London, and others such as La Goutte d'Or in Paris, which is home to workers of Arab origin, with families and – usually – jobs, though facing strong social pressure and experiencing the accelerated deterioration of their physical space.

Finally, it is paradoxical that it should indeed be in the areas for socializing and leisure, alongside the business centres and international hotels of European cities, that marginalized groups, in both social and cultural terms, proliferate in the street, precisely because only by being spatially visible can the excluded groups survive their exclusion.

The new European urban landscape is thus made up of a superposition of socio-economic processes and historical time periods working on a space that has been built up, knocked down and built up again in successive waves of urban transformation. The specific result of globalization is the acceleration of this continuous process of urban restructuring in step with requirements and objectives that are increasingly external to the local society. Thus city centres are becoming connectors to the global, with central spaces experiencing permanent restructuring, and the suburban peripheries becoming areas of withdrawal for various social groups and economic activities, either by segregation or by the spatial demarcation of their sphere of existence. Ultimately, European cities are maintaining their façade of an urban history that is deep-rooted in cultural terms, though they are increasingly being inhabited by global capital flows and by cosmopolitan élites dependent on the Internet. And it is perhaps in their metropolitan suburbs with their social and functional diversity where the new local society is being generated, one that articulates itself globally through the reconstituted space of the historical city.

TOWARDS THE DUAL CITY?

In our first chapter we pointed out that the new techno-economic model is characterized simultaneously by its great productive dynamism and by the way it excludes large territorial and social sectors. In a way this dichotomy is expressed territorially on a planet-wide scale. For example, Sub-Saharan Africa, with the major exception of South Africa, seems to be increasingly excluded from the dominant economic and technological circuits of the world system. But the excluding model also appears through cumulative regional inequality processes, eg as between the south-east and the north-east of Brazil, or between Catalonia and Extremadura in Spain (Cuadrado Roura et al, eds, 1994). However, the relatively new factor is that the deepest social exclusion processes manifest themselves in an intra-metropolitan duality, particularly in the large cities of nearly every country: in different spaces within the same metropolitan system there exist, with no articulation between them and sometimes without them even seeing each other, the most highly valued and the most degraded functions, the social groups that produce information and appropriate wealth contrasting with the excluded social groups and people in a marginalized state. These processes exist in nearly all large cities, because the logic behind them is part of the new model for techno-economic development. Yet these effects can be softened, and in fact they are in many cases, by social and urban policies aimed at integration. However, in designing such policies, the starting point must be a recognition of the phenomenon of the growing intra-metropolitan duplication which occurs, to varying quantitative extents, in different contexts.

To illustrate this analysis we will refer to a number of cities in the north

BOX 2.3 SÃO PAULO, CITY OF INEQUALITY

In 1993 the Fundacao Sistema Estadual de Analise de Dados (SEADE) Foundation of the state government of São Paulo carried out a study for the International Institute for Social Studies of the United Nations' International Labour Office on social inequality in the metropolitan area of São Paulo. Taking a representative sample of 5,500 households, the study focused on analysing the segmentation of the labour market, working on the hypothesis that the labour relationship determined social integration and exclusion processes. The researchers classified the population into four groups – A, B, C and D – along a scale of indicators for income, education, employment and housing conditions. Group A took in 20.5 per cent of the population, B 37.2 per cent, C 19.7 per cent and D 22.6 per cent. The disparity in conditions between groups A and D was extreme. The unemployment rate among the poorest was five times higher than among the best off. Thus in Group D, 39 per cent of the families were below the poverty threshold, being dependent on income from their children's labour for 30 per cent of their income. The illiteracy rate was seven times higher in Group D than in group A; over half the heads of family in Group D had not finished their primary education, and 87 per cent of the family members of over seven years of age had not taken or had not finished their secondary schooling. As regards housing, over 37 per cent of São Paulo families were living in conditions well below habitable standards, while 13 per cent were living in 'very satisfactory' conditions. Taken as a whole, a total of 11.3 per cent of families in the metropolitan area were in a state of extreme poverty, with income levels of just 26 per cent of the family average, large families, and in many cases living in shacks (illegally in 15 per cent of cases), with a higher proportion of Blacks or mulattos (42 per cent of families living in poverty), and with a higher level of recent immigration to São Paulo. According to the study, the great economic dynamism of São Paulo in recent years has led to growing social inequality for its inhabitants.

Source: SEADE (1994)

and the south of the planet, some of these cases being shown in separate boxes (see Box 2.3 São Paulo and Box 2.4 Madrid). It is important to note, in analysing intra-metropolitan duality, that at least four processes of differing natures are mixed up in the process:

1. the housing and urban-services crisis which, in most developing societies, affects a high proportion of the urban population, including sectors with regular employment and average income – the informal city is not the same thing as the marginal city;
2. the persistent and growing social inequality in large cities, from London or Madrid to São Paulo or Mexico;
3. the urban poverty affecting a good deal of the population, on account of the general state of the country, as is the case with most African cities;

Box 2.4 Change and Continuity in Social Inequality in the Metropolitan Area of Madrid, 1986–1991

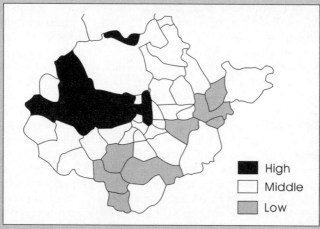

High
Middle
Low

Source: Leal (1994) p77

In the second half of the 1980s, the city of Madrid experienced a significant process of economic growth, associated with Spain's full membership in the European Community and with foreign capital investments gravitating towards the capital of the country – ie associated with the qualitative transformation of Madrid's role in the network of global cities. Even though living standards of the population as a whole rose considerably, the distribution of that wealth was unequal, and maintained a marked pattern of spatial segregation, the forms and locations of that segregation were modified (see map).

In the only empirical study on the subject, the prominent sociologist Jesus Leal points out: 'these processes have consecrated a decisive change in the social structure of the urban space of Madrid marked by the difference between a bourgeois centre and a proletarian periphery, the image of the fifties... The present-day city is more complex, and the social changes arising from the rejuvenation of the middle classes directly affects the structure through the improving social condition of recently built areas, which in general has tended to counteract differentiating processes out in the periphery. However, the social distance between the north-west and the south are still very great, and is even on the increase on the whole. This can clearly be seen in differences in education levels among people living in those areas'.

Source: Jesus Leal, 'Cambio Social y desigualdad espacial en el área metropolitana de Madrid (1986–91)' in 'Economía y Sociedad', issue 10, June 1994; quotation, p77

4. social-exclusion phenomena themselves, ie significant segments of metropolitan society being reduced to survival conditions, they being of little economic, social and political interest for the dominant logic of the social system.

New York, which is probably the world's economic capital in terms of capital-ist-élite settlement, is a deeply dualized city, as was shown by a research project on the subject directed by Mollenkopf and Castells between 1987 and 1990 (Mollenkopf and Castells, eds, 1991). What is significant is that this duplication should have become more marked precisely in the 1980s, the heyday of the city's finance- and property-related prosperity, particularly in Manhattan. Much of the process is due to the transformation in occupa-tions: between 1977 and 1987 some 140,000 industrial jobs were lost, while 342,000 jobs were created in advanced services at various levels. Professionals and technicians came to account for 31 per cent of the active population, a similar increase also coming about in lower-skilled services workers. In addition, what was really significant in terms of social polariza-tion was the exclusion from the workforce of a growing proportion of young people from the poorer sectors, mostly Blacks and Hispanics. 37 per cent of those in secondary education left school without finishing their studies, and then found it very hard to get a steady job. As a result, the activity rate for the population of New York stood ten points below the national average. Yet those young people, as well as a great mass of illegal immigrants, did not remain inactive: they swelled the ranks of those engaged in the informal economy and, in many cases, the criminal economy, centring on drugs, that being one of the essential mechanisms of the economy and society of New York. Furthermore, Sassen (1988) has shown how the new consumption model of the broad stratum of professionals at the top of the social structure is complemented by an informal workforce, in so far as the capital intensive consumption model that is typical of the suburbs (the electro mechanical home) has been replaced by labour intensive urban consumption among the élite (domestic service, childminders, restaurants and bars, security, personal services). Hence some of those excluded from society are occasion-ally reintegrated, though being kept always in temporary work circuits with scant prospects for social mobility (Sassen, 1991b).

Harris (1991) has shown empirically how this social duplication is expressed in spatial terms in New York. After carrying out a detailed study on spatial segregation by social groups during the 1980s, he concludes:

'Restructuring of the economy of New York over the last thirty years has created greater social inequality. The contrast between the rich and poor districts has become greater. Different zones of the metro-politan area have been affected in different ways, with the city centre having undergone the greatest transformation. The loss of industry has affected the outskirts more, while the growth of offices has been concentrated in Manhattan. The changing geography of employment has shaped the emerging social geography of the metropolitan area. Major parts of Manhattan have been gentrified, while most of the outlying districts have experienced a social decline. The result of this process is a new pattern of accentuated

*contrasts between Manhattan, the outlying districts and the subur-
ban areas ... Many classes of informal work have been developed
to provide a response to local needs. In the South Bronx, informal
work means survival. In Soho, it means a fashionable lifestyle. In the
new ethnic communities dispersed about the city, informality is the
way in which people build a home far from what was once their
home. Life on Long Island or in Fairfield County (as in many North
American suburbs) largely depends on unpaid housework. But
Manhattan, with its skyscrapers of apartments and condominiums is
– even more than in any other city of the continent – designed on
the exclusive basis of paid work. The homes and workplaces of New
York thus make up a complex geography which incarnates the polar-
ities of class, sex, ethnicity and race.'*

Thus the urban dualization of New York does not reflect a simplistic distinction between the rich and the poor, and nor is it limited to contrasting images
of luxury limousines on the one hand and homeless people sprawled out on
the sidewalks on the other. More fundamentally, it reflects an urban social
structure that is based on interaction between opposite and equally dynamic
poles of the new informational economy, whose developmental logic polar-
izes society, segments social groups, isolates cultures and segregates the
uses of a metropolitan space that is shared by differing functions, classes
and ethnic groups.

Urban social dualization characterizes cities in poor countries too, where
it also stems from the segmentation of the labour market, drawn along
ethnic, sexual and educational lines. In this context a well documented statistical analysis of the social structure and the labour market in Ouagadougou,
carried out in 1992 (Lachaud, 1994), shows that 25 per cent of the active
population is unemployed, that most of those who have work are not in
regular employment, and that 58 per cent live in poverty, as measured by
average standards prevailing in Burkina Faso. There is a close link between
employment circumstances and poverty, and also between level of education
and obtaining regular employment. More significant still is that 60 per cent
of wage earners get their post through the intervention of a friend or a
member of the same ethnic group, which lends decisive weight to control of
the civil service (the chief resource-holding institution) by ethnic groups.
Access to specialized education is likewise dependent on personal relations.
And even the possibility of setting up a business, whether formal or informal
and whatever its size, depends on access to capital and to official permits,
which in turn depends on systems of contacts drawn on ethnic lines. Social
segmentation in Ouagadougou, expressed in a pattern of spatial segregation between a formal centre and an informal periphery, is governed by a
labour market that is dominated by the contradictory processes of social
exclusion and ethnic inclusion. Other African capitals show similar situations
and processes, as can be seen in Figure 2.4.

The dialectic between local development and local dualization can be
seen in a particularly clear way in the Lima of the 1990s (Chion, 1995). To
begin with, Lima experienced extraordinary economic growth during the
period 1992–95, it being directly linked to the internationalization of its
economy and the modernization of its communications and management

systems. Peru, whose economy was spiralling uncontrollably downwards in the 1980s, was the country with the highest GDP growth rate in the world in 1994 – 13 per cent – even though in absolute terms 1994's GDP was still lower than that of 1987. The economic growth was determined essentially by the sale of Peruvian assets, particularly public companies, at low prices, in a political climate that was relatively stable, and with guerrilla activity being repressed, under the controversial but effective presidency of Fujimori. Foreign capital flowed to Peru in the form of both direct asset acquisitions and Stock Exchange investments. The market capitalization of shares quoted on the Lima Stock Exchange was multiplied by ten between 1990 and 1994. International trade increased by 80 per cent between 1988 and 1990. Together with the traditional markets of South and North America, Peruvian trade was geared to the Asian Pacific, business with that area growing by 90 per cent between 1987 and 1993. In 1994 a number of Chinese companies made significant investments in Peru, notably the acquisition of Hierroperu airport by the Shougang Corporation. The Chinese government paid out 38 million dollars in loans for agricultural development. Peru's new international connections were facilitated by substantial modernization in its telecommunications in the wake of the purchase of the Peruvian state telecommunications system by the Spanish telephone company Telefonica, which invested 800 million dollars in 1994–95, installing 450,000 telephone lines and also a fibre-optic network in the business centres of the coastal cities. To set those data in perspective, it may be noted that the total number of telephone lines existing in Peru in 1993 was 611,000. At the same time, Telefonica set up new global connections through the use of a satellite shared with Argentina and Chile, whose telecom companies were also acquired by Telefonica. Two-thirds of the lines are concentrated in Lima, and the fibre-optic network serves mainly the financial district of Lima. In parallel with this, a network for scientific and technological exchange was set up in Lima, with connections to the country's main scientific centres and direct access for 450 institutions to the Internet. The Ministry of Education provided the infrastructure required through the link with the Panamsat 1 transponder. The urban space of Lima reflects this far-reaching change in the Peruvian economy. The Miraflores district, which is the traditional residential base of the upper middle classes, became consolidated as the centre for international business, with new complexes of 'intelligent' buildings, shopping centres and service providers for companies located in the area. A motorway connection to the airport facilitates its global exchange. Significantly, the councillor representing Miraflores was elected as mayor of Lima in 1995, defeating the candidate President Fujimori in the elections.

As Peru proceeded with the globalization of its economy and Lima became one of the nodes of the new South American economy, living conditions for the majority of the population in the country went on deteriorating. According to the study carried out by Figueroa, Altamirano and Sulmon (1996) for the International Labour Office (ILO), the percentage of Lima's population living below the poverty line grew from 26 per cent in 1980 to 78 per cent in 1993. According to their calculations, average monthly salaries in Lima in 1994 ranged from 7,800 dollars for senior executives, 2,500 for junior executives, 700 dollars for office workers, 300 dollars for industrial workers and 60 dollars as the minimum salary, which is earned by over half the population. Accordingly, they conclude that:

> 'We note the reinforcement of duplication in the world of work
> around the organizations of the modern sector, public and private
> alike, with higher qualifications based on higher levels of vocational
> and technical education. [At the same time] people will have to
> carry on creating their jobs in subsistence activities.'

This occupational and social duality is manifested in the urban space. Lima's outer districts, built up over decades of urban land invasion, have been consolidated and are becoming dense and overpopulated at their periphery, a 'shantification' process taking hold in the peripheral districts and particularly visible in 'Villa el Salvador', a district that was baptized 20 years ago in the populist ideology of the military regime as 'the first self-suggested city of Latin America'. Solidarity networks and religious groups are the main survival mechanisms for these urban areas whose conditions of hygiene and habitat are becoming more and more precarious and which are home to the majority of the metropolitan population of this latest node of the wealth-concentrating and managing global network. The global city and the informational city are also the dual city.

CONCLUSION: THE SPACE OF FLOWS AND THE SPACE OF PLACES

The transformation of our societies by the processes of globalization and informationalization have a spatial dimension, the empirical manifestations of which we have examined in this chapter. Yet at a deeper level what this transformation amounts to is the setting up of a new spatial logic that is characteristic of the new processes of capital accumulation, production organization, market integration, and of communication for the messages and the exercise of planetary power. We can put forward the idea that this spatial logic is characterized by domination of the space of the flows, structured in electronic circuits that link together, globally, strategic nodes of production and management (Castells, 1996a). But that logic is not the only spatial form in our societies, just the dominant one. In contrast with it we still find, as was the general rule throughout history, the space of places, as the territorial form of organization of everyday living and the form experienced by the great majority of human beings. Yet while the flow space is globally integrated, the place space is locally fragmented. One of the essential mechanisms for dominance in our historical time is the dominance of flow space over place space, giving rise to two distinct universes in which the traditional relations of exploitation are fragmented, diluted and naturalized. Cities can only be recuperated by their citizens to the extent that they rebuild, from top to bottom, the new historical relationship between function and meaning through articulating the global and the local.

Chapter 3

The City of Women

INTRODUCTION

The city, as society, has throughout history been based on the work of women, subordinated to men in the patriarchal family structure. The current processes of transformation on a planetary scale are deeply altering the relationship between city and women, raising a new set of urban problems. On the one hand, large numbers of women have been taken into paid employment, thereby altering the day-to-day organization of the city while at the same time changing power relations between sexes within the family unit. On the other hand, the accelerated process of urbanization under the new conditions of globalization has given rise to new needs in family life which, over much of the world, rest on women's ability to manage the difficulties encountered by city inhabitants in gaining access to the complex network of urban services. In some parts of the world these tasks include dealing with the school systems or the health bureaucracies, weekly shopping in the supermarket or the maintenance and repair of the household electrical infrastructure. In other urban areas, female responsibilities take in carrying of water and maintenance of public hygiene, without which the large conurbations would break down under a chain of epidemics. The 'feminization' of such tasks is clearly not a matter of natural law or eternal curse, since men can, must and should take on many of the functions outlined. Our analysis must nevertheless take the present situation as its point of departure in order – without accepting that situation – to propose paths of urban policy which help to make cities into more egalitarian social structures, more equal not only between classes but also between sexes. In this chapter we will therefore look firstly at the functions of women in the productive urban economy, and then pinpoint their specific relationship with housing. We will go on to look at the problems women encounter in urban transport and in coping with the urban infrastructure and environment. We will then look in some detail at the new problems faced by children in the city, a subject which is clearly of equal concern to men, though in the current social division of work it occupies a primordial place in the lives of women. We will look, finally, at the leading role played by women in urban social mobilizations, an essential factor in potential policies of reform of the urban condition of women which can result from such mobilizations in conjunction with the will to transform governments as they pay heed to the interests and wishes of one half of the population.

WOMEN'S WORK

One of the most significant social effects of the new global international economy has been the enormous numbers of women joining the economically active populations of all countries, both as wage-earning employees and as self-employed workers. Women have, of course, traditionally carried out socially productive work in the household and in childcare, in cultivation of the land and in the paid activities of the man/head of the family. The new factor is that – while retaining most of the activities just mentioned – the majority of women in nearly all the industrialized countries and a rapidly rising proportion in the urban economies of the developing countries have joined the employment market, as shown by the evolution of the female employment rate for selected countries between 1970 and 1994, and the proportion of women in the workforce, according to the information presented in Tables 3.1, 3.2 and 3.3.

Table 3.1 Women's Economic Activity Rate, Selected Countries

Country	1970	1994
Canada	47	63
USA	53	65
France	53	64
Spain	22	31
Italy	37	44
United Kingdom	51	60
Japan	60	64
Argentina	33	38
Brazil	27	38
Chile	27	39
Mexico	21	37
South Korea	47	52
Singapore	36	58
Malaysia	45	55
China	74	81
Botswana	61	49
South Africa	47	54
Namibia	28	30
Zimbabwe	56	49
Kenya	70	62
Zaire	65	52
Arab States	12	21
East Asia	73	80
Latin America and Caribbean	27	37
South Asia	35	35
South-East Asia and Pacific	57	56
Sub-Saharan Africa	65	58
Least Developed Countries	63	57

(Index: Males = 100)   Source: UNDP (1995)

Table 3.2 Women as a Percentage of the Labour Force

Region	Percentage
North America	38
Latin America	24
Western Europe	34
Asia	34
Africa	32
Oceania	33

Source: Vickers (1991)

By adding paid work to household work, women in all countries work more hours than men: taking 100 as the index of male working hours (paid and non-paid), the index for women is 127 for Italy, 111 for France, 112 for Columbia, 109 for Indonesia, 106 for the United States and Venezuela (UNDP, 1995).

But what specific relationship is there between the new type of economy and the mass influx of women into paid work? On the one hand, globalization has penetrated the economies of all countries, breaking down the structures of traditional sectors, commercializing life models and bringing together into large urban conurbations a proportion of the population which will soon be in the majority (Satterthwaite, 1995). But the call for mobilization of the labour reserve made up of women the world over has arisen mostly out of a rising need for labour in the new information economy (thus giving the lie to prophesies concerning structural unemployment). It is true, too, that cultural changes in women world-wide – encouraged in large measure by feminist and women's rights movements – have increased women's desire for independence, and this, in our times, involves a paid job. But even more important than this demand from women has been the offer of work from companies, government departments and production and distribution circuits. Why, though, has the expansion in employment taken on a female complexion in the new economy? Interpretations of a

Table 3.3 Women's Economic Activity Rate, 1994 (% of women in paid work)

Region	Percentage
Arab States	18
East Asia	69
Latin America and the Caribbean	30
South Asia	29
South East Asia and the Pacific	49
Sub-Saharan Africa	52
European Union	40
Nordic Countries	56

Source: UNDP (1995)

Table 3.4 Women's Non-Agricultural Wage as a per cent of Men's, Selected Countries

Country	Percentage
Tanzania	92.0
Vietnam	91.5
Australia	90.8
Sweden	89.0
Kenya	84.7
France	81.0
Italy	80.0
Brazil	76.0
Germany	75.8
USA	75.0
Mexico	75.0
United Kingdom	69.7
Thailand	68.2
Switzerland	67.6
Canada	63.0
China	59.4
South Korea	53.5
Bangladesh	42.0
Average	*74.9*

Source: UNDP (1995)

biological order, relating to the smaller physical effort required in the services economies, are pure ideology: the history of humanity has been the history of exhausting agricultural work carried out by women the world over, just as the history of industrialization has been largely written by women working in factories, except when male subcultures (such as the miners) barred women from access to direct production. It is not women's physical strength, nor their deft hands, nor their ready smiles which have brought about women's working situation. What has made women highly desirable workers in the new global information economy is their capacity to provide an equivalent service at a lower wage and under much more insecure working conditions than their male counterparts. And this is for one reason only: society's discrimination, reproduced in laws and retained by the trade unions of many countries. Table 3.4 shows the average wage differences between women and men in the mid-1990s.

But there is yet another factor still more important than wage levels: job flexibility. In a changing economy, with constant global interactions and interactions between the local and the global, companies and the employment markets have needed to free themselves from the constraints of a social legislation won through the labour disputes of industrial society. Part-time work, subcontracting, fixed contract work and the processes of informalization of the economy are essential mechanisms of the new model of flexible production. In Japan, for example, the maintenance of lifelong employment within the large companies related mainly to men, while female employment

Table 3.5 Age of Export Processing Zone (EPZ) Workers and Share of
Women in Work-Force

Country	Age of EPZ workers	Share of women in EPZ industries (%)	Share of women in non-EPZ manufacturing industries (%)
Malaysia	Average age 21.7 years	85	32.9
Brazil	Average age 21.7 years	48	24.8
Macao	88% below age 29	74	48.1
Mauritius	70% below age 25	79	10.0
Tunisia	70% below age 25	90	48.1
Philippines	88% below age 29	74	48.1
Dominican Republic	83% below age 26	68	17.6
Sri Lanka	83% below age 26	88	17.1

Source: Rosa (1994)

(with 49 per cent participation of women in the working world) occupied a secondary employment market, usually insecure and part-time, which provided companies with a cushion in times of crisis (Gelb and Pillay, 1994). The ILO's documented research into fixed contract and part-time work in the developed economies shows that this type of working relationship (the one with the fastest growth rate at the end of the century) is predominantly female (Bosch et al, 1994). In the newly industrialized countries, the role of young female labour, subjected to the dual patriarchal authority of the company and the family, has been decisive in ensuring the competitiveness of multi-nationals which have decentralized into those countries (Rosa, 1994). Table 3.5 shows the preponderance of women in the workforces of the export processing zones (EPZ) of selected countries. Research by Beneria and Roldan (1987) into the recruitment of women in Mexico's informal companies reveals the reasons behind this preference on the part of companies: women's income is considered as supplementary; fixed contract and part-time work is seen to be the rule; it is assumed that women have a more submissive attitude, accept orders more easily and have a lower tendency to join trade unions; furthermore, women do not get drunk like men and have lower absenteeism rates. The real situation, however, is more complex: after a while women do react, struggle and impose working conditions. But in so far as the companies have a large reserve of female labour available to them, recruitment of women ensures equal work for a lower wage and under more insecure conditions than for men until, with one generation passed through, recourse is had to the next.

In developing countries women make up the bulk of the work-force of the informal urban economy, the other side of globalization, a sector which is essential to ensure the life of cities over most of the world. Thus, according to the United Nations Development Programme (UNDP) (1995), in Bolivia women account for half of the workers in the informal sector and only one-quarter in the formal sector. Similarly, in the Congo and in Zambia two-thirds of informal service workers are women, while in Nigeria 94 per cent of street vendors are women. The aforementioned study by Beneria and Roldan (1987) on Mexico City shows the organization of women's informal employment in modern industrial sectors, including exporting sectors, ranging from clothesmaking and textiles through to packaging and the production of electronics accessories. The structural adjustment programme which has been rocking many developing economies has aggravated the wage and employment conditions of women, while at the same time increasing their competitive advantage over men from the companies' viewpoint, due to their greater social vulnerability. Thus in Mexico women's income compared to that of men fell from 71 per cent in 1984 to 66 per cent in 1992, while at the same time the deterioration in living conditions and cutbacks in social services have made the role of women more vital still in their contribution to family income and their day-to-day management of austerity.

The processes of informalization and globalization of the economy and the policies of business restructuring and macroeconomic adjustment have thus been largely based on massive incorporation of women into paid work, under conditions of discrimination, and in maintenance of the multiple function of women as producers and educators of children, runners of the home and agents of the organization of daily life, more important than ever under the conditions of the new model of urbanization.

WOMEN AND HOUSING

Housing policies are usually based on two increasingly questionable suppositions: that they affect men and women equally; that the basic norm of collective life is the nuclear family formed around the couple. In reality, access to housing is in turn conditioned by the difference of income and discrimination against women. And the family exists under an increasingly wide range of forms (Dandekar, 1992). In a phenomenon which is global in its scope (Aliyar and Shetty, 1992), there has in recent times been a significant increase in the number of households headed by a woman. According to Moser (1987):

> 'It is estimated that one-third of the world's households are headed by women. In urban areas, particularly in Latin America and Africa, the figure exceeds 50 per cent ... and globally, the phenomenon is on the increase.'

The failure of housing policies to take account of this phenomenon leads to discrimination against women in access to housing, for the fact of taking male income as the basis of minimum income for access to subsidized housing places considerable obstacles in the way of female households. Indeed, 70 per cent of the world's 1,300 million poor are women (UNDP, 1995). And what is more, the criteria for eligibility for subsidized housing are based on regular income from formal employment, while women's income often comes from casual work and unstable jobs. As an illustration of this, we might cite the example of the housing programme implemented in Solanda, Ecuador, started in 1982 with the aid of the United States government and aimed at 6,000 low-income families. Only 175 of the families which could opt for the programme were headed by women, and the vast majority of these could not have had access to housing had the general eligibility criteria been applied (Aliyar and Shetty, 1992).

In the United States 44.6 per cent of single mothers are poor, while a further 14.8 per cent are on the threshold of poverty (Sprague, 1991). The living conditions of female households are lower across the board than in male households in terms of the quality of the dwelling itself and security in the legal conditions of occupation (see Table 3.6).

Housing policies in societies subject to rapid processes of cultural and demographic change should be adapted to take account of the increasing diversity of types of household: traditional nuclear families, people living alone, adults sharing accommodation, and families composed of a woman or women and children. In the United States, for example, one-third of all households were headed by women in 1988, of whom 50 per cent were from ethnic minorities (Frank and Ahrentzen, 1989; Caplow et al, 1991).

Contrary to what is believed, the extended family is not only not disappearing, but is actually developing in many societies as a response to the economic crisis. An interesting study carried out in Zimbabwe in 1991 and 1992 showed a rise in the number of family dependents living in households, as a form of family solidarity in times of economic crisis (Kanji, 1995). In another context, Leal showed the family's role in cushioning the effects of high youth unemployment in Spain (Leal and Cortes, 1993). But increased numbers of family members, or offspring remaining in the parental home as adults (in Spain, the average age of emancipation has reached 27 years), shows itself in an equivalent increase in household obligations, mostly taken on by women.

Again in respect of housing, the discrimination suffered by women varies according to whether the housing is in the formal private sector, in council housing or in informal housing. In the formal private market the main obstacle is a mismatch between prices and the purchasing power of families headed by women. For example, in a study on the suburbs of the city of Durban, in South Africa, of a total of 1,600 private dwellings on the census only 15 per cent were owned by women, and even this was because these women were mostly schoolteachers and nurses receiving a government housing subsidy. By comparison, in the informal market in the same zone 40 per cent of the dwellings were in the name of women (Todes and Walker, 1992).

In the case of public housing, too, the methods of access to public or subsidized housing usually discriminate against women involuntarily, due to their being less well-informed, with less access to information sources and with restricted mobility in time and space resulting from their childcare responsibilities (Moser, 1987).

For the greater part of the world's urban population, the informal housing market is the main way of getting a roof over one's head. According to Hardoy (1992), in the 1970s, in a survey of 13 large metropolitan areas in Africa, Asia and Latin America, it was estimated that over 41 per cent of the population lived in irregular settlements. And this proportion has contin-

Table 3.6 Housing Quality, United States, by Household 1993

	All households	Female households	Female households as % of all households
Total	94,724	27,856	29.4
New construction	4990	902	18.1
Per cent	5.3	3.2	
Mobile homes	5655	1615	28.6
Per cent	6.0	5.8	
Severe Physical Problems	1901	626	32.9
Per cent	2.0	2.2	
Moderate Physical Problems	4225	1555	36.8
Per cent	4.5	5.6	

(figures in thousands)   Source: US Dept of Commerce (1995)

ued to rise over the last two decades (Fonseka and Malhota, 1994). This is the habitat for the large majority of households headed by women, a habitat characterized by scant services, difficult maintenance conditions and insecurity of legal occupation status (Moser and Peake, 1987).

But the housing difficulties of women do not come to an end when, as is still the most common situation, they belong to a family of the traditional type. The financing of housing by public institutions or financial bodies is frequently negotiated by women in their role as family managers, but they need the guarantee and signature of their husbands, even when the latter can offer no greater financial guarantees than their wives. Some international experiences, such as the Grameen Bank Project in Bangladesh, have achieved good results by centring their housing finance programmes on loans preferentially granted to women with very low incomes (Aliyar and Shetty, 1992). Servon's (1995) doctoral thesis on programmes of micro-loans for women as a way of stimulating the run down urban districts of San Francisco, New York and Boston also placed the emphasis on the greater financial responsibility of women in the administration of loans received.

The geographical location of housing within the spatial structure of the city also has an influence on the female condition, in that women have to make a day-to-day calculation of their various functions in the home, at work and in relation to services at different points of the urban area. The processes of suburbanization have placed increasing distance between city facilities and places of work and residence, forming an obstacle to the spatial-temporal organization of these functions in the daily life of women. And this in spite of the fact that in some countries, such as the United States, office work has been suburbanized to take partial account, amongst other factors, of the existence of suburban female employment markets, with women who wish to work in their zone of residence, even for lower wages, in return for simplifying their spatial life patterns (Nelson, 1984). Changes in the spatial structure of cities usually affect women more than men, precisely due to this need for daily organization of different functions. Between 1975 and 1977 in New Delhi, for example, there was mass displacement of 700,000 people living in 17 irregular settlements, and subsequent impact studies showed that women suffered much greater effects than men from this displacement. Many women, moved far from their employment, were unable to combine their housework and their jobs, and the cost of transport made it still more difficult to see to all the family business. While the men's employment rate fell by 5 per cent, that of the women fell by 27 per cent (Singh, 1980, quoted by Moser and Peake, 1987).

In much of the world, furthermore, the home is a place of paid work for women. Although this is especially the case for developing countries, the teleworking future may extend the phenomenon to the more advanced countries (Graham and Marvin, 1996). The studies by Mahajan (1992) on Bombay and by Beneria and Roldan (1987) on Mexico City show the essential role of paid home work in the industrial structure of the informal economy, while Miraftab (1992) has pointed to the link between this type of work and the large multinational companies, and Tinker (1992) showed how the production of home-cooked meals for sale is a vital part of family income and an essential mechanism in feeding the population in many of the developing world's large cities.

The importance of the home as a way of linking paid employment and housework for women is brought into question by land-use plans and municipal by-laws which impose a strict division between residential, commercial and industrial functions in many urban areas. In the Dandora Residential Project in Nairobi, for example, urban zoning restrictions were identified as the main cause of the economic deterioration of the resident families, leading to generalized delayed payment for loans received (Nimpuno-Parente, 1987). Moreover, in many other cases, the differential application of planning legislation on the location of activities is a source of discrimination against women and a constant threat to the survival of many families (Moser, 1993). It is based, in the last resort, on a failure to recognize the economic and social situation of the city, and on the utilization of that mismatch between the real city and the legal city as a source of power and, frequently, abuse of power. This statement should not be seen as a defence of the atrocious living and health conditions which frequently exist in these multi-use dwellings. But a recognition of the spatial convergence of the many activities of women should lead to an integrated industrial and services zoning in residential areas so that organization of urban life is bearable for women, while conditions are created for a new economy and a new society.

Another housing problem specific to women relates to the architecture and organization of dwelling areas. We might note, on the one hand, a reproduction of the patriarchal model of the family in organization of household space, according to the critique levied for some time by feminist architects such as Hayden (1981). But, on the other hand, it is also a matter of the scant consideration accorded the specific nature of female work in the home in the design of residential units throughout much of the world. Thus, for example, the cooking and cleaning area is frequently treated as a leftover space in many residential projects in developing countries. As a result, it is estimated that 70 million women suffer respiratory and other health problems due to high levels of household pollution from kitchen stoves (Sehgal, 1995). One study on household environment problems in Jakarta found that 28 per cent of women interviewed had respiratory illnesses, the most common causes of which were the use of firewood as the main household fuel, lack of ventilation in the kitchen, the use of toxic smokes to kill mosquitoes and the unhealthy conditions in the dwelling (Surjadi, 1993).

Other aspects of dwelling design which fail to consider the needs of women include the lack of privacy in bathing and hygiene arrangements, room layout as a function of social representation rather than functional needs, and difficulties of access to urban services in relation to the location of residential units (Bhatnagar, 1992).

The culture and traditions of each society have to be taken explicitly into account in dwelling design. As Miraftab (1992) points out in the research for her doctoral thesis from the University of California:

'The role of the home for women is even more important in Muslim societies, which favour the privacy of women ... In these cases, a lack of sensitivity on the part of designers to the role of the home for women and in relation to the different spatial needs of men and women can give rise to serious psychological effects in women. One survey on two public dwelling schemes in Tunis revealed that the design of very small interior courtyards increased the neurosis and suicide rates amongst the women living in them.'

Lack of attention to dwelling design in relation to the specific needs of women in different cultures has also been documented by Moser and Peake (1987), according to whom:

'The space and design requirements for commercial activities vary according to the cultural context. In some cases, women wish to run a shop from their main rooms, in which case they need a large room with storage facilities and different power socket outlets for appliances such as refrigerators. In other cases, especially in hot climates, what they need is a spacious verandah so that they can combine paid activities such as sewing and craft work or commercial sales with childcare.'

In the last resort, the participation of women of different cultures and urban conditions in the design of the multifunctional space which is their general lot would appear to be essential to make built zones suitable for the sex differences which lie at the foundations of urban social structure in all societies.

A View of Urban Transport, Infrastructure and Environment from the Female Condition

Although women are the primordial agents of linkage between household units and the urban structure, cities are usually developed and planned without taking account of the specific needs raised by such linkage. Urban transport planning, for example, has traditionally focused on organizing patterns of mobility between the home and the workplace, which does not permit reflection of the diversity of journeys which women have to make in taking on their many daily tasks. A study of Belo Horizonte found that urban transport was organized around the needs of men. Buses ran along routes from the outskirts into the city centre at the beginning of the day, and from centre to outskirts at the end of the working day, to transport the male work-force in regular employment. But the daily travel needs of women were much more diverse: taking the children to school, shopping, going to health services and, above all, reaching their part-time jobs over a wide spectrum of area and time, at times when there were no longer buses. This resulted in the daily travelling time of the women being three times longer than that of the men (Schmink, 1982).

The case of the United States is paradigmatic (see Box 3.1). Equipped with one of the world's most highly developed transport systems – though one centred on the automobile – mobility in metropolitan areas has reached crisis point since, over the last two decades, women began a generalized taking up of employment (without leaving aside many of their previous responsibilities), coming into contradiction with a transport system organized around the needs of white middle-class males. As in the case of Brazil mentioned above, the urban mobility of the vast majority of men is structured around the journey between home and workplace. Women, on the other hand, must undertake different tasks and fit them all in on the trip to and from work, for which reason they need a much more flexible means of transport which is, nowadays, the car. The incorporation of women into employment has therefore multiplied the number of vehicles on the urban freeways, leading increasingly to their saturation. Transport statistics show that women make many more intermediate stops than men along their routes between home and workplace (McKnight, 1994). Furthermore, the traditional suburban model of the American city has entered functional crisis in that it was implicitly based on a full-time driver able to provide mobility for the entire family (taking the husband to the suburban railway station and picking him up after work, taking the children to and from school and their various activities, doing the shopping in large stores, carrying out the necessary paperwork and other procedures for the entire family at various points of the metropolitan structure). Only with this family mobility taken on individually by the housewife could the suburbs extend and ensure the daily life quality today yearned for by the middle-classes of many countries (even those that did not experience it, but contemplated it in the idealized view portrayed in Hollywood productions). But when those housewives became, in addition, workers with set times and places, American women could not continue to provide their services as family driver, and this situation meant a reconversion of the metropolitan transport structure in which connection between the suburbs, and not only the link between centre and outskirts, enforced the construction of new freeways and the development of a denser fabric of collective intra-metropolitan transport.

Similar trends have been observed in European countries. A study carried out in France showed the influence of transport on women's work, chosen to cut distance from the home containing the children to the care of whom

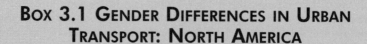

Box 3.1 Gender Differences in Urban Transport: North America

Difference between men and women drivers in annual mileage in the US, 1983

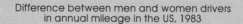
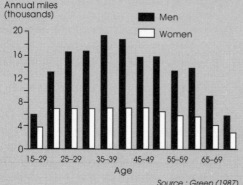

Source : Green (1987)

Drivers Licenses by gender

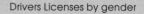
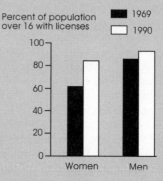

Source : McKnight (1994)

Percentage of Parents who link trips to work

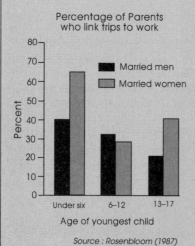

Age of youngest child

Source : Rosenbloom (1987)

Percentage of Parents who make trips solely for their children

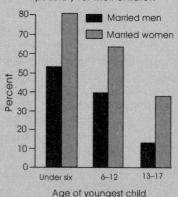

Age of youngest child

Source : Rosenbloom (1987)

The transport system in North American cities is based on providing mobility of services workers from the residential suburbs to the city centres and the metropolitan nodes where most jobs are still concentrated. The strict spatial separation between residence and work has made it difficult for women to travel daily to their work in addition to taking their children to school and going shopping and carrying out other tasks. The result is that women now use cars almost as much as men, as is shown by convergence in the number of driving licences between both sexes. Men drive almost double the annual mileage of women, but women make more trips per day (3.13) than men (3.05). Indeed, women (whose employment rate is still lower than that of men) make fewer journeys to work but more trips for personal and family reasons. A typical pattern of mobility for a woman is one of daily trips with various stops, carrying out various errands and taking family members to and from work/school. Women make many more children-related trips than do men. One reason is the aforesaid pattern of trips with several stops, which is easier with a car, given the scant flexibility of public transport systems, organized around journeys between home and work. But another powerful reason is the feeling, and the reality, of being much more exposed than men to insecurity on public transport. In New York, 52% of women are afraid of using public transport after 8 o'clock in the evening.

mothers still devoted much of their attention. Thus, women with at least one child younger than 14 years old had an average weekly travelling time to work of 3 hours and 15 minutes, compared with 4 hours and 5 minutes for women without young children, and 4 hours and 45 minutes for men (Grieco et al, 1989). In England, men have a much higher proportion of work-related travel than women (except, significantly, among the younger ages of both sexes, when the women have not yet married), while the women have a much greater frequency of journeys for other activities (see Table 3.7).

In short, the city of women is temporally and spatially diverse, calling for a flexible and dense transport structure, in contradiction with most metropolitan transport systems organized around the regulated working day of traditional male employment. However, as the economy, society and job market become increasingly oriented towards flexibility and diversification of times, spaces and activities, there would seem to be some convergence between the interests inherent in the female condition and the most likely future outlook for urban transport. If the suburbs of the developed countries'

Table 3.7 United Kingdom: Percentage of Journeys Made by Men and Women for Various Purposes, by Age

Journey Purpose	Age 16–20	Age 21–29	Age 30–59	Age 60–64	Age 65 and over
Journey to work					
Men	25	31	35	33	5
Women	25	19	22	10	2
Shopping/Personal					
Men	20	22	24	29	53
Women	26	35	40	55	62
Escort and other					
Men	1	3	6	4	2
Women	1	11	8	1	1

Source: Hamilton and Jenkins (1989)

large metropolitan areas depend for their expansion on the work of women as agents of urban mobility, many territorial conglomerations in the developing countries depend on women's work for their more day-to-day survival. Indeed, the insufficient urban infrastructure of water, electricity, sanitation and basic services means that families largely depend for their supplies on the work of women, who thus become indispensable agents of management of the current process of accelerated urbanization. In Mozambique, women spend 15 hours a week transporting water, while in Senegal they spend 17.5 hours on that task (UNDP, 1995). Another study in India assessed women's work in providing water for their families at four hours daily (Bhatnagar, 1992). A group of researchers analysing the condition of women in Ecuador in 1992 noted that the school attendance figures amongst the young girls in state schools fell sharply each time water or electricity supplies were cut, the girls being recruited immediately by their families to obtain and transport water and/or solve other problems deriving from the lack of urban services (Moser and Peake, 1987). And numerous studies in irregular urban settlements the world over point up the decisive role of women in coping with the health conditions deriving from the lack of drainage networks, preventing epidemics of even greater proportions than those which do in fact arise (see Box 3.2).

Management of an urban environment on the edge of ecological catastrophe is perhaps the greatest responsibility taken on by women in many of our world's cities. When we consider that in Brazil only 3 per cent of urban waste is suitably treated (Blanc, 1994), that in Bangkok 25 per cent of solid waste is not collected (Hardoy et al, 1990), that in Khartoum only 20 per cent of the population has the use of some kind of latrine (Omer, 1990), and that in 1988 there were 170 million urban inhabitants without access to water and 331 lacking sanitary facilities of any type, then day-to-day survival depends on family discipline and the attention to survival provided by the women of such settlements. The constant struggle against dirt, the creation of clean zones around the dwelling, constant sterilization of water and foodstuffs, the education of children and husbands, the discipline imposed on the household community, are daily actions tirelessly repeated in an ongoing battle against environmental decay and for the dignity of the habitat.

THE CITY OF CHILDREN

Children are the responsibility of men and women alike and, in the last resort, of society as a whole, which creates or destroys their future through the care taken of those children. The social division of work in the patriarchal system which characterizes our societies nevertheless means that the production, care and upbringing of children form an essential part of the city of women as it exists at present. All the more so when urban childhood is currently at a critical juncture.

Indeed, the mass incorporation of women into paid work and the attendant limitation on their availability for the care of children has not, barring a few exceptions, been accompanied by a greater responsibility of men in their parental duties or by society's recognition of the need to institutionalize childcare, at least in the market economies. The socialist economies, which needed full mobilization of the female workforce, took on the socialization of childcare, while at the same time retaining the family structure. But in so far as market mechanisms have extended throughout the world by the process of globalization, and the welfare state has been stricken with crisis by a downward levelling of the rules of competition, kindergarten, school and child welfare have been subjected to heavy pressure in the world as a whole. The situation is of course more critical still for poor children and for children in the large cities of the developing countries. A major United Nations Children's Fund (UNICEF) report on urban children, Blanc (1994), noted a worrying scenario:

> 'The current social transformations and conditions in the world are creating a youth population which is relatively unhealthy, despondent and disturbed, which is growing up with problems of social adaptation which are more severe than ever. Social decline is chronic in the urban areas of the developing world ... Urban children are more likely now than in 1980 to be born into poverty, to be premature, to die in their first year of life, to be underweight at birth, and to have mothers who have received no prenatal care. They are also more likely to have unemployed or severely underemployed parents, to see their parents die or go to prison, to live in a single-parent family, to live in a substandard dwelling, to suffer physical abuse, to leave primary school early, to never go to secondary school and still less to university. They are also more likely to work in an exploitative environment, to take drugs, to engage in prostitution, to be exposed to street violence and to suffer armed conflicts.'

In the United States, since the 1960s, one child in five lives in poverty, and the proportion continues to rise. This poverty affects nearly half of black children (4.3 million) and one-sixth of white children (8.1 million). Infant mortality in the ethnic minority districts of New York or Washington is as high or higher than in the Latin American countries. The number of single mothers is rising at a dizzying rate, and single mothers are nine times more likely to be poor than young women living alone without children (Blanc, 1994). There is a direct relationship between poverty, residence in the run down urban areas of the large American cities, dropping out of school, membership of gangs, drug trafficking and use and violence, including armed violence, increasingly frequent amongst adolescents.

A combination of crisis and economic restructuring, accelerated urbanization and family disintegration have created a massive phenomenon of child labour in the world, together with millions of children living in the streets some or all of the time (see Box 3.3). Although these different phenomena are not equivalent, together they make up a scenario of increasing infantilization of urban poverty which constitutes perhaps the most flagrant denial of the notion of progress in a segregating global economy. As a proportion of the representative sample of urban children, the aforementioned UNICEF study puts the number of children living on their own resources in the streets in various censused countries at 11 per cent in the Philippines, between 2 and 16 per cent (according to widely varying

Box 3.2 Invisible Work: Women as Free Providers of Urban Services and Household Supplies

Women carry out much of the work which makes cities function and keeps households running, but most of their efforts are scantly acknowledged and rarely paid. If all unpaid labour, most of which is women's unpaid labour, was included in national accounting procedures, it would account for an estimated 72 per cent of GDP in Australia, 53 per cent in Germany and 45 per cent in Finland. The UNDP has estimated that if unpaid work was accounted for at the average wage-rate for each country, then the overall global gross product would rise by US$16 trillion, of which $11 trillion would correspond to the invisible work of women (UNDP, 1995).

In the cities of the developing world, where much of the population does not have access to water and sanitation, women supply the basic services of the urban infrastructure, such as obtaining water and fuel, carrying out waste treatment and ensuring sanitation where there is no sewer system. Thus, for example, while in many lower-class settlements families cook and get heat from firewood, municipal ordinances usually prohibit cutting firewood for ecological reasons. The result is that women have to undertake arduous and frequently illegal work to get firewood, for there is no alternative to it as a household fuel (Lee Smith and Trujillo, 1992). Women have also organized inter-family solidarity in settlements in order to survive in times of crisis. In Lima in 1989, for example, it was estimated that there existed some 3,000 communal kitchens run by women, together with 7,000 'glass of milk committees' for the children in the shanty towns (Barrig, 1991).

GNP Gender Gap

Country	1990 GNP per capita ($)	Women's unpaid labour ($)	Adjusted GNP per capita ($)
Guatemala	910	649	1,559
Thailand	1,470	345	1,815
Algeria	2,360	1,976	4,336
USSR	8,865	1,598	10,463
United States	21,970	6,443	28,413
Sweden	24,060	5,257	29,317

Percentage of Urban Population with Access to Water and Sanitation Services in Selected Asian Countries		
Country	% access to water	% access to sanitation services
China	85	
India	76	31
Indonesia	60	40
Republic of Korea	90	100
Philippines	49	
Thailand	67	84
Vietnam	67	48

Source: UNICEF (1995)

estimates) in Brazil, 27 per cent in Nairobi, 10 per cent in Mexico, 20 per cent in Honduras, etc (Blanc, 1994). These children leave their homes incapable of bearing situations of violence and family breakdown, frequently drawn by the friends already living in the streets and forming their support group. Once in the street they work (including work as beggars), frequently searching through rubbish or as street sellers, almost always on behalf of adults who employ them. They are exposed to all kinds of physical, sexual and economic abuse, and even in some cases to human hunts, such as have occurred in Bogotá and Rio. But the phenomenon of children in the street goes far beyond that of children abandoned or who have fled their homes. There are tens of millions who, while living more or less regularly with their families, work in the street, bringing back the bulk of their earnings to their families and engaging in a number of tasks, the main ones of which are shown in Table 3.8.

The main impact of their presence in the streets is their absence from school, with the waste of human resources this represents. In India, for example, 60 per cent of the urban children interviewed had never attended school; in Kenya, three-quarters of those interviewed were out of school and most had left school at the primary level; in the Philippines, half were not in school; in Brazil, three-quarters were in school, but very behind in their studies (Blanc, 1994). Some categories of children are subjected to particularly tough conditions. The UNICEF report specifically mentions three of these: child houseworkers, who are kept by medium- and high-income families under a system of servitude, living in the house and submitted to constant demands for services of all types in exchange for their survival; the children of building workers who follow their parents from site to site in different cities, living with them, often at the construction site itself; and children engaged in prostitution. Child prostitution is a widespread and growing phenomenon in many cities in the developing countries, and in some cases, such as Bangkok and Manila, is organized as part of specialized tourist circuits in the new global market for specialized goods and services (see Box 3.4).

Box 3.3 Street Children: Brazil

Brazilian cities became sadly famous in the 1980s for the thousands of children who thronged their streets seeking out their subsistence apparently on the fringes of their families. Empirical studies carried out nevertheless showed that most of these street children were not abandoned, but were simply poor and contributed to the family income with the agreement and support of their parents, naturally to the detriment of their education. Almost all these children return to their homes at the end of the day of work in the street. On the basis of another study Lusk (1989) set out a typology of the street children of Rio de Janeiro: a) children living with their families and working in the street on behalf of the family (21.4 per cent of the total surveyed); b) children who retain links with their families, but who work in the street independently and occasionally sleep in the street (50.5 per cent); c) children of homeless families, who live with their families in the street (13.6 per cent); d) children who live in the street without contact with their families (14.6 per cent). This last category of children is older in average age and does not usually go to school; 60 per cent engage in illegal activities and 80 per cent take drugs.

Street children are particularly vulnerable to violence. Murder and suicide are in fact the most common causes of death amongst Brazilian adolescents. A reliable study found that in São Paulo, Rio and Recife, 457 street children were killed between March and August of 1989. Many of the killings were related to drug trafficking in the streets, since the children are frequently used as intermediaries by the traffickers, so that they can operate without risk and at low cost. In other cases, para-police groups and 'right thinking' persons determined to 'clean up the streets' kill children in order to frighten poor people off.

Sources: Rizzini et al (1994); Cupertino (1990)

On a more general level, there is the survival of non-regulated child labour in large companies, in family businesses and in the services sector of the informal urban economy, in proportions of some 100 million jobs, to take an average of the various estimates made. This phenomenon represents a backward step with respect to the labour legislation achieved in the workers' struggles of the early period of industrialization (ILO, 1991). An ILO estimate of the minimum numbers involved is shown in Table 3.9.

Taken as a whole, these social conditions experienced by the urban children of a large part of the world show themselves in a number of serious physical, psychological and social effects which are summed up by the UNICEF report.

The main problem in drawing up urban policies to remedy the situation lies in it being impossible to legislate for poverty. The labour of urban children is an essential part of the survival strategies of the poor in many of the world's cities. Leaving home early, dropping out of school, early

Table 3.8 Work Activities, Place and Structure of Work of Street Children and Working Children Living at Home

Sector	Street children (on their own) On streets	Working children (living at home)	
		On streets	Not on streets***
Vendor			
Lottery tickets	▲	▲	
Newspapers	▲	▲	
Food (sweets, peanuts, candy)**	●▲	●▲	●
Other small items**	●▲	●	●
Flowers** (F)		●	
Pottery and other handicrafts**	●	●	●
Illegal items (drugs,** home-brewed beer,** contraband cigarettes, counterfeited or stolen goods)	●▲	●▲	●▲
Services			
Car washer, windshield cleaner (M)	●	●	
Parking attendant (M)	●		
Shoe shiner (M)	●	●	
Shop helper*	▲	▲	▲
Stevedore (M)	●▲	●▲	
Delivery boy (M)	●		
Scavenger and garbage sorter (steel, plastic, paper, rags, bottles, etc)	●▲	●▲	
Mechanic (M)		▲	
Domestic worker (F)*		▲	
Surrogate mother (F)			●
Prostitute (M/F)*	●▲	●▲	●▲
Other			
Member of crime syndicate	●▲	●▲	
Pickpocket and purse snatcher	●▲	●▲	
Beggar	●	●	

* Activity usually carried out in the homes/work places of other people; ** also home-based production (including piece work); *** activity carried out in the home and immediate community; (M) prevalently male occupations; (F) prevalently female occupations; ▲ predominantly with employer; ● predominantly self-employed.

Source: Country studies

BOX 3.4 CHILD PROSTITUTION: A NEW GLOBAL INDUSTRY

Child prostitution has received a new boost in the large cities of the developing world as a joint result of processes of globalization of wealth and localization of poverty. Recent years have seen the creation of companies in the rich world which organize 'sex tours' in Asia and Latin America. Amongst the most popular destinations of this new industry are Thailand, the Philippines, Brazil, Colombia and Benin. In Thailand, the number of boy and girl prostitutes (including minors of under eighteen years) is estimated at 800,000. Sri Lanka has 10,000 child prostitutes, many of them in the service of foreign men.

Fear of AIDS is contributing to raise the price of virginity, thereby reducing the age of sexual initiation, in many cases right down to eight years. International reports point to the sale of thousands of children in India and Bangladesh to brothels and Middle East pornographic companies. Often, as in Calcutta, girls are prostituted by their prostitute mothers, taking the latters' places when age puts them out of work. There is documentation for many countries of sale or hire of children by their own families to intermediaries of the sex industry. Medical reports on Asia and Latin America point to a significant increase of venereal diseases amongst under fourteens. Taken as a whole, the child sex industry generates thousands of millions of dollars and is expanding fast.

Source: Blanc et al (1994)

pregnancies, addiction to drugs, alcohol or glue, and gang violence, are direct consequences of the premature exposure of still-delicate beings to the daily harshness of our cities.

Going beyond poverty, children of all social conditions and in almost all urban contexts find their existence frequently ignored in the design of cities and in the organization of urban services. The studies of child care carried out at Massachusetts Institute of Technology (MIT) and Berkeley by the city planner Michael Southworth show the need for childrens' autonomy in use of the city, though indeed within a network of protection. In cities where mobility is car-based, children and young people are deprived of urban diversity, except in controlled family situations. Children's playgrounds are set out in modules preconceived by bureaucracies and frequently antiquated, without any real knowledge of the evolutive psychology of boys and girls at various stages of development and in different societies. When cities such as Barcelona and Paris take initiatives in running festive street activities or educational play areas designed for children, the citizens immediately feel the positive effects of such services on the quality of city life in general. One symbolic gesture was the reopening of Sarajevo to urban life at Christmas 1995, led by a troupe of clowns and mimics from Barcelona, who managed to bring children's laughter back to the streets of a city tortured by years of warfare.

Table 3.9 Labour Force Participation of Children 10–14 Years Old

Region	% of children	Total number (thousands)
Africa	22.0	16,681
Americas	7.9	4,723
Asia	15.3	49,287
Europe	0.3	90
Oceania	6.9	148
World Total	13.7	70,929

Source: Grootaert and Kanbur (1995)

Cities have throughout history been built with scant consideration for the specific needs of children, and modern city planning has in general added only a few symbolic elements in the form of city gardens and nurseries. And in recent times the uncontrolled urbanization linked with the new global economy has taken still further the negation of the urban existence of children by forcing them into the productive world of adults in conditions of servitude, or by casting them into the street without the protection needed for childhood. Amongst the urban middle-classes, the television is often the main childcare facility, as women's incorporation into the working world outside the home has not been acknowledged socially with any parallel development of urban services for children. The city of children, as present-day negation and future promise, is thus one of the most important challenges facing cities worldwide, with different problems and different levels of dramatism according to the levels of development and family conditions.

WOMEN, URBAN SOCIAL MOVEMENTS AND LOCAL POLITICS

The social division of work, reserving for men the productive and power spheres and for women management of overall daily life, has had the paradoxical effect that in various times, zones and cultures women have been, and are, the main figures in community organizations and urban social movements at the foundations of local politics (Castells, 1983; Massolo, 1992). This relationship between women and territorial and urban pressure groups has been further reinforced in recent times by the rapid process of urbanization and by disturbance of the traditional patterns of family life. Not only are community organizations platforms of pressure to obtain services, but they also form the basis of the solidarity and support networks to which women have recourse to overcome daily difficulties in running the home and, above all, in child care (Miraftab, 1992).

Popular resistance to technocratic economic adjustment policies in many countries in the 1980s (the 'revolts against the International Monetary Fund', as they were termed in the classic study by Walton in 1990) were likewise headed by women, in movements such as those in Santo Domingo in 1984 and 1985, Brazil in 1983, Chile in 1983–85 (Datta, 1990) and Mexico City in 1988–90 (Massolo, 1992).

Table 3.10 Women in Local Politics: Municipalities or Equivalent, Selected Countries

Country	Female Council Members (1990–94) (%)	Female Mayors (1990–94) (%)
Industrialized Countries		
France	17	5
Germany	20	–
Japan	3	0
New Zealand	35	13
Norway	28	23
Russian Federation	30	0
United Kingdom	25	–
USA	21	16
European Union	16	5
Nordic Countries	29	17
OECD	16	6
Developing Countries		
Cuba	14	5
Ghana	8	–
Indonesia	12	1
Republic of Korea	1	–
Mexico	–	3
Mozambique	27	–
Nicaragua	13	10
Paraguay	10	5
Philippines	13	8
South Africa	–	6
Thailand	6	7
Venezuela	16	6
Vietnam	22	–

Source: UNDP (1995)

A new phenomenon of social organization linked with the conditions of the new informal urban economy also has women as its protagonists. These are the associations of homeworkers set up to claim their rights and enhance their negotiating capacity with the networks of companies which subcontract them. In India, for example, the Khadi and Village Industries Commission (KVIC) organizes women who work from home in the textile, leather, food processing and even electronics industries, being particularly active in the state of Kerala. A similar organization, the Self-Employed Women's Association, organizes homeworking women in Ahmedabad, combining labour claims with the cooperative movement and requests to the municipality relating to housing and urban services (Kusow, 1992). It should be noted that Ahmedabad is one of Asia's urban nuclei of fastest economic growth in the 1990s, as an expression of the new global organization of the Indian economy, thus underlining the direct relationship between economic stimulation, computerization of production and new forms of social mobilization. A similar type of organization of women tailoring workers arose in Mexico City in the second half of the 1980s, the Union of 19th September, to obtain economic compensation for the damage caused by the 1985 earthquake (Rowbotham and Mitter, 1994). In another context, the new information technologies permit at the same time the extension of homeworking and the organization of working women in Holland, where the Union of Women Homeworking Support Centres provide help and information to 166,000 industrial women homeworkers (Tate, 1994).

The mobilization of women through urban movements could show itself gradually in greater female influence on local politics, though we are still far from equality in this field (Nelson and Chowdhury, 1994). Table 3.10 shows the proportion of women mayors and town councillors out of the total respective populations of selected countries. It can be seen that of the countries analysed, in different contexts and with different levels of development, only Norway exceeds 20 per cent of women mayors, and only Russia and New Zealand have some 30 per cent of women town councillors. On average, in the OECD countries only 6 per cent of mayors and 16 per cent of town councillors are women. It would nevertheless seem reasonable to think that only a greater direct presence of women in municipal government bodies could carry forward the construction of a city which, unlike the present-day city, would also be a city of women.

Chapter 4
The Multicultural City

INTRODUCTION

Our world is ethnically and culturally diverse, and cities concentrate and express that diversity. In the face of the homogeneity affirmed and imposed by the State throughout history, most civil societies have historically been formed on the basis of a multiplicity of ethnic groups and cultures which have generally resisted bureaucratic pressures in the direction of cultural standardization and 'ethnic cleansing' (see Box 4.1). Even in societies which are highly homogeneous ethnically, such as the Japanese and Spanish societies, regional (or national, in the Spanish case) cultural differences mark out territorially specific traditions and ways of life which are reflected in diverse behaviour patterns and, at times, in intercultural tension and conflict (Alonso Zaldivar and Castells, 1992). The management of this tension and the building of peaceful coexistence based on respect for differences have been and remain amongst the most important challenges facing all societies. And the concentrated expression of that cultural diversity, of the attendant tensions and of the wealth of possibilities which is also contained in that diversity is perfectly manifested in cities, the receptacles and melting pot of cultures which combine in the construction of a common citizen project.

In the last years of the twentieth century, the globalization of the economy and the acceleration of urbanization processes have increased the ethnic and cultural diversity of cities through national and international migration processes which lead to the interpenetration of populations and dissimilar ways of life within the sphere of the world's main metropolitan areas. The global becomes localized, in a socially segmented and spatially segregated manner, by human movements provoked by the destruction of old productive methods and the creation of new centres of activity. The territorial differentiation of the two processes – that of creation and that of destruction – increases the unequal development of regions and countries and brings a growing diversity to the urban social structure. In this chapter we will analyse the process of formation of ethnic-cultural diversity in its new manifestations and the consequences of this diversity for the running of cities.

GLOBALIZATION, MIGRATORY MOVEMENTS AND URBANIZATION

The acceleration of the urbanization process in the world is largely due to an increase in rural-urban migratory movements, frequently caused by the expulsion of agricultural workers as a result of modernization of tasks, though it is also a result of industrialization processes and of growth of the informal economy in the metropolitan areas of the developing countries (Papademetriou and Martín, eds, 1991; UNDIESA, 1991; Kasarda and Parnell, eds, 1993). Although the statistics vary from country to country, Findley's (1993) calculations for a number of developing countries (see Table 4.1) indicate on average that, while from 1960 to 1970 the contribution of rural-urban emigration to urban growth was 36.6 per cent, over the 1975 to 1990 period this rose to 40 per cent of the new urban population, and the contribution to metropolitan growth, in both periods, was greater still. In almost all countries, the influx into the cities of emigrants from rural zones markedly accentuates the cultural diversity and, in ethnically varied countries like the United States and Brazil, the ethnic diversity.

Globalization has also given rise to major population shifts between countries, although international migratory movements are complex in pattern and do not follow the stereotyped views held by public opinion. Thus, almost half of the 80 million international migrants in the whole world are concentrated in Sub-Saharan Africa and the Middle East (Campbell, 1994). Some 35 million migrants are to be found in Sub-Saharan Africa, making up 8 per cent of its total population. These migratory movements in Africa are of two types. On the one hand, there is the migration of workers, on their way to countries of greater economic dynamism, especially South Africa, the Ivory Coast, Gambia and Nigeria. On the other hand there are extensive migratory movements of refugees from hunger, war and genocide, in the Sahel, in the horn of Africa, in Mozambique, in Rwanda and Burundi, amongst other zones; in 1987 alone, it was estimated that 12.6 million people were displaced by wars or catastrophes in Africa (Russell et al, 1990). In Asia, Malaysia is the country with highest immigration, with almost one million foreign workers, mostly from Indonesia. Japan, too, has nearly one million foreigners on the census, and several thousand illegal workers whose numbers are rising fast; most of the foreigners in Japan, however, are Koreans who have been living in the country for several generations. Singapore has some 300,000 immigrants, who account for a high proportion of its population, while Hong Kong, Korea and Taiwan have smaller contingents, of less than 100,000 each. As the development of these countries continues apace, however, and demographic pressure mounts in China, India and Indonesia, an increase of international migration is to be expected, this in addition to the increase of rural-urban migration throughout Asia. Thus, while in 1975 Japan had an annual immigration of some 10,000 foreigners, by 1990 that figure had risen to some 170,000 per year, most of them from Korea (Stalker, 1994).

Latin America, a land of immigration during the twentieth century, has gradually become an area of emigration. While during the 1950 to 1964 period the region as a whole had a net migratory balance of +1.8 million

Box 4.1 A Multicultural World

Country	Ethnic Groups	Language
Angola	Ovimbundu 37%; Kimbundu 25%; Bakongo 13%	Portugese; various Bantu languages
Argentina	White 85% (Spanish, Italian); Mestizos, Indians	Spanish, English, Italian
Australia	Caucasian 95%; Asian 4%; Aborigines 1%	English, Aboriginal languages
Brazil	Mulatto 49%; Caucasian 23% (Portugese, Italians, Germans); Black 17%	Portugese; Spanish, French
Canada	British 40%; French 27%, other European 20%; Indigenous 1.5%	English, French
Chile	European and Euro-Indian 95%; Indian 3%	Spanish
China	Han Chinese 91.9%; Mongol; Korean; Manchu; others	Mandarin; Yue; We; Hakka; Xiang; Gan; Minbei; Minnan
Côte d'Ivoire	Baoule 23%; Bete 18%; Senoufou 15%; Malinke 11%	French; Dioula; Akan; Kru; Voltaic; Malinke
Cuba	Mulatto 51%; White 37%; Black 11%	Spanish
France	Large majority European; significant North African minority	French; Breton, Alsatian German, Flemish, Basque, Catalan
Germany	German 95%	German
Guatemala	Mestizos 56%; Indian 44%	Spanish; Mayan languages
India	Indo-Aryan groups 72%; Dravidian 25%; Mongoloid 3%	16 languages, including Hindi and English
Indonesia	Javanese 45%; Sudanese 14%; Madurese 7.5%; Malay 7.5%	Bahasa Indonesian (Malay); English; Dutch; Javanese
Malaysia	Malay 59%; Chinese 32%; Indian 9%	Malay; English; Chinese
Mexico	Mestizo 60% American Indian 30%; Caucasian 9%	Spanish; Amerindian languages
Peru	Indian 45%; Mestizo 37%; White 15%; Black, Asian	Spanish; Quechua; Aymara
Senegal	Wolof 36%; Serer 17%;	French; Wolof; Serer;

	Fulani 17%; Diola 9%; Tousouieur 9%; Mandingo 9%	Peul; Tukulor
Singapore	Chinese 77%; Malay 15%; Indian 6%	Chinese; Malay; Tamil; English
South Africa	Black 75%; White 14%; Coloured 9%; Indian 3%	Afrikaans; English; Nguni, Sotho languages
Spain	Spanish 72.8%; Catalan 16.4%; Galician 8.2%; Basque 2.3%	Spanish; Catalan; Galician; Basque
United Kingdom	English 81.5%; Scottish/Irish/ Welsh 14%; Indian/West Indian/ Pakistani over 2%	
United States	White non-Hispanic 74.1%; Black 12.5%; Hispanic 9.9%; Asian/Pacific Islanders 3.5%; American Indian 1%	English; Spanish
Venezuela	Mestizo 67%; White 21%; Black 10%; Indian 2%	Spanish

Source: United Nations Centre for Human Rights (1991)

people, by the period 1975 to 1985 that balance had become negative, at −1.6 million. The most significant changes were the drastic reduction of immigration to Argentina and the considerable increase of emigration from Mexico and Central America, towards the United States in particular. Now, at the end of this century, immigration movements in Latin America are generally from other Latin American countries; in Uruguay in 1991, for example, of the total of foreign residents, 40 per cent were from Argentina, 29 per cent from Brazil and 11 per cent from Chile. The highest proportion of foreign population is to be found in Venezuela (7.2 per cent), followed by Argentina (6.8 per cent).

In the more developed countries, in Western Europe and in the United States, there exists amongst the population a feeling of there having been an unprecedented influx of immigrants over the last decade, a genuine invasion in the terminology of some of the media. The figures show a different situation, however, varying between countries and historical moments (Stalker, 1994). It is true that unequal development at a world scale, economic and cultural globalization and transport systems favour large shifts of population. To this must be added the exoduses provoked by wars and disasters, as in the case of Europe the pressure of the peoples of Eastern Europe, who now enjoy the freedom to travel while at the same time suffering the impact of the economic crisis. But immigration control, strengthening of frontiers between the OECD countries and the rest of the world, the falling rate of job creation in Europe and the increasing xenophobia in all societies pose formidable obstacles to the shift of population which could result from the trends mentioned above. Let us look, therefore, at the real profile of recent migration from the South and the East to the North and the West.

Table 4.1 World's Foreign-Born Population by Region, 1965–1985

Region	Millions of persons		Percentage of total population	
	1965	1985	1965	1985
World	75.9	105.5	2.3	2.2
Industrial countries	31.0	47.4	3.5	4.5
Europe	15.6	23.0	3.5	4.7
Former Soviet Union	0.1	0.2	0.1	0.1
North America	12.7	20.4	6.0	7.8
Oceania	2.6	3.9	14.8	16.0
Low- and middle- income countries	45.0	58.1	1.9	1.5
Caribbean and Central America	0.5	0.9	2.0	2.7
China	0.3	0.3	0.0	0.0
East and South East Asia	7.6	7.5	1.9	1.2
North Africa and West Asia	5.5	13.4	4.0	5.7
Gulf Cooperation Council States	0.7	5.8	11.0	34.2
South America	5.4	5.6	2.4	1.5
South Asia	18.7	19.2	2.8	1.8
Sub-Saharan Africa	7.1	11.3	3.0	2.7

Source: United Nations (1994)

In the United States, a society made up of successive waves of immigration, there has indeed been a major increase of immigrants in absolute numbers since reform of the immigration law in 1965 to permit immigration for reasons of family reunification. But even so, as shown in Figure 4.1, current levels of immigration trail very far behind the historical peak reached between 1904 and 1914 (in which year 1.2 million immigrants arrived in the United States). Furthermore, while in terms of the proportion of the population those 1.2 million immigrants in 1914 were equivalent to 1.5 per cent of the population, total immigration in 1992 represented only 0.3 per cent of the population. What has changed substantially, however, is the ethnic make-up of the immigration, which instead of coming from Europe and Canada, now comes for the most part from Mexico, the Caribbean and other Latin American countries and Asia (see Figure 4.2). A similar phenomenon has taken place in other countries such as Canada and Australia characterized, like the United States, by having higher proportions of foreign immigrants in their populations. In Canada in 1992 over 40 per cent of immigrants came from Asia, particularly from Hong Kong, while only 2.8 per cent came from the United Kingdom. Vancouver, Canada's third largest city, has been transformed over the last decade by the arrival of 110,000 Hong Kong Chinese, taking the proportion of Chinese population to 27 per cent of the city's residents. That immigration, by the way, has meant an inflow of 4,000 million dollars per year into the local economy. In Australia

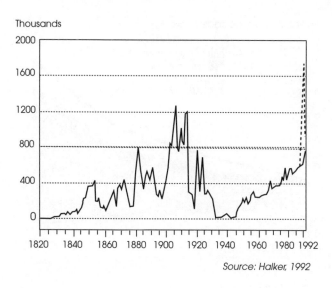

Thousands

Source: Halker, 1992

Figure 4.1 United States, immigration 1820–1992

in the 1990s, 21 per cent of the population was born abroad, and 40 per cent have at least one parent born abroad. Of the new immigrants who arrived in Australia in 1992, 15 per cent came from Asia.

Western Europe presents a diversified picture in respect of migratory movements. Taking as an indicator the percentage of the foreign resident population in relation to the total population, and observing its evolution between 1950 and 1990 (Table 4.2), we can see that France and England, for example, had a lower proportion of foreign population in 1990 than in 1982, while Belgium and Spain had shown hardly any variation (from 9.0 to 9.1 per cent, and remaining at 1.1 per cent, respectively). If we leave aside the anomalous case of Luxembourg, the only European country whose foreign population exceeds 10 per cent is Switzerland, also a special case due to the high degree of internationalization of its economy. And the average for the total European population is only 4.5 per cent of foreigners. The most significant increases during the 1980s took place in Germany, Austria, Holland and Sweden, basically due to influxes of refugees from Eastern Europe. But this influx, too, would appear to be much more limited than the Western European countries had feared. A European Commission report (Council of Europe, 1993) for example, estimated that 25 million citizens from Russia and the Soviet republics might emigrate to Western Europe by the year 2000. Now, however, in the middle of the 1990s, it is estimated that Russian emigration is around 200,000 people per year, this despite the frightful economic crisis which Russia is going through. For those acquainted with the mechanisms of emigration, the reason is simple: emigrants travel by means of previously established contact networks, which means that the colonial metropolises are the places which receive the waves of immigrants from their former colonies (France and the Maghreb, for example). Then there are the countries which deliberately recruit cheap labour in selected countries (Germany in Turkey and Yugoslavia, for

Arrivals in each decade (millions)

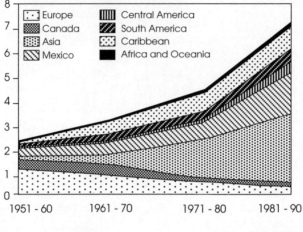

Source: Halker, 1992

Figure 4.2 United States, immigration by region of last residence

example). Russians and ex-Soviets, on the other hand, having had travel prohibited them for seven decades, lacked and still lack support networks in emigration countries – with the exception of the Jewish minority, precisely the population group which does in fact emigrate. Leaving one's family behind and launching out into the void of a hostile world without any support network is thus something which is only decided upon by masses of people when it is enforced by a catastrophe (famine, war, Nazism).

Now, if the figures indicate that immigration into Western Europe does not reach such massive proportions as is perceived by public opinion, why does such a feeling exist? And why the social alarm? What is really occurring is an increasing transformation of the ethnic composition of European societies, on the basis of immigrants imported during the period of strong economic growth of the 1960s. Indeed, as shown in Figure 4.3, the fertility rates of foreigners are very much higher than those of the nationals of the European countries of residence (except, significantly, in Luxembourg and Switzerland, where the majority of foreigners are of European origin). And for demographic reasons, the fertility gap will continue to increase with the passage of time. This is the true source of social tension: growing ethnic diversity in a Europe which has not taken aboard that diversity and continues to speak of 'immigrants' when, increasingly, it is a matter of nationals of non-European ethnic origin. Table 4.3 shows that the population increase in the United Kingdom between 1981 and 1990 was only 1 per cent for Whites, while it was 23 per cent for ethnic minorities. Even so, there are 51.847 million Whites, while the minorities account for only 2.614 million people. There nevertheless exists a clear awareness of the inevitable process of formation of a society with large ethnic minorities, of the North American type. Something similar is happening in other European countries, as shown in Table 4.4. Two-thirds of the foreigners in France, and three-quarters of those in Germany and Holland, are of non-European origin. To this must be

Table 4.2 Foreign Resident Population in Western Europe, 1950–1990 (in thousands, with percentage of total population)

Country	1950		1970		1982[1]		1990	
	No.	%	No.	%	No.	%	No.	%
Austria	323	4.7	212	2.8	303	4.0	512	6.6
Belgium	368	4.3	696	7.2	886	9.0	905	9.1
Denmark	–	–	–	–	102	2.0	161	3.1
Finland	11	0.3	6	0.1	12	0.3	35	0.9
France	1765	4.1	2621	5.3	3680	6.8	3608	6.4
Fed. Rep. of Germany	568	1.1	2977	4.9	4667	7.6	5242	8.2
Greece	31	0.4	93	1.1	60	0.7	70	0.9
Ireland	–	–	–	–	69	2.0	90	2.5
Italy	47	0.1	–	–	312	0.5	781	1.4
Liechtenstein	3	19.6	7	36.0	9	36.1	–	–
Luxembourg	29	9.9	63	18.4	96	26.4	109	28.0
Netherlands	104	1.1	255	2.0	547	3.9	692	4.6
Norway	16	0.5	–	–	91	2.2	143	3.4
Portugal	21	0.3	–	–	64	0.6	108	1.0
Spain	93	0.3	291	0.9	418	1.1	415	1.1
Sweden	124	1.8	1.8	411	406	4.9	484	5.6
Switzerland	285	6.1	1080	17.2	926	14.7	1100	16.3
United Kingdom	–	–	–	–	2137	3.9	1875	3.3
Total[2]	5100	1.3	10,200	2.2	15,000	3.1	16,600	4.5

Source: Fassman and Munz (1992)

1 1982 is a reference year, rather than 1980 since the data are better for 1982.
2 Includes interpolated figures for the missing (–) data.

added, in the case of France, the rising proportion of population of non-European origin born in France and entitled to French nationality upon reaching the age of 18 years. It can also happen, as in the German case, that the law refuses the right of nationality to those born in national territory of foreign parents, a situation in which thousands of young Turks who have never known any land other than Germany find themselves. However, the cost of such a last-ditch defence of autochthonous nationality is the creation of a permanent caste of non-citizens, thus setting under way an infernal mechanism of social hostility.

One additional factor is important in the perception of an ethnic diversity which goes beyond the direct impact of immigration, and that is the spatial concentration of ethnic minorities in cities, particularly in large cities and in specific districts of large cities, in which they can even make up the majority of the population. The spatial segregation of the city on the basis of the ethnic and cultural characteristics of the population is thus not a heritage of a discriminatory past, but rather a characteristic and increasingly common feature of our societies. The era of global information is also the era of local segregation.

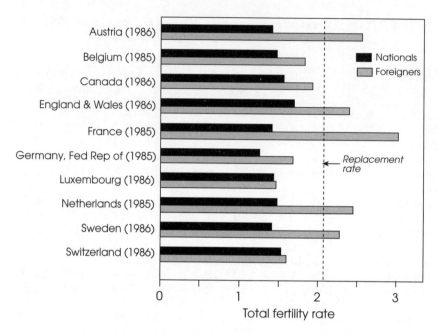

Source: Stalker, 1992

Figure 4.3 Total fertility rate for nationals and foreigners, selected
OECD countries

ETHNIC DIVERSITY, SOCIAL DISCRIMINATION AND URBAN SEGREGATION

In all societies, ethnic minorities suffer economic, institutional and cultural discrimination, which usually results in their segregation within the space of the city. Inequality of income and discriminatory practices in housing markets lead to a disproportionate concentration of ethnic minorities in certain urban zones within the metropolitan areas. Furthermore, defensive reaction and specific culture reinforce the pattern of spatial segregation, in that each ethnic group tends to utilize its concentration in districts as a form of protection, mutual aid and affirmation of its specific nature. There thus arises a double process of urban segregation – on the one hand, that of the various ethnic minorities with respect to the dominant ethnic group and, on the other hand, that of the different ethnic minorities amongst themselves. This spatial differentiation must be understood in statistical and symbolic terms, that is, as a disproportionate concentration of certain ethnic groups in certain areas, rather than as the exclusive residence of each group in each district. Even in extreme situations of urban racial discrimination, as was the case of the apartheid regime in South Africa, a strong socio-spatial differentiation in class terms can be observed from the time of dismantling of institutionally imposed segregation (see Box 4.2).

Table 4.3 United Kingdom Ethnic Minorities, 1981–1990

Ethnic Minority	1990 (000s)	1981–90 (% change)
Afro–Caribbean	474	–5
African–Asian	256	40
Indian	584	5
Pakistani	457	58
Bangladeshi	109	110
Chinese	136	47
African	171	98
Other/mixed	428	18
All ethnic minorities	2614	23
White	51,847	1

Source: Stalker (1994)

The most widely known and studied model of urban ethnic segregation is that of United States cities. Segregation has persisted throughout the history of the United States and has actually been reinforced over the last two decades with the location of new immigrants in their corresponding ethnic minority segregated areas, thereby constituting true ethnic enclaves in the main metropolitan areas and thus in historical practice giving the lie to the famous myth of the 'melting pot', which is only applicable (and with limitations) to the population of European origin (Blakely and Goldsmith, 1992). Thus, in Los Angeles county, 70 of the 78 municipalities existing in 1970 had less than 10 per cent of residents belonging to ethnic minorities; by 1990, however, the 88 municipalities which then made up the county had more than 10 per cent ethnic minority population, though 42 municipalities had

Table 4.4 Non-European Union Source of Foreign Residents in Selected Western European Countries, 1990

Country	No. (thousands)	% of total foreign	Largest non-EU country	% of total foreign
Belgium	354.1	39.1	Morocco	15.7
France	2298.7	63.7	Algeria	17.2
Germany	3916.4	74.7	Turkey	32.0
Netherlands	524.0	75.7	Turkey	29.4
Norway	102.7	71.7	Pakistan	8.0
Sweden	246.2	50.9	Yugoslavia	8.5
Switzerland	340.1	30.9	Yugoslavia	12.8
United Kingdom	986.0	52.6	India	8.3

Source: Stalker (1994)

Box 4.2 Race, Class and Urban Segregation in South Africa: The City of Apartheid and its Future

The extreme case of urban segregation in the twentieth century was the apartheid system in South Africa. The origins of the system lay in the spatial control of black workers by the white colonists particularly, from the time of discovery of the gold and diamond mines in the first half of the nineteenth century. Apartheid was institutionalized by the Urban Areas Act of 1923, which established strict separation of residential zones between black and white people. In 1948 a new territorial separation was established between black people already living in towns and those resident in rural areas, which last were permanently denied the right to live in the cities, although their presence could be authorized for limited periods to fill particular labour needs.

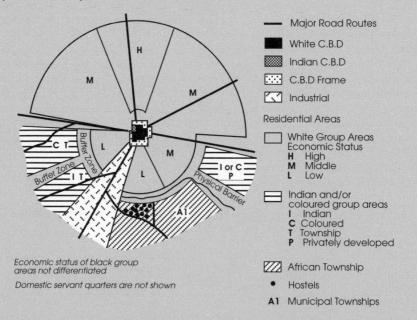

— Major Road Routes

▨ White C.B.D

▨ Indian C.B.D

▨ C.B.D Frame

▨ Industrial

Residential Areas

☐ White Group Areas
Economic Status
H High
M Middle
L Low

▤ Indian and/or
coloured group areas
I Indian
C Coloured
T Township
P Privately developed

*Economic status of black group
areas not differentiated*

Domestic servant quarters are not shown

▨ African Township

● Hostels

A1 Municipal Townships

In planning the city of apartheid separate residential areas were established for whites, blacks and indians. White residential areas were divided off from black and indian zones by buffer zones and industrial areas. Municipal governments were also separate. Economic activity was concentrated in the white city, which was the one which received most of the taxes and consumption (even of the blacks), while social problems and urban poverty were, and are, concentrated in the black areas. The intensification of industrialization and urbanization during the 1970s led to an explosion of irregular settlements in rural areas adjacent to cities.

Their inhabitants, workers in the city centres but without permits to live in them, had to resign themselves to illegal dwelling in miserable conditions and to travelling long distances daily without suitable transport systems. Although in 1980 urban residence in black settlement areas was permitted, the acceleration of urbanization showed itself in an increase of the (exclusively black) irregular settlements, which form a substantial part of the urban population, as shown in the table below:

Population of Informal Settlements in Selected Areas, 1990

Area	Total Black Population	Informal Settlement Population
Gauteng (Johannesburg area)	5,213,000	2,260,000
Durban	2,600,000	180,000
Port Elizabeth	580,000	330,000
Bloemfontein/ Botshabelo	470,100	1,000,000
East London	342,800	105,000

Source: South African Institute of Racial Relations

A certain racial mixing has taken place in the cities over the last few years. Saff (1994) classifies this under two main processes:

> *'The first, which occurs in some "white suburbs" and in the central parts of the city, may be described as desegregation ... It is characterized by the immigration of blacks with income levels equal to or higher than those leaving the district ... The second process consists in the expansion of the peripheral cities and the irregular settlements into the municipal territories of the "white" areas. The residents of these settlements have a very much lower socio-economic level than the residents of the white areas; thus, although the racial structure of the city is being changed by this process, the social conditions of the blacks in these settlements persist in that they are still excluded from the services and institutions of the "white zone".'*

On the other hand, extensive areas of Johannesburg which were once white areas have now been desegregated or have even become predominantly black, such as Joubert Park and Hillbrow. Extreme social inequality between races remains, however. In 1993, the black city of Alexandra had a population of between 250,000 and 300,000 inhabitants, a density of 60,000 persons per square kilometre and an operating budget of 15 million dollars, while neighbouring Sandton (white) had a popula-

tion of between 110,000 and 145,000, a density of 1,000 inhabitants per square kilometre and an operating budget of 53 million dollars. Throughout the country as a whole, it is estimated that between seven and eight million persons have no house. And in the first year of the new government, only 20,000 houses could be built. Although the end of apartheid has permitted desegregation processes, it has reinforced ethnicity as an element of cultural definition and of social and political mobilization. During the struggle against apartheid, inter-racial themes of social liberation predominated in the urban movements of South African settlements. Under the new post-apartheid democratic system, ethnic and racial identity take on a predominant role in popular organization and in local political control objectives. The explosive KwaZulu/Natal conflict is strongly conditioned by tribal loyalty, to the point that the African National Congress, traditionally inter-racial and focusing on social liberation, has suffered intense internal conflicts in some zones such as the Western Cape. All the more so in that, as Saff (1994) points out:

'The number of South African residential areas that are desegregated is hard to assess. It may nevertheless be stated that the vast majority of the South African population is excluded both from the process of desegregation and from deracialization of space.'

In short, the end of apartheid has not meant the end of urban segregation, but rather its deinstitutionalization. And the end of the racist State opens the range of identities as a perennial foundation of social mobilization and political organization (Mare, 1993; Wilmsen et al, 1994). The city freed from apartheid is not a culturally and ethnically uniform city. Racial democracy and urban equality are built upon differential identities, and it is not possible to affirm the abstract principle of cultural uniformity and lack of racial difference.

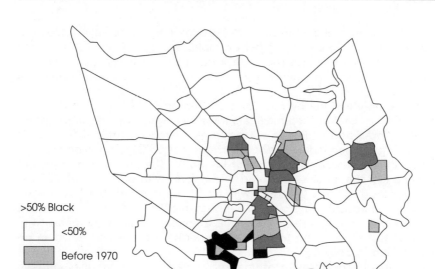

>50% Black

☐ <50%

▨ Before 1970

▩ 1970-1979

■ 1980-1989

Source: Bullard et al ,1994

*Figure 4.4 Expansion of Houston area black settlement by decade
(1970–1990)*

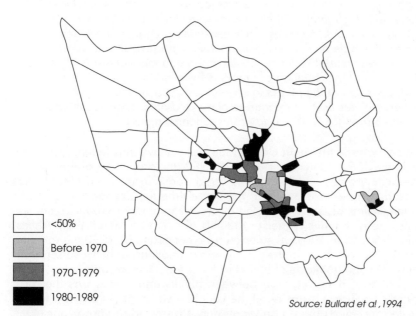

☐ <50%

▨ Before 1970

▩ 1970-1979

■ 1980-1989

Source: Bullard et al ,1994

*Figure 4.5 Expansion of Houston area Hispanic settlement by decade
(1970–1990)*

more than 50 per cent of ethnic minority groups in their populations (Bullard, Grigsby and Lee (1994)). In another example, Figures 4.4 and 4.5 show the evolution of the zones of Houston (the Texan metropolis) with concentrations of black and Hispanic populations, along adjacent axes of spatial settlement between 1970 and 1990.

The complete study by Massey and Denton (1993) on urban racial segregation in United States cities shows the high levels of segregation between blacks and whites in all the large cities (see Table 4.5). For an absolute segregation index of 100, the average is 68.3, rising to an average of 80.1 for the metropolitan areas of the north. The three main areas are also amongst the most segregated: New York, with an index of 82; Los Angeles, with 81.1; and Chicago, with 87.8. The index of 'black isolation', too, which measures interaction between blacks and other non-black groups (100 being the level of absolute isolation) shows high values, with an average of 63.5, rising to 66.1 in the northern areas and reaching an index of 82.8 in Chicago.

The spatial concentration of underprivileged ethnic minorities leads to the creation of real 'black holes' in the urban social structure, in which poverty, the running down of housing and urban services, low employment levels, lack of professional opportunities and criminality mutually reinforce each other. In his study on segregation and crime in urban America, Massey (1995) concludes that:

> 'The coming together of high levels of poverty amongst blacks and high spatial segregation indices create ecological niches in which there arise high indices of criminality and violence and of risk of falling victim to said crimes ... Unless a desegregation movement arises, the cycle of violence will continue. Paradoxically, however, the perpetuation of violence makes desegregation more difficult, for it means that the isolation of blacks is beneficial for the whites in that, by isolating the blacks in segregated districts, the rest of society isolates itself in relation to crime and other social problems resulting from the high poverty rates amongst blacks.'

Criminality rates in the main United States cities have thus fallen, in general terms, in the 1990s. Between 1980 and 1992, the proportion of the number of American homes which have suffered some form of criminality has decreased by one-third, while at the same time the probability of Blacks being the victims of crime has risen at an extraordinary rate. Black adolescents have a nine times higher probability of being murdered than Whites; while in 1960, 45 in 100,000 suffered a violent death, by 1990 the rate had risen to 140 in 100,000. In their study on the relationship between segregation of blacks and homicide of Blacks in 125 cities, Peterson and Krivo (1993) found that spatial segregation between blacks and whites was the most statistically significant factor of all the variables which might account for the homicide rate, much more important than poverty, education or age. One kills those close at hand. And when a society, breaking with its liberal traditions and with its racial integration laws, adopts the cynical attitude of shutting its impoverished racial minorities away in increasingly run-down ghettos, it provokes the exasperation of violence in those zones. But from

Table 4.5 Black Segregation and Isolation in United States Cities with
Largest Black Population, 1980

Metropolitan Area	Black–White segregation	Black isolation
Northern Area		
Boston	77.6	55.1
Buffalo	79.4	63.5
Chicago	87.8	82.8
Cincinnati	72.3	54.3
Cleveland	87.5	80.4
Columbus	71.4	57.5
Detroit	86.7	77.3
Gary-Hammond-E. Chicago	90.6	77.3
Indianapolis	76.2	62.3
Kansas City	78.9	69.0
Los Angeles-Long Beach	81.1	60.4
Milwaukee	83.9	69.5
New York	82.0	62.7
Newark	81.6	69.2
Philadelphia	78.8	69.6
Pittsburgh	72.7	54.1
St Louis	81.3	72.9
San Francisco-Oakland	71.7	51.1
Average	80.1	66.1
Southern Area		
Atlanta	78.5	74.8
Baltimore	74.7	72.3
Birmingham	40.8	50.2
Dallas-Fort Worth	77.1	64.0
Greensboro-Winston Salem	56.0	50.1
Houston	69.5	59.3
Memphis	71.6	75.9
Miami	77.8	64.2
New Orleans	68.3	68.8
Norfolk-Virginia Beach	63.1	62.8
Tampa-St Petersburg	72.6	51.5
Washington, DC	70.1	68.0
Average	68.3	63.5

Source: Massey and Denton (1993)

that time on, the ethnic minority is condemned to live entrenched behind
police protection and society is condemned to earmark for the police and for
prisons a budget which is as large as that for education, as is the case in the
state of California.

Although racism and urban segregation exist in all cities, their outlines
are not always as clear-cut or their consequences so violent as those to be

found in United States cities. Brazil, for example, is a multiracial society in which blacks and mulattos occupy the lowest positions in the social scale (Aguiar, 1994), but although its ethnic communities are likewise spatially segregated, both between the regions of the country and within the metropolitan areas, the index of dissimilarity, which measures urban segregation, is very much lower than that of the North American metropolitan areas (see Box 4.3). Likewise, although economic inequality is influenced by ethnic origin, institutional barriers and social prejudices are much less deep-rooted than in the United States. Two societies with an equally slave-based past have thus evolved towards different patterns of spatial segregation and racial discrimination, in function of cultural, institutional and economic factors which favoured the mixing of races and social integration in Brazil, but hindered it in the United States, a comparison which invites analysis of the historical variation in a human nature which is not immutable.

What does appear to be established is the tendency towards segregation of ethnic minorities in all cities, and particularly in the cities of the more developed parts of the world. Thus, as European cities have received new groups of immigrants and have seen their ethnic minorities grow on the basis of the groups established over the past three decades, the pattern of urban ethnic segregation is accentuated. In the United Kingdom, although London accounts for only 12 per cent of the population, it has 42 per cent of the ethnic minority population. Concentrated particularly in certain districts, those ethnic minorities are characterized by a lower level of education, higher unemployment rate and economic activity rate of only 58 per cent, compared with 80 per cent for whites (Jones, 1993). In the London district of Wandsworth, with some 260,000 inhabitants, some 150 different languages are spoken; to this ethno-cultural diversity is added the dubious privilege of it being one of England's most socially deprived districts. In Göteborg (Sweden), 16 per cent of the population is of foreign origin and lives concentrated in the north east of the city and on the island of Hisingen. In Zurich, which has seen its foreign population (especially Turks and Yugoslavs) rise from 18 per cent in 1980 to 25 per cent in 1990, 44 per cent of this population is concentrated in the industrial zones of the urban outskirts. While in Holland foreigners account for only 5 per cent of the total population, that proportion rises to 15–20 per cent in Amsterdam, Rotterdam, The Hague and Utrecht, while in the older quarters of these cities it rises to 50 per cent. Foreigners form 9 per cent of the population of Belgium, but their proportion in Anderlecht is 26 per cent, while in the most run-down district, La Rosee, foreigners account for 76 per cent of its 2,300 inhabitants (Council of Europe, 1993). In short, European cities are largely following the path of urban segregation of ethnic minorities characteristic of the North American metropolises, although the spatial form of urban segregation is diverse in Europe. While the French banlieue form outlying metropolitan ghettos, central European and British cities tend to have their ethnic minorities concentrated in the inner cities, in a spatial model similar to the North American one, which can contribute to the decline of the urban centres if the living conditions of ethnic minorities in Europe are not improved. The importance of gangs and the expansion of criminal activities is less marked in Europe than in North America but if the

BOX 4.3 TEMPERED URBAN SEGREGATION: BRAZIL

Brazil is a multiracial society in which the black and mulatto ethnic groups occupy the lowest places in the social scale, while the ethnic groups of white origin occupy the higher places. There is a sharp regional ethnic diversity, too, with blacks concentrated in the northeast (the centre of the slave-based economy up to 1888), while most whites live in the industrialized south. There is likewise urban segregation between whites and blacks, particularly marked in the northeast (see Table B). The indicators which measure segregation – both the index of dissimilarity and that of interaction between social groups – nevertheless show much less segregation in Brazilian cities than in those of the United States, with values between two and three times lower on a scale from 1 to 100, depending on points of comparison (see Table A). New York, for example, shows a dissimilarity index of 82, compared with 37 for São Paulo. The measurement of social interaction (with value of 0 for total absence of urban spacial interaction between racial groups) assigns a 16 to New York and a 63 to São Paulo. Racial differences and their expression in urban segregation persist across societies, but history, culture and institutions attenuate or accentuate racism and discrimination in the city.

A: *Indexes of Dissimilarity in Metropolitan Areas: Brazil, 1980*

Region and Metropolitan Area	Index of Dissimilarity			
	White vs Black	White vs Brown	Brown vs Black	Per cent White
Northeast	0.509	0.405	0.434	30.1
Recife	0.499	0.389	0.424	37.1
Salvador	0.534	0.488	0.353	22.8
Central-East	0.381	0.367	0.344	61.3
Rio de Janeiro	0.427	0.383	0.312	60.0
Belo Horizonte	0.419	0.427	0.341	54.1
São Paulo	0.402	0.380	0.364	78.3
São Paulo	0.412	0.394	0.364	71.5
South	0.467	0.433	0.476	86.4
Porto Alegre	0.422	0.407	0.421	85.3
Curitiba	0.477	0.417	0.467	84.1
Mean	0.450	0.397	0.407	58.1

Source: Telles (1992)

B: Indexes of White/Black Dissimilarity and Interaction in 10 Largest
Brazilian and Selected United States Metropolitan Areas, 1980

Metropolitan Area	Dissimilarity	Interaction
São Paulo	37	63
Rio de Janeiro	37	50
Belo Horizonte	41	42
Porto Alegre	37	77
Recife	38	30
Salvador	48	18
Fortaleza	40	25
Curitiba	39	75
Brasilia	39	43
Belém	37	23
New York	82	16
Los Angeles	81	17
Chicago	88	13
Miami	78	21
San Francisco–Oakland	72	30

Source: Telles (1995)

tendencies toward social exclusion continue to become accentuated it
would seem reasonable to suppose that similar situations will lead to
similar consequences, cultural and institutional differences aside. The
multicultural city is a city enriched by its diversity, as Daniel Cohn Bendit
noted in his introductory address to the Frankfurt Conference on multiculturalism sponsored by the Council of Europe (Council of Europe, 1993).
But as that address made clear, a segregated city is a city which breaks
with social solidarity and is one in which the reign of urban violence will
eventually take hold.

DRIFTING POPULATIONS IN CITIES

The variable geometry of the new world economy and the intensification of
the migratory phenomenon, both rural–urban and international, have led
to a new population category divided between the rural, urban and metropolitan settings: a drifting population which moves with the economic tides
and according to the permissiveness of the institution, seeking out its
survival with variable temporal and spatial features according to countries
and circumstances.

Although due to its very nature the phenomenon is difficult to study, an
increasingly broad current of research is providing data on its scale and on
the consequences it has for the functioning and running of cities (Goldstein,
1993; Wong, 1994).

Perhaps the society with the largest drifting population is China over the last decade. For a long time in China population movements were regulated by a 1958 law according to which each Chinese citizen was registered as the member of a *hukou* (home) and classified on the basis of that residence. Under such regulations, any change of residence from rural to urban was extremely difficult: journeys needed prior permission and the rationing system meant that only the coupons issued in the place of residence and work could be used in shops and restaurants. The '*hukou* system' was thus an effective method of controlling spatial mobility and reducing rural-urban migration (Wong, 1994). With the economic liberalization of China in the 1980s, however, immobility became dysfunctional for the assignment of human resources according to dynamics partially governed by the laws of the market. Furthermore, the privatization and modernization of agriculture increased productivity and expelled from the land thousands of millions of peasants who then became surplus labour (Kirkby, 1985). Unable to cater for the needs of this economically displaced rural population, the Chinese government decided to lift the restrictions on population movements and/or to apply them less strictly according to the regions in question and the political situation of the time. This policy change resulted in mass rural–urban migration over the last decade, especially towards the large cities and towards the exporting industrial centres in the south of China. But those cities and regions, despite their extraordinary economic dynamism (they being, indeed, the centres with the world's highest economic growth rates over the last decade) could not absorb the millions of recent arrivals into the stable work force nor provide them with accommodation and urban services, so that many of the urban immigrants live without fixed abode or on the rural outskirts of the metropolises, while many more have adopted a pendulum of seasonal migration, coming and going between their villages of birth and the metropolitan centres (Day and Ma Xia, 1994). Guangzhou, for example, a city of some six million inhabitants, had in 1992 1.34 million temporary residents plus a further 260,000 daily 'tourists'. Guangdong province is estimated to have at least six million temporary migrants. In Shanghai, there were 1.83 million 'drifters' by the end of the 1980s, while in 1993, following development of the industrial zone of Pudong, it was estimated that a further one million drifters had arrived in Shanghai that year. The only reliable migratory survey carried out in the last decade, in 1986, put the proportion of 'temporary residents' amongst the populations of the 74 cities surveyed at 3.6%. Another survey at nationwide level estimated the number of drifters in 1988 at between 50 and 70 million. What would appear to be beyond question is that the phenomenon has increased. Peking's central railway station, built for 50,000 passengers daily, is currently used by some 170,000 to 250,000 passengers, depending on periods. The municipal government of Peking estimates that each additional 100,000 daily visitors to the city leads to increased consumption of 50,000 kilos of grain, 50,000 kilos of vegetables, 100,000 kilowatts of electricity and 24,000 litres of water, while those persons use 730 public buses. Such numbers of visitors generate 100,000 kilos of garbage and 2,300 kilos of waste for the drainage system. The living conditions of this drifting population are far lower than those of the permanent population (Goldstein, 1993), and it falls easy prey to crime and the refuge of criminals, thereby increasing the prejudices harboured by the resident population against the drifters. Although on a smaller scale than in China, the drifting population phenomenon is characteristic of most of the developing world, and especially Asia (Day and Ma Xia, 1994). In Bangkok, for example, of the emigrants arriving in the city between 1975 and 1985, 25 per cent had already lived in three different cities and 77 per cent of those questioned were not planning to stay in Bangkok for more than one year, while only 12 per cent of the migrants had regularly put Bangkok down in the census as their place of residence, a fact which points to an existence spent between their zones of origin and the various urban labour markets. The scale of the phenomenon, and its spread to other areas of the world, make the distinction between rural and urban increasingly inoperative, in that the truly significant factor is the mesh of relations established between the dynamism of the large cities and the flows of population located at different moments in different times and with varying intensities according to the rates of linkage between the global economy and the local economy.

The cities of the developed countries are also witnessing an increase in the drifting population, though of a different type. In an interesting study Martinotti (1993), stressed the importance of populations of visitors who use the city and its services without being residents there. These are not only people from other localities within the metropolitan area, but also people from other regions and other countries; on any particular day, tourists, business travellers and urban consumers make up a considerable proportion of the urban users of the main European (and North American and South American) cities, though they do not show up in the statistics and are not reckoned in the fiscal and institutional base for the urban services which they nevertheless use intensively.

Drifting populations give rise to three main problems in the running of urban areas. Firstly, their existence increases the pressure on urban services to an extent which cities cannot take on without at least receiving special aid from higher government levels, in consonance with their true populations and the actual use made of their infrastructures. Secondly, the lack of suitable statistical accounting for that mobile population, and the irregular nature of its movements, prevent sound planning of urban services. Thirdly, distortion is set up between the people present in the city and the citizens able to deal with the city's problems and running. This situation is negative both for the 'drifters', who lack rights and are even occasionally rendered 'illegal', and the residents, who find citizen solidarity broken by the existence of differences of legal status and of community membership within the real population of the city. The development of shifting population groups, directly related with the globalization of economic and communication flows, thus constitutes a new urban reality for which cities have not yet found answers.

MULTICULTURALISM AND URBAN SOCIAL CRISIS

In May 1991 there gathered in Frankfurt, under the auspices of the Council of Europe, representatives of various European municipal governments to discuss municipal policies for the multicultural integration of Europe. In the declaration published at the end of that meeting (Council of Europe, 1993) it was noted that the European countries had as a consequence of decades of immigration and emigration, become multicultural societies. Likewise, to the extent that the immigrants and the resulting ethnic minorities were concentrated in the large cities, policies on the treatment of immigration and of respect for multiculturalism constituted an essential component of the new municipal policies. Those attending concluded with the statement:

> 'Only a genuinely democratic Europe capable of carrying forward a
> policy of multiculturalism can be a factor of stability in the world
> and can effectively combat the economic imbalances between the
> North and the South, the East and the West, which lead to disor-
> derly emigration.'

A similar statement could be made for North American society and for the world in general. Xenophobic reactions in all countries, however, and the increase in racism and religious fanaticism worldwide, would not appear to augur any easy handling of the new urban situation. Immigrants and ethnic minorities appear as the scapegoats of economic crises and social uncertainties, according to an old historically established reflex, regularly exploited by irresponsible demagogic politicians. Even so, the stubborn new reality of an interdependent global economy, of socioeconomic imbalances and of reproduction amongst ethnic minorities already resident in the more developed countries make multiculturalism and pluri-ethnicity inevitable throughout nearly the whole world. Even Japan, one of the world's most culturally homogeneous societies, is experiencing a rapid increase of its foreign population, while it is witnessing increased numbers of *yoseba* (casual workers, without fixed jobs or abode) and their spatial-temporal location in urban ghettos such as Kamagasaki in Osawa. There are those – the authors of this book amongst them – who think that pluri-ethnicity and multiculturalism are sources of economic and cultural wealth for urban societies (Alund and Schierup, 1991). But even those who are alarmed by the disappearance of social homogeneity, and the social tensions to which it gives rise, must accept the new reality: our societies, in all latitudes, are and will be multicultural, and the cities (especially the large cities) are the places in which the greatest diversity is concentrated. Learning to live with this situation, succeeding in managing cultural exchange on the basis of ethnic difference and remedying the inequalities arising from discrimination are essential aspects of the new local policy in the conditions arising out of the new global interdependence.

Chapter 5

Cities as Political Agents

CITIES AS THE PROTAGONISTS OF OUR EPOCH

Cities are taking on an increasingly prominent role in political, economic, social, cultural and media life. Cities may be described as complex and multidimensional social agents. Cities as social agents should not be confused with local government, though they clearly encompass it. The city best expresses itself as social agent in that it forms a link between public administrations (local and others), public and private economic agents, social and civic organizations, intellectual and professional sectors and social communication media, that is, between political institutions and civil society.

This link is implemented through collective and joint action, which can take various forms and objectives:

- resistance to, or confrontation with, an external agent such as a higher government body, a multinational, etc;
- the definition of products in which they are interested, in their production or sale, various urban agents (eg tourism promotion, cultural range, headquarters of an international organization, etc);
- campaigns based on public–private cooperation (for example, safety, image, urban refurbishment, etc);
- large-scale urban development projects linked to an event or deriving from a broad-consensus political–civic programme;
- socio-political mobilization having its main basis in an affirmation of collective identity and a will for political autonomy (which also takes specific form in particularly urban objectives).

In recent years the signs of this increasing protagonism of the cities have multiplied. Let us look at a few examples.

In Europe, the economic recession of the 1970s provoked a reaction from local governments and the main urban economic and social agents. The former went far beyond their legal obligations in an effort to attract investments, generate employment and renovate the city's productive base. They acted in concert with the urban agents to promote the city. Some years later a conference of European cities (Rotterdam, 1986) was entitled: 'The cities as motors of economic development'. The Eurocities movement had been born, to be constituted formally at the next Conference (Barcelona 1989), and that movement now brings together Europe's fifty largest cities.

With the creation of the Committee of Regions (Maastricht 1993), made up of representatives of the regional governments and cities, the European Union has finally acknowledged regional governments as part of its institutional fabric, something which was in no way envisaged in its founding treaty (Rome 1957).

The new economic protagonists often have the names of cities. The Eurocities have been defined as 'the European multinationals' and as the European 'force de frappe', by Delors (president of the European Commission), Maragall (President of the Council of Municipalities and Regions of Europe) and others.

The economic protagonism of cities is clearer still in other continents, and especially in Asia: Seoul, Taipeh, Hong Kong, Singapore, Bangkok, Shanghai, Hanoi, etc. Economic statistics are issued for the cities and there exists in them a strong complementariness between the government of the city and the economic agents as a whole, all of them oriented towards the external markets. The Asian cities have shown that in the world of the global economy speed of information about international markets and adaptation to same, flexibility of productive and commercial structures and a capacity to form part of networks determine success and failure, much more than the positions acquired in the past, accumulated capital, natural wealth or geographical location. The secret lies in the speed of innovation of the web of small and medium companies linked with the large companies in a network with the exterior and with domestic political power. This ensures major information and promotion functions and guarantees the city system's planning and provision of services, since the economic and urban fabrics naturally merge. In the case of the cities of Asia, urban political power has developed a model with low overheads (unlike the European model), but with high social costs. It would not appear to be a model that can be borne for long, for its persistence introduces dissuasory factors for the attractiveness of the city and does not make its human resources sufficiently qualified.

In the United States cities have played a major role in political change and economic policy. The extreme neoliberalism of the Reagan and Bush presidencies not only harshly suppressed much of the social provision which covered the minimum needs of one-third of the urban population but also favoured deindustrialization and underemployment in the cities and a fall of income amongst local governments. Some cities nevertheless reacted and set under way ambitious strategic projects, combining objectives of economic growth and urban development with responses to the problems generated by environmental decline, increasing social inequalities and citizen insecurity. Cities such as Los Angeles, San Francisco, Detroit, Seattle, etc. (together with the states of Florida and Wisconsin) used strategic planning and public–private partnerships to demonstrate at once the negative nature of an aberrant neoliberal policy and the cities' response capability. The great demonstration called by the mayors who brought together half a million people in Washington announced the fall of Bush (1992) and the start-up of new policies for cities: new infrastructures, 'enterprise zones', the relaunching of social programmes based on the generation of employment and on education, the taking of health care into the public sector, urban environmental protection, etc.

This political protagonism of cities manifested itself spectacularly in Eastern Europe. The collapse of State based communist systems found its main expression in cities: Berlin, Budapest, Prague, Warsaw, etc. Almost always, the politico-social movements which expressed the rebellion of civil society were called 'civic movements'. And it is in the cities that both democratic organization and the competitive economy have been reconstructed.

In Latin America the processes of political democratization and decentralization of the State enhanced over the course of the past decade the role of cities and of local government. But the limitations of these very processes, the social effects of the adjustment policies coming on top of the inherited inequalities and marginalities, the weakness of the sociocultural fabric of the cities and the serious shortfalls in infrastructure and public services have nevertheless delayed the emergence of cities as protagonists. The situation has changed in the 1990s. On the one hand, the economic reactivation which has stimulated the start-up of large-scale urban projects (in some cases encouraged by privatizations) and has breathed dynamism into the construction sector has, on the other hand, sharpened the inherited contradictions and deficits in physical infrastructure and communications, lack of public resources and, in general, of capacity for action of the local governments, the weak social integration in the cities and the scant cooperation between the public and private sectors. Furthermore, the consolidation of internal democratic processes and the increasing economic opening up to the exterior have multiplied social demands and accentuated a sensation of a functional crisis in the large cities. The intensity and visibility of urban problems (traffic congestion, citizen insecurity, air and water pollution, shortfalls of housing and basic services) have lent focus to this sensation of crisis. At the same time the dynamics of the economy (reactivation), of social life (participation) and of politics (democratization) have created the conditions for coming up with responses. Such responses have not been lacking: the passing of political and financial reform projects in Latin America's figurehead cities (Mexico DF, Bogotá, Buenos Aires and those emerging from Brazil's new constitution), the political and media protagonism of the mayors of the large cities, who have even become national leaders, the start of strategic plans for economic, social and urban development based on broad civic participation, decentralization of local governments, the start-up of large-scale urban projects under public and/or private initiative and the cooperation between public and private sectors, etc. The consolidation of these emerging factors will depend on whether they can stimulate large city projects which enjoy the active participation of the main public and private agents and can win broad consensus amongst the citizens (DeForn et al, 1991; La Terra (9), 1995; Roncayolo, 1990; Roncayolo et al, 1993; Paquot, 1994; Choay, 1994; Fortier, 1995; Sennet, 1994; Ajuntament de Barcelona, 1990).

We have seen recently how some large-scale projects in the process of conception evolve from a sectoral and administrative approach towards a global concerted urban development proposal. An example might be some large-scale communication infrastructure projects in Bogotá (47 kilometre perimeter or ring road, proposal for a Metro and mass intermodal transport system) or the 2004 Olympic Games candidature proposal of Rio de Janeiro (which defines six large areas of urban centrality).

The Latin American cities have also expressed their wish to define concerted development projects amongst each other, to defend together the principles of political decentralization and local autonomy and to take part in the building of supranational institutions of regional or continental scope. Though these do not attain the associative level and multiplicity of networks which exist in Europe (Council for the Municipalities and Regions of Europe, Eurocities, etc, as described in Chapter 9), there have been some notable recent initiatives such as the creation of *Mercaciudades* (or cities of the Mercosur), the consolidation of the Unión de Ciudades Capitales Iberoamericanas (UCCI) or proposals for the coordination of projects between cities in order to form urban axes or systems (such as the Valparaíso–Santiago–Mendoza–Córdoba–Rosario–Asunción–São Paulo axis). In this context the municipalist associative movement has had an infusion of life at both national and continental levels (Red Latinoamericana de Asociaciones de Municipalidades – IULA), as has cooperation between the cities of Latin America and those of North America and of Europe (such as through Ciudades Unidas Desarrollo – Federación Mundial).

CITIES WITH PROJECTS: THE STRATEGIC PLAN. AN OVERVIEW OF EUROPE AND LATIN AMERICA

The European Precedent

Large cities have to respond to five types of challenge: new economic base, urban infrastructure, quality of life, social integration and governability. Only by generating a capacity for a response to these challenges can they on the one hand be competitive vis-à-vis the exterior and find their place in the global economic spaces and, on the other, guarantee their populations the minimum levels of wellbeing necessary to allow the consolidation of peaceful democratic coexistence.

The response to these challenges calls for a strategic plan city project (Box 5.1). The construction of this project may rest on different factors. In some cities, the sensation of crisis led to a joint reaction on the part of the local government and the main economic agents to undertake transformation of the urban infrastructure to facilitate a transition from the traditional industrial model towards the skilled tertiary centre.

In the case of Birmingham, which through a strategic plan obtained major aid from the European Community, it had its urban centre refurbished and has become England's most dynamic city. Other cities such as Amsterdam and Lyon anticipated the crisis and promoted changes of infrastructure and image through strategic plans to bring themselves into line with the new requirements of the global economy and of international competitiveness. In other cases, however, such as Projetto Milan, the impotence of local government prevented the strategic proposals from becoming specific lines of action.

The response to the awareness of crisis has been facilitated in some cities by their ability to attract and make use of a major international event. Barcelona has become a paradigmatic example of this (Box 5.2). The strate-

Box 5.1 Strategic Plans: Methodological, Communication and Marketing Guide

The strategic plan is an integral planning tool for the economic and social development of a territory. It is drawn up on the basis of analysis of the current situation and of participatory objective-setting systems. The plan sets out the future concept of a territory and the key lines of action to achieve its objectives in order to promote joint, coordinated action of all institutional, economic and social agents in the territory, to achieve the collective support of the population for a future project which that population feels to be its own, and to ensure systematic and effective external dissemination of the future concept of the territory in extraterritorial settings with a view to attaining its objectives.

In order to bring these processes to a successful conclusion, the organizational and communicative conditions to permit such work must be set out. From the outset, the proposal for a strategic plan calls for a number of preconditions, amongst which we might highlight the following:

* expansive vocation of the city (under way or as a project);
* existence of urban agents who accept linkage;
* widespread feeling of growth crisis or of loss of opportunities to permit confrontations between agents connected with the day-to-day conflicts to be overcome;
* leadership (one person and shared).

In cities such as Barcelona, Valencia, Rio, Bogotá and Lisbon, there have arisen these circumstances in which political initiative from City Hall has combined with active receptivity by the economic and professional organizations, universities and social organizations, and outside technical support to permit the transfer of know how.

Organization of a strategic plan always includes the following points, although the specific form taken may vary from one city to another and are adapted to their own economic, social and institutional circumstances. All strategic plans have a promoting core group which brings together the main public and private bodies and their highest representatives. These are the agents which will make up the Management Committee or Governing Council of the plan. Depending on the number of members of the Council, an Executive Committee is formed to include the Plan technical management team (the governing council meets every two or three months, while the Executive does so every two or three weeks). The technical team will be formed by an independent office which nevertheless has links with Mayor's department or equivalent. There may also be other supplementary technical teams based in other bodies. Finally, there is the General Council which represents the Assembly of institutions involved. This may have between 100 and 400 members and meets seven or eight times, in line with the broad phases of the plan.

The standard calendar of a strategic plan is as follows, including organization of the plan, the marketing plan and the first phases of the diagnosis.

Start of the plan (a fortnight)
- Designation of the person in charge of the plan politically and technically.
- Designation of the Management Committee.
- Setting out the scope and subject area of the plan.
- Designation of the technical team and structure of functions.
- Work sessions with the advisory group to set out the overall structure, methodology, objectives, etc (these sessions include meetings with the main plan agents).

Up to the third month
- Meetings with the members of the Management Committee.
- First meeting to form same.
- Drawing up of the call to the city to create the General Council.
- Organization and structure of the technical team, setting out of individual functions, computer back-up, working method, meetings method and management, etc.
- Setting out of the general communication and marketing criteria.
- Design of the corporate image of the plan and its application.
- Launch of the plan in the media.
- Structuring of dissemination systems.
- Drawing up of lists of people and institutions to bring into the plan in function of the different levels of participation (meetings, surveys, members of councils, etc).
- Meetings with municipal managers in order to explain the scope of the plan to them, obtain their agreement and go on to define the broad themes and projects.
- Meetings with the institutional heads and members of the Management Committee to obtain information and incorporate it into decision-making processes.

Then, at the end of this phase, holding of the First General Council. This stage will have been backed by two working sessions with the advisors to cover the organizational and marketing aspects.

1st Phase of the diagnosis
- Drawing up of the diagnostic index.
- Selection of secondary sources of information.
- Drawing up of the two stage qualitative survey for the city's main economic and social agents.
- Drawing up of a more general survey of all city organizations.
- Drawing up of possible scenarios related to evolution of the setting.
- Commissioning of sectoral diagnoses to find out the state of the art in the various themes.

- Possible commissioning of sectoral themes on which information is lacking.

At the end of this stage, drawing up of the pre-diagnosis or general schema with which to orient and set out the plan objective. This stage will have been backed by a working session with the advisors in order to specify the diagnostic tools.

Finally, we should highlight the various possible sources of financing. From the experiences to date, we note the existence of international financing (usually complementary), local public financing (indispensable for the start-up), and private financing (which must back the greater part of the process). This financing can take the form of contributions from economically promoting companies and institutions, contributions in kind, or the sponsoring of specific events of the Strategic Plan, especially communication and marketing events.

Communication and marketing play essential roles in drawing up and implementation of the strategic plan.

- During the phase of drawing up:
  – to achieve sufficient levels of knowledge and understanding of the objectives and processes of the strategic plan amongst the population as a whole;
  – to generate an outlook favourable to participation on the part of the main institutional, economic and social agents.
- Once drawn up:
  – to achieve sufficient knowledge, understanding and involvement of the population as a whole with the future concept and lines of implementation proposed by the plan;
  – to promote a thorough understanding and active participation commitment in the start-up of the lines of work and measures recommended by the institutions and other relevant agents in the territory.
  – to achieve sufficient levels of knowledge and understanding of the future concept of the territory amongst the relevant extraterritorial audiences.

The communication plan is structured in the following phases:
- drawing up of the communication target audiences;
- drawing up of the messages;
- selection of communication channels and media;
- operation action plan.

All target audiences, both internal and external, which are important for achievement of strategic plan objectives will be identified and classified. The internal audiences are those attached to the cities and their settings, while outside audiences are all the audiences in the country and abroad included within the external dissemination objectives. The communication or response objectives sought – in terms of knowledge, understanding, involvement and participation – are set out for each one of the audiences. These objectives are planned in time-scales. Likewise, for the purposes of allocation of funds, the various audiences are placed in order of priority of their importance for achievement of the objectives emerging from the strategic plan.

The messages to be given out must be classified and set out in function of the target audiences of the communication and the content of that communication. Target audiences can be global or specific, while the content may relate to the city or spheres and activities of same (economy, city planning, culture, etc). The messages may thus be classified as follows:

• Global message: The one the city must convey about itself to the target audiences.
• General segment messages: Those which the city must convey about itself as a whole and specifically to each of its target audiences.
• General sphere/activity messages: What each sphere or activity must communicate to each specific target audience.

Once these messages have been drawn up, an integration strategy for the messages must be set out in function of the degree of support which the global message must lend to each of the other types of message. On the basis of the information-source habits of the different target audiences of the communication, the most suitable personal and impersonal communication channels and media must be identified, to convey to them the messages which have been drawn up and to achieve the responses sought or communication objectives defined. The priority levels of the target audiences and selection of the most suitable communication media will be decisive factors for allocation of the budgetary allowances. A time-scales operational communication plan will be drawn up as a result of integration of the three previous stages. Integrated into the plan, specific communication measures and media for achievement of the objectives posited will be specified and designed. The measures and media will be implemented in the form of briefings to commission implementation thereof by local suppliers. Each briefing will specify: the name of the media/measure, the target audience, the communication objective, the content and structuring of the message, the back-up measures and media and the timing of the work.

gic plan would probably not have been the framework for an ambitious urban transformation project, now partly implemented, without the spur of the 1992 Olympic Games. But this is not a unique case. Lisbon, a city which was immersed in a vicious circle of melancholy and marginalization, has boosted a major process of urban transformation and economic dynamization through being a cultural capital (1994) and through preparation for its universal exhibition (1998). Glasgow, too, used its designation as a cultural capital to modernize its urban infrastructure and make itself an attractive venue for international congresses and meetings and to attract tourists and visitors (especially with its summer cultural festival). More recently, Manchester has followed down this path (candidature for the Olympic Games, Global Forum, etc).

But a positive response can hardly be provided where there is no personalized leadership. The figure of the mayor has often been decisive, as in the cases of the aforesaid cities, especially Lisbon (Sampaio) and Barcelona (Maragall). The crisis of government of most Italian cities in the 1980s likewise explains the failure of their strategic projects (eg Milan and Turin after Tognoli and Novelli). The international competitiveness and good image of cities which are not large capitals – such as Lille, Montpellier or Strasbourg in France – cannot be understood without taking into account the strong personalities and dynamism of their mayors (Mauroy, Frêche and Trautman). In other cases, full advantage has not been taken of exceptional opportunities, precisely due to a lack of local leadership, as with the Expo Universal of Seville in 1992, and Madrid as European cultural capital in the same year. But in Spain, too, some cities which had been left on the sidelines of the great projects of the glorious years (1986–1992) have managed to react through shared leadership (between public institutions and private agents), setting strategic plans in motion, as in the case of Valencia and Bilbao. Local leadership does not always initially lie with the political authorities, though they must in any case be present and must contribute towards the building of shared leadership.

In all these cities, the urban transformation project is the sum of three factors:

1. a sensation of crisis sharpened by a growing awareness of globalization of the economy;
2. a coming together of the urban public and private agents, and the generation of local leadership (political and civic);
3. a joint will and citizen consensus for the city to take a leap forward, from the physical, economic, social and cultural points of view (Arias and Gago, 1989; Thomas, 1990; Heinz and Jeannot, 1993; Gibelli, 1992; Bouinot and Demils, 1993; Godet, 1991; Hall, 1989; Ascher et al, 1992; DeForn and Pascual, 1995; Porter, 1992; Conseil Communes et Régions Europe, 1994).

But can this analysis be applied today to Latin America and its large cities? Counterparts of the European examples quoted can be found in Latin America, though running some years behind Europe. Though the challenges may appear to be greater, conceptually they are the same. It is true that demographic growth, the extension of the 'illegal' city, the burden of social marginality, the lack of modern infrastructure and the weakness of local governments are differentiating factors. But there are other factors which are more positive than in the case of Europe: lower unemployment, greater economic dynamism, flexibility of productive structures, good quality–cost ratio of human resources and high potential of the regional economic area. Some decisive questions which must currently be confronted by Latin American cities can probably be tackled and resolved with the urban agents: joint action by public and private agents, the creation of central provision and well-planned public spaces, the reconstruction of civic culture, political-

Box 5.2 Barcelona 2000 Economic and Social Strategic Plan

One of the initiatives which has awoken most interest and demand, both in terms of information and of advisory services, is the Barcelona 2000 Economic and Social Strategic Plan. Started in 1988, the Barcelona 2000 Plan has involved a process of collaboration and consensus of all the public and private economic and social agents acting in the city in order to achieve a common vision and a guide for action, particularly in order to continue and enhance the dynamism generated by the 1992 Olympic Games.

Barcelona City Hall is the plan-promoting institution, to which are added a further 10 bodies to form the Executive Committee, and another 187 to form the General Council. The Executive Committee is made up of Barcelona City Hall, the Official Chamber of Commerce, Industry and Navigation of Barcelona, the Círculo de Economía, Comisiones Obreras trade union, the Zona Franca consortium, Barcelona Trade Fair Centre, Fomento al Trabajo employers' association, the Autonomous Port of Barcelona, Unión General de Trabajadores trade union and the University of Barcelona.

The plan was drawn up over the September 1988 to January 1990 period, and included: diagnosis; analysis of city strengths and weaknesses; setting out of the general objective and possible strategic lines; drawing up of strategies and actions by over 560 persons (technicians, executives and businessmen from the city); classification, reduction and priority levels of strategies; and, finally, drawing up and approval of the plan. The central objective of the plan, approved in March 1990, is for its practical application to act upon the city in such a way that, by changing its main variables, it becomes a more attractive and competitive territory with a better economic base and permitting a modern life quality. The three strategies can be summed up as:

1. Connection of Barcelona with the European cities network by boosting communication and transport infrastructure and by internal linkage of the metropolis, seeking equilibrium thereof and improving mobility and accessibility.
2. Improving the life quality of the inhabitants, measures in the fields of the environment, housing, training, culture and social wellbeing.
3. Balanced economic development, creation of economic activity assistance infrastructure, measures to make the industrial fabric and advanced services sector more competitive, and measures for the development of economic sectors with potential.

The implementation phase began in March 1990, with each sector or institution assuming responsibility for execution and forming commissions to promote activities calling for support. Most of the measures are currently being promoted, while some have already been completed. The achievement of these objectives, the staging of the Olympic Games and the high level of internationalization achieved by Barcelona led, by mid-1992, to starting the second version of the plan to adapt to growth of the city on the basis of the new level already in place.

Apart from those which emerge from the changes undergone by the city, the main consequence has been the dissemination of strategic thinking amongst the city's agents, which has permitted overall synergies through decisions taken along the same direction and towards the same objective. Also there was the fact of having a structured version of the city's requirements as a highly operative element for discussions with state and supra-state organizations and with the large investors. Thus was fulfilled one of the basic objectives sought: to improve the attractiveness of Barcelona for carrying out activities and as a place of residence, thereby contributing to improving the quality of life of the citizens. In 1991 the plan was awarded the European Communities' Special Planning Prize.

Barcelona is currently drawing up its Second Strategic Plan, which is to allow its economic area to become part of the world economic context. The plan evaluates Barcelona's factors of competitiveness, sets out the activities calling for a priority boost, and the geographical zones upon which Barcelona can disseminate its influence, which include Latin America as an area of considerable future, and the Pacific as the new central axis of the world economy. The basic strategies proposed by the second phase of Barcelona's plan are structured around three priority objectives:

1. Facilitating the integration of companies in the area of Barcelona in the global setting, through measures in the fields of support infrastructures for specialized services, communications and telecommunications, access to the markets of Latin America and the regions of the Pacific, and the use of Community programmes.

2. Resituating the factors of competitiveness, especially in the field of human resources, innovation capacity, new products, imagination and creativity, quality, industrial organization, quality of public services, efficiency of public administration, business strategies and management capacity.

3. Sustainable development to avoid degradation of the environment, with special emphasis on the prevention of pollution, markets for new green products, promotion of eco-industry, control of products, etc.

administrative reform to make local governments more efficient and more participatory and, above all, modernization of the urban infrastructure (public services, communications and business areas).

Can the cities of Latin American be said to be reacting now? Undoubtedly they are. In the first place, the democratization and decentralization of the state have reinforced and lent legitimacy to local governments. This has in turn created the conditions in many cases for expression of the local public leadership capacity of mayors, intendants or governors.

Secondly, the economic opening up, a factor which instils fear and yet generates opportunities, has mobilized economic agents. These agents have become aware of the need to have a competitive city which is attractive and functional, provided with modern infrastructures and ensuring minimum levels of quality of living and security. This awareness has led them to posit objectives and measures of a collective nature compatible with local government.

Thirdly, the dominant public and private agents have begun to understand that a city which excludes or marginalizes a major part of its population is not viable or, to be more precise, creates living conditions which can only be endured with difficulty. An urban economic development based on high social costs does not necessarily lead to low overheads. Citizen insecurity, the time taken up with day-to-day mobilization and the running down of public areas and the urban environment in general also have economic costs. A competitive city must have capacity for the socio-cultural integration of the large majority of its population. Thoroughgoing urban measures of a social nature today appear to be necessary and urgent and, therefore, liable to find the political and economic support which was lacking some years ago.

Fourthly, and as a consequence of all the foregoing, the conditions are created for the existence of broad areas of citizen consensus with the political, intellectual and professional sectors and with the people's social organizations.

The lack of links between the various urban agents, which has been characteristic of the Latin American cities, appears to be on the way to being overcome.

Finally, the city needs to be understood not only as a territory which concentrates a large human group and a wide diversity of activities, but also as a symbiotic area (political power–civil society) and a symbolic area (integrating culturally and lending its inhabitants collective identity, with a trademark value or change value towards the exterior) becomes a sphere of potential responses to the economic, political and cultural challenges of our epoch. Let us cite three of these. First is the need to provided integrated non-sectoral responses to the problems of employment, education, culture, housing, transport, etc. Second, the setting up of public–private commitments amongst the requirements of economic growth and the environment. Third, the configuration of new spaces and mechanisms to stimulate political participation, facilitating relations between government bodies and the governed and promoting organization of the social groups.

The reaction of the city tends to take specific form in the drawing up of a 'Project for the Future' or strategic plan concerted between the main public and private agents. In addition to some Colombian cities (Bogotá (Box 5.3), Medellín, Cartagena), other Latin American cities have undertaken this path or have announced their intention to do so, amongst them Rio (Box 5.4), Porto Alegre, Salvador de Bahía and Recife in Brazil, Santiago and Concepción in Chile, Córdoba and Rosario in Argentina, Asunción in Paraguay and Caracas in Venezuela. Others such as Mexico DF and Buenos Aires have had to place their pending political reform at the forefront in order to put in place local government with leadership capacity. In yet other cases promotion of the city, urban and economic transformation and public–private cooperation have expressed themselves in lending metropoli-

Box 5.3 Strategic Plan: Bogotá 2000

The Bogotá Strategic Plan arose out of an expanding city which nevertheless faced considerable functional and socio-political obstacles to its development. It was an initiative from the Chamber of Commerce and other public and private entities, and from the United Nations Development Programme (UNDP), which ensure the technical and economic instruments necessary for its start. The plan immediately found support from City Hall, and later from central government.

Organization

The Consultative Committee is composed of over 300 bodies which take in a wide spectrum of Bogotá society, including business or economic development organizations, community and grass-roots organizations and the city's large non-governmentalk organizations (NGOs), all represented on this organ for the drawing up, consultation and dissemination of work on the plan. The same broad institutional and social base is reflected in the composition of the Management Committee, made up of 35 members and constituting the highest body for management and approval of the broad phases of the plan. Included are government departments (Council of the Presidency for Bogotá and Ministry of Development), local government (City Hall and Municipal Council, key departments, etc), the main economic institutions, city companies and trade unions (Chamber of Commerce, Banks Association, Federación de Trabajadores trade union, Industrial Association, etc), universities, the media (El Tiempo, El Espectador, Radio Caracol), large civic organizations (Viva la Ciudadanía, Fundación Compartir, Fundación Social, etc) and the neighbourhood social organizations.

The plan is promoted permanently by the Management Board, including representatives from ten of the institutions on the Committee. The base of the Management Board, along with City Hall and the UN Programme, is made up of the main employers' associations, trade unions and cities and media organizations. Its role is to act as the true promoting nucleus of the plan, promoting measures and facilitating implementation of the initiatives arising out of the debates of the various working groups.

The other novelty which Bogotá brings to the standard structure is the Technical Board, which monitors the plan on a day-to-day basis by means of weekly or fortnightly meetings. The Technical Board is made up of managers of executive type from some of the institutions of the Management Board: Technical Team, Ministry of Development, Architects Society, Chamber of Commerce, Viva la Cuidadanía (NGO) and the odd guest depending on the agenda. The Technical Board is the link between the Management Board and the Technical Team, playing a dual evaluation and promotion role.

Diagnosis and Objectives

The diagnosis work for the Bogotá plan is organized around five commissions, in which a total of 317 bodies take part. The result of their work was identification of seven critical issues which permitted structuring of the diagnostic summary and progress in formulation of the central objective and strategic lines.

- Central Objective: to make Bogotá a city in which its inhabitants find quality of life and friendly co-existence, with an integrated urban structure which develops its potential as a national and regional point of linkage and which projects its attractiveness in the economic and cultural fields.
- Strategic lines:
  1. City quality, life quality. The subject matter tackled looks at management and orientation of social policy and specific problems regarding housing, education, health, the environment and vulnerable population groups.
  2. Citizen peaceful coexistence. Work boards have been formed for the spheres of security, citizen communication and use and perception of public space.
  3. Governability of the city and public–private cooperation. Debate has been structured around the themes of administrative reform, local finances and community participation.
  4. Connected urban structure. The broad axes of the line are the planning function, regional integration, large-scale urban transformation and structure of public space.
  5. External accessibility and internal mobility. Themes were analysed concerning public–private management of internal mobility and external accessibility as medium for regional development.
  6. Competitive economy at national and South American regional levels. Bogotá as a competitive platform for a diversified industrial and services economy, though one shaken by opening up of the economy.

Projects and Campaigns

The Bogotá 2000 Strategic Plan has developed with originality a line parallel to the diagnostic line and the laying down of strategic lines: the boosting, support or intermediary work in large strategic projects considered a priori as projects of broad consensus, including:

- cleaning up of River Bogotá;
- public transport plan and Metrobus and Underground Metro projects;
- airport: 2nd runway;
- roads plan, especially Ring Road;

- public spaces plan linked with citizen culture campaign;
- citizen security plan;
- 'Bogotá beautiful with you' campaign.

The interest of this (perhaps rather unorthodox) line is that on the one hand it encourages the active participation of some public or private sectors especially sensitive to or interested in any of these projects or campaigns, while on the other hand it allows a mutually reinforcing dialectical relationship to be established between the active diagnosis and the strategic lines (which run the risk of appearing to be generic or not very viable) and the specific or ad hoc projects (which outside of the global framework of the strategic plan may not be fully reasonable as priority cases which are a logical part of the whole).

Development of the Strategic Plan and Drawing up of Projects

In addition to the large projects already set out in the process of drawing up the plan, approval of the diagnosis and of the strategic lines involves the formation of 18 groups which work on a list of almost 200 projects, which must be reduced or added to, given priority and allocated resources if they are to be coherent and viable. All the work carried out has as a common objective the according of priority to clusters of projects which permit progress to be made on transformation of the city towards the model posited by the central objective of the plan. The following have so far been identified as the most important measures:

- a thorough transformation of the municipal administration to permit better running of social policy and planning and progress of the decentralization process under way;
- linkage of the metropolitan space by the adoption of partial agreements which allow for its subsequent institutionalization;
- modification of citizen behaviour patterns and increased security;
- improvement of Bogotá's international image in order to consolidate its economy and attract new activities.

Sources: Avendaño, 1994; Strategic Plan Technical Unit, 1995; Borja and De Forn, 1994

tan or territorial master plans a more executive and participatory content (as in San José in Costa Rica and Quito in Ecuador), in economic promotion and international city marketing campaigns (eg Monterrey, Mexico) or in urban operations of refurbishment and promotion of the central areas (eg Buenos Aires, São Paulo and, again, Bogotá).

The City Project

The efficacy of these plans or projects depends on many factors. We would

Box 5.4 Strategic Plan: Rio de Janeiro

The Rio de Janeiro Strategic Plan has the objective of making Rio a metropolis with increasing quality of life, socially integrated, friendly and with a confirmed vocation for culture and joyful living. An entrepreneurial and competitive city with capacity to be a centre of thought, of business generation for the country and of privileged connection with the exterior. The strategic plan is a joint initiative of the Prefeitura, the Industrialists Federation and the Commercial Association of Rio de Janeiro, which constitutes a promoting committee in the form of a consortium of 60 companies responsible for financing of the Plan. Simultaneously, a Management Council of 22 members was chosen, on which the Consortium, the municipality and the social, professional and academic bodies are represented. The General Council is composed of over 340 members representing all the city's economic and social agents. The General Council approved the strategic plan for Rio de Janeiro in September 1995. The technical team includes the coordinator of the Plan, the technical director and a team of experts financed by the Consortium and with the complementary backing of the Prefeitura. External advisory services have likewise been contracted, with the support of a local consulting company.

On the basis of the general objective set out above, the plan laid down seven strategic lines, including quality of life, linkage of the city, social integration, critical infrastructures, development of the productive base, development of the city's specific propensities and employment. These strategic lines (outlined below) took specific form in 24 objectives.

- Quality of life: improving the life of Rio inhabitants, with special attention to the city's critical problems regarding mobility, violence and the development of networks of public services, recognizing the diversity of the citizenry and showing concern for high risk groups.
- Linking of the city: strengthening the centre of Rio de Janeiro and its central features, reinforcing the identity of the districts (primary social integration space) as a well connected, harmonious and balanced whole.
- Social integration: affirming the value of the citizens by restoration of social integration, recognition of obligations to the city and improvement of peaceful urban coexistence.
- Critical infrastructures: improving systems of accessibility and transport logistics, developing communication infrastructures and services for production, and development of internal and external trade.
- Development of the productive base: developing urban industries and advanced services and consolidating the industrial sectors already set up in Rio and its hinterland.
- Development of the city's specific propensities: boosting and improving the cultural, leisure, sport and tourist activities for which the city has a vocational propensity.
- Employment: creating new jobs, promoting training and in-service training of human resources and concentrating efforts on youth employment.

Analysis of Proposals

The working groups decided on a number of strategies and objectives, which can be summed up as follows:

- The 21st century Rio inhabitant: strategy which aims to offer people a range of opportunities and facilities for access to work and to social and cultural goods with the objectives of finding Rio de Janeirans places in the formal employment market, boosting the educational system, facilitating access to and improving the quality of health services, and bringing a broad diversity of people into day-to-day life.
- Welcoming Rio: aims to improve the city's relationship with its hinterland so that Rio can be identified as a receptive, functional city able to promote and extend peaceful coexistence and neighbourliness.
- Participatory Rio: has the objectives of achieving decentralized and participatory administration, the development of citizenry and improvement of citizen security, reorganizing the structure of government and citizen participation.
- Integrated Rio: aims at urban normalization by improving internal mobility, creating new central features and refurbishing the Centre to achieve better linkage of the city and a territorial balance which facilitates the dissemination of urban quality for all citizens.
- Gateways of Rio: is a strategy oriented at laying the city out as the linking centre of the metropolitan region, with improvements in accessibility, improvements of the operational capacity and efficacy of goods transportation, and special emphasis on advanced telecommunications.
- Competitive Rio: centres on improving infrastructures and services and developing the productive fabric in order to recover the city's competitiveness in a globalized world.
- Rio 2004, regional, national and international pole: consists in implementing a number of projects within fixed periods and relating to the internal and external image of the city (Rio city centre as cultural market, sports city, marketing city, etc).

PROJECT EXAMPLE

Strategy: Competitive Rio
Objective: Improved services infrastructures
Actions: Supporting commercial activity
              Promoting overseas trade
              Creating the International Financial Centre
              Attracting companies

STRATEGIC SUB-OBJECTIVE

Providing the city with backing for commercial activity through the implantation of infrastructure suitable for staging trade fairs and conventions.

IMPACT INDICATORS
Number of events staged in the city.
Number of overnight stays to which the events give rise.
Average number of participants.
Exhibition area.

PROJECTS
Riocentro

Description:	Complementing Riocentro so that it extends its capacity for staging events and creates a permanent Trade Fair Centre.
Bodies responsible:	City Hall (RIOTUR) Private sector
Financing:	Yes
Status:	Being executed.

Conventions Centre of the Hotel Nacional

Description:	Revitalization of the CCHN in order to create a space for the staging of medium-sized events in the city.
Bodies responsible:	City Hall Private sector
Financing:	Yes
Status:	Being executed.

Creation of new spaces for medium-sized trade fairs and exhibitions.

Description:	Support for public and private initiatives for the creation of medium-sized spaces for trade fairs and conventions located in Copacabana, Flamengo and Plaza Mauá.
Bodies responsible:	City Hall (RIOTUR) Federal Government (MAer/INRAERO/MEx) Private sector
Financing:	No
Status:	Under study.

STATUS OF THE PROJECTS (6 months after approval of the Plan)

Being executed:	60 (38%)
In portfolio:	17 (10%)
At project stage:	22 (14%)
Under study:	22 (14%)
To be developed:	38 (25%)

Sources: Final List of the Strategic Plan. Rio Sempre Rio. Presentation by the Technical Director: Rodrigo Lopes, September 1995 Notes by the Urban Technologies Advisory Team – Consultores Europeos Asociados

like to place special emphasis on three of these which strike us as specially important, not because they are actually more important than other factors, but rather because they are sometimes not taken sufficiently into account.

In the first place, the drawing up of a future project will be efficacious only if it mobilizes the public and private agents right away and takes specific form in actions and measures whose implementation can start immediately. Only thus will the viability of the plan be verifiable, confidence be generated amongst the agents promoting it, and a citizen consensus be built on the basis of civic culture and city patriotism. This will form the main strength of a strategic plan.

Secondly, a strategic plan must build and/or modify the image which a city has of itself and the image it has from the outside. In so far as it is a response to a sensation of crisis, resulting from a will to enter new global economic and cultural spaces and an aim to draw in a population which often feels excluded or taken little into account, the city project is a project of citizen communication and mobilization and of internal and external promotion of the urban area.

Finally, a strategic plan brings into question local government, its powers and organization, its mechanism of relation with other government levels and with its citizens, its international image and projection. Without a radical political reform – as much or more in the way of acting than in the legal base – only with difficulty will the objectives of response to the current challenges outlined above be achieved (Rolnik, 1994; Polèse and Wolfe, 1995; Sorkin et al, 1987; Grimberg, 1994; Fernández de Luco, 1995; Fernández, 1995; Singer et al, 1993; Reese, 1995; Marianacci, 1995).

CITIES AND THEIR GOVERNMENT: TOWARDS A PROMOTING LEADERSHIP

The historical claim for local autonomy which characterizes municipalism, the call for the processes of political and administrative decentralization and modern democratic culture to be taken further, and the allocation of greater public resources for the suitable exercise of its powers, are no longer sufficient proposals. A local government able to provide a response to the current urban challenge and construct and lead a city project must be a promoting government.

Local autonomy has been understood as legal protection of the capacity for self-organization, as exclusive and specific powers, as the right to act in all spheres of general interest to the citizens and as the availability of own resources without conditions attached to them. The legitimating principle of autonomy is that of proximity, which permits the establishment of a direct and immediate relationship between the representative organization and administrative structure and the territory and population. The principle of proximity remains valid, as does the call for local autonomy. In Latin America the constitutions of unitary and federal states alike (with the addition for the latter of provincial or departmental constitutions) place considerable restrictions on self-organization and local powers. Local public funding is scandalously insufficient (we are very far from the 50:25:25 ratio between the three levels to which Europe tends), and legal defence of autonomy before the law courts is practically unviable. The question of autonomy has therefore not been resolved. But the present times call for rather more to be posited, for city and local government are not what they used to be.

In the first place the city is today a plurimunicipal or metropolitan city, tending to lend structure in functional terms to a discontinuous and asymmetric regional area. It is difficult to put a figure on the urban population, since the users of the city centre can sometimes be as numerous or more numerous than its residents. There are many public and para-public government bodies acting in the city and their powers and functions are sometimes shared, sometimes concurrent and sometimes melt into each other (or mutually explain their omission). In New York alone, for example, it has been calculated that over 100 public or para-public bodies act with little or no coordination between them and with their powers and actions quite often overlapping. That is, the three classic elements on which local government is based – population, territory and organization – no longer provide sufficient clarity of definition. This is due above all to the fact that a large city is defined by its centrality, and local government must deal with functions for a population and a territory which goes beyond what historically and legally corresponds to it. And, it goes without saying, these functions cannot be exercised as a monopoly.

From all that has been outlined, we can deduce some consequences for approaches to autonomy and organization of local government. Firstly, a new type of relationship with the public government bodies considered to be 'higher' (especially central government). Without prejudice to wider recognition for the sphere of local autonomy, it is advisable to draw up contractual relations for joint exercise of those powers and functions which call of necessity for inter-government cooperation (eg communications infrastructure and the financing of public transport, economic promotion of the territory, citizen security, large-scale urban development operations, environmental policies and policies to combat poverty, etc). Urban contracts are destined to become a new paradigm of relations between government authorities. In the metropolitan sphere, government of the territory almost always calls for going beyond the contractual relationship, without this necessarily involving the creation of a new local or departmental government body which does away with or subjects municipal governments. We will look below at some proposals which facilitate joint scheduling of public action and shared management of services in the metropolitan sphere.

Secondly, local political organization cannot be based as it now is on an executive legislative dichotomy, on a centralized government and on a rigid separation between the public and private sectors. Management and contracting methods must ensure responsiveness and transparency and be in response to criteria of economic efficiency and social efficacy and not of political or bureaucratic control.

Finally, local government must assume a share of responsibility in the exercise of powers and functions traditionally reserved for the state (eg justice and security) or to the private sector (eg business activity in the market). This share of responsibility may consist in recognition of the right and of the resources to act, in the attribution of specific legal powers or in the capacity to exercise a role of leadership or coordination with respect to other government levels and the private sector.

Before putting forward some political and administrative reform proposals, we feel it more advisable to specify the novel functions facing local governments. Organization comes after the definition of objectives. What do we understand by the promoting role of local government?

- External promotion of the city by developing a strong and positive image based on a range of infrastructure and services (communications, economy, culture, security, etc) which attract solvent investors, visitors and users to the city and facilitate their 'exports' (of goods and services, of their professionals, etc). This range would by no means have to be wholly financed, implemented or managed by local government. The promoting role is precisely that of creating the conditions which facilitate their implementation by public or private agents (by means of planning, policy campaigns, economic compensation, etc).
- Joint arrangements with other government bodies and public–private cooperation as means to carry out both the aforesaid external promotion and those works and services required by the accumulated deficits, new urban requirements and the change of scale of the city. Joint arrangements and cooperation call for political initiative, legal and financial innovation and citizen consensus.
- Internal promotion of the city in order to instil 'civic patriotism' in its inhabitants, a sense of belonging, a collective wish to participate and confidence in and optimism about the future of the city. This internal promotion must be based on visible works and services, both those of monumental or symbolic character and those directed at improving the quality of public areas and the wellbeing of people.
- Political administrative innovation to generate multiple mechanisms of social cooperation and citizen participation. The promoting role of local government largely consists in stimulating and orienting the energies of the population towards collective wellbeing and peaceful civic coexistence, three examples being employment, citizen security and maintenance of public facilities, services and spaces. These are three types of problems which call for treatment at local level (whatever the causal factors and the competent bodies) and a considerable capacity for innovation and cooperation. Neither state or unilateral public action nor the magic hand of the market will resolve them.

Democratic innovation is probably the most exciting aspect of the role which local governments are increasingly taking on themselves. We believe that this innovative obligation is a response to three different challenges: that of citizen participation, that of social cooperation and that of integration of urban policies.

There is undoubtedly a crisis of the collective identities and of participation in the representative institutions and the political parties. The local setting (district, city, region) is a suitable framework for experimenting with and developing new electoral formulae, forms of territorial and functional decentralization, of participation in the running and execution of public programmes, etc. Democracy will be renovated from the principle of proximity, an indispensable adjunct of the supranational constructions today set in motion. To this end, the right to diversify and the duty to invent must be taken on board. Why, for example, can cities not regulate their own electoral systems, as long as they respect certain basic principles?

Social cooperation is today an essential need in facing up to sets of problems new in their nature or in their intensity. Some of these – such as employment, security and the maintenance of public spaces – were mentioned earlier, and others might also be mentioned, such as social care of the elderly, care for the environment, or the promotion of cultural activities which bring in a heterogeneous population, part of which is vulnerable to marginalization. Public policies are insufficient, since they will never be able to make available all the resources necessary and they cannot build up management methods suited to these social demands. Public action must support and stimulate social initiative. To take the example of employment, only by multiplying the creation of jobs in sectors outside international competition (such as those of social character and those related with urban ecology, etc.) will we be able to overcome the contradictory dynamics which occur, even in periods of growth, between active population and jobs available. Innovation must take specific form in the taking on of powers and functions at local level to permit the application of integrated policies. The problems of housing, poverty, the environment, education, economic promotion, culture, etc, cannot be tackled efficaciously by sectoral policies and bodies. And this brings us to a need to create new blocks of powers and new forms of management of local governments (*International Social Science Journal*, 1996; Borja, 1988 and 1996a; Wilheim, 1983; Tulchin, 1995).

NEW SPHERES OF COMPETENCE AND FUNCTIONS OF CITY GOVERNMENT

The spheres of competence and functions of local government cannot be laid down by uniformist state legislation nor can they be based on a rigid separation according to criteria of exclusivity. We believe that such competence and functions have to be laid down in accordance with other criteria such as proximity, capacity, joint agreement, social demand and diversity. Cities and territorial entities have to be able to exercise all those spheres of competence and functions whose very nature means that they cannot be exercised over broader areas: the principle of proximity is an essential part of democratic legitimization. Cities differ in size, population, activities, quality of human resources, etc. The principle of capacity means that certain types of cities can take on or attribute to themselves certain spheres of competence because they generate political, economic, social or technical resources which permit them to tackle them with guaranteed efficacy. One example might be the drawing up of an approach to, or coordination of, the forces of public order.

The principle of joint agreement leads us to accord primacy to contractual over hierarchical relations in respect of links between public government bodies (state and territorial governments) and with private agents. This is a matter of developing formulae such as consortiums, mixed company contract programmes, etc. The expression of social demand must always be taken very much into account. No local government can make a case that it has no competence when serious problems exist on subjects such as employment or citizen security. Legislation must permit and facilitate the action of local government in all those cases where social demand and political will are agreed upon facing up to challenges which in theory or due to legal inertia involve the spheres of competence of the state or are inherent to private action. All this leads us to press for the principle of diversity. Cities are and must be different in their forms and their activities. They must also be different in their organization and their spheres of competence. Below, we will outline succinctly a possible extension of the field of action of city government.

Economic Realm

The only municipal companies have traditionally been companies providing public services under a monopoly system. Economic promotion work has almost always been limited to definition of areas or zoning via planning and to tourist publicity for the city. Economic promotion of the city will now call for local government to have powers and means – in collaboration with other public and private agents, but at its own initiative – to develop business activity zones, to create banks with lines of venture capital, to promote public and joint-venture companies which compete with the private sector, to undertake international campaigns to attract investors and visitors, to promote and run trade fair precincts and congress centres and business and technological parks, set up information and advice offices for local and international businesses and investors, etc.

Town Planning, Housing and Environment Realms

Although these do pertain to the more traditional local government realms, the main decisions are in practice taken by national governments (financing of large-scale public works, use of central areas or areas suitable for urban property development, state or national enterprise management, subsidized housing programmes, penalizing powers in respect of environmental offences) or the private agents (who take decisions about whether or not to invest in urban areas and about drawing up the constructional projects and specific uses of the areas built up). All this without prejudice to local government using the theoretical power accorded it by its competence in respect of territorial planning, but rather than using this power to force the public and private agents into negotiation, priority should be accorded to joint arrangements with them.

This is one of the principal aspects of strategic planning. The promoting and local leadership role can thus take concrete form in establishment of the large public works projects financed by the State, in the salvaging of obsolete areas in the possession of port and military authorities or diverse ministries, in the management of housing programmes, in the delegation or transfer of disciplinary competence on all urban environmental matters, in the definition of new planning spheres which link planning with the execution of projects, in the possibility of creating holding companies, consortiums or mixed companies for implementing large urban development operations jointly with other government bodies and with the private agents, in the taking into the public domain of the subsoil, in the refurbishment of the old quarters, in use plans, etc.

Citizen Safety and Justice Realm

In this realm, local government must take upon itself competence to exercise:

*   A coordinating function on the basis of its capacity and the proximity principle. This might include coordination of the forces of public order or the police forces as a whole acting in the city (open area and public building security, traffic, petty urban crime, etc.). In some cities the national police force reports operationally in such cases to City Hall (without prejudice to the existence of a local police force).
*   An innovating function to implement preventive and/or repressive policies to deal with new sets of problems such as drug trafficking and rehabilitation of drug addicts, the development and application of environmental protection regulations, the repression of racism, xenophobia and other forms of social, ethnic or religious discrimination. In some cities the need has now been raised to set up their own system of judges and prosecuting attorneys: municipal justice.
*   A complementary function of justice and of the State police in order to take advantage of local government's greater potential for social cooperation. This is the easiest way to start to take on powers in this sphere.

Social and Cultural Realm

The powers and capacity for action of local government in social and cultural policy is usually widely acknowledged. In this sphere it is a question of resources rather than a legal matter. Lack of resources means that in practice higher layers of government replace local government, through sectoral programmes or individual projects. In other cases action is taken by the private sector, without such action being integrated into a coherent urban programme. In yet other cases, a major area of the city and of its inhabitants are simply left without any cultural facilities or social services. The powers which have to be won here are those of management and/or coordination of public or mixed programmes and projects and the implementation of all necessary forms of public–private cooperation.

Three fields of action strike us as particularly important:

1. Social programmes of housing and basic city planning with the cooperation of the inhabitants themselves. Prior recognition of the informal popular habitat. Building the city out into the periphery (with monuments, communications, central urban features and political-administrative decentralization).
2. Job creation programmes in sectors on the sidelines of international competition – personal services, maintenance of urban services and infrastructure, urban ecology.
3. Cultural range, both in respect of the range offered to outside audiences (attractiveness) and inside audiences (integration).

Education and health lie under municipal competence in some countries, while in others is a state or shared competence. In general, such provision cannot be of exclusively local competence (programming and financing must be at state level in order to avoid the creation of greater inequalities), though it is advisable to leave running of the basic network (non-university education and primary health care) to local government.

Realm of Urban Services, Transport and Communication Infrastructure

This realm raises at least three sets of problems:

1. Financing of the infrastructure and maintenance of basic services – such as public transport, water supplies and sewage networks – calls for contractual agreement with the state, and perhaps also with the concessionaires, along programme contract lines.
2. Relations with state or para-state public companies acting under monopoly systems, such as telephone companies and railways. Local government must achieve a favourable position from which to negotiate under good conditions. A strategic plan can lend legitimacy to an intermodal transport and communications plan which integrates the regional railway network with the urban network or obliges the telephone company to cofinance services galleries.
3. The possibility of taking on political and business powers in novel fields, such as communications towers, cabling the city, authorizing radio and local television stations, multi-media experiments in relationships with the citizens.

Conclusion: New Spheres of Competence, New Resources and New Management Modes

Many local governments say that they do not want further powers and more obligations, but rather more financial and other resources. And it is indeed true that a gap has formed between the growth of functions and demands made of the city government and the resources they have to provide a response.

But more power, more freedom and greater autonomy are needed in many cases. In the order of economic activities (even in aspects as simple as shop opening hours), for example, the application of penalizing powers in environmental themes (eg against polluting agents) or local radio and television authorization licences do not call for major financial resources (and can even provide income). Sometimes it is a question of being able to organize differently in order to make the contracting of goods and services more flexible (as long as this shows itself in greater transparency) or in order to innovate in administrative procedures (to facilitate relations with the citizens). In short, a greater degree of freedom and independence. One thing is certain: new policies and further spheres of competence cannot be taken on without reviewing old organizational structures and procedures designed for control rather than for action.

THE POLITICAL AND ADMINISTRATIVE REFORM OF LOCAL GOVERNMENTS

It would now appear to be clear that present local political structures and their organizational schemata and management resources are not the ones best suited to the building of this local leadership and taking on of the proposed new spheres of competence and functions. Though we cannot go into the matter in depth here, we would simply like to point to five lines of reform.

Metropolitan Government of the Territory and Decentralization of the Greater City.

Metropolitan structures must be created for territorial and strategic planning, joint scheduling of urban development investments and management of services at supramunicipal level. Metropolitan government must be understood more as a contractual or consortium relationship between levels of government rather than as a hierarchical relationship, even though its agreements are imposed upon all. Government of the metropolitan territory cannot be the task of a single level of the State, but rather of all (central, provincial or county and municipal). In parallel, the greater city must be decentralized into districts or localities, at both political and administrative levels.

Political Organization

Political organization which acknowledges the personalization of leadership, the need to go beyond a legislative executive confrontation and ensure continuity of municipal management. Amongst others, the following reforms are proposed:

- Direct election of mayors, including local mayors or district presidents.
- Homologation between executive majority and legislative. The mayor may, for example, be the head of the electoral list with most votes or on the list of the mayor with most council posts.
- Suppression of impediments to re-election or extension of mandates by four to six years.
- Assignment of executive or professional posts by open competition, without the contract being linked to the duration of political mandates.

Local Government Financing

International doctrine and experience – at least those oriented in accordance with federal and decentralizing stances – propose a public expenditure distribution with a 50:50 split between central government and territorial governments (municipalities and provinces, departments or regions). Local government financing must be largely automatic (own income plus share of national taxes such as income tax and value added tax (VAT)), the state contribution being of a compensatory nature (policy of re-equilibrium) or via programme contracts or other end oriented instruments.

The financing of urban development projects must involve a major element of self-financing through public appropriation of urban capital gains generated and through public–private cooperation.

Business Management of Services and Public Activities

It is not our aim to impose a single model, and still less sweeping privatization, but rather to advocate a diversity of management modes in order to achieve the greatest economic efficiency and social transparency. We are nevertheless convinced that a promoting form of local government cannot work according to the management and contracting methods inherent to traditional government. So some proposals might be:

- Autonomous management centres (which can take various forms: institutions, boards or foundations, public companies or consortiums, etc) for those activities or services which can be materially separated from the general services. Such centres would have their own funds and would themselves monitor expenditure, hiring or personnel and outside services, etc. Administrative control would be carried out subsequently.
- Mixed or private companies entrusted via concession or contract with an activity or the provision of a public-domain service. This is perfectly acceptable as long as the public government body lays down the conditions for provision of the service or the quality of the activity and as long as business-style management is shown to be most efficient.

Much of municipal activity can be implemented by means of such functional decentralization formulae as those just proposed, from management of cultural activity to economic promotion, from implementation of urban development projects to public transport management. When such decentralization is not possible, then it is advisable at least to make management and goods and services contracting procedures more responsive.

Relations with Those Administered, Communication and Participation

This is probably one of the fields in which innovation is most necessary and most possible. We might note three types of reforms:

1. Facilitating citizen access to government bodies and public services companies, for example by single service windows, telephone procedures, oral statement value, house-to-house surveys, etc.
2. Communication based on the generalized use of the new technologies (eg multimedia to permit citizen feedback or response) on the one hand, and personalized relations resting on direct elections and territorial and functional decentralization, on the other.
3. Citizen participation by concerted programmes based on cooperation of the users, support for grass-roots social organizations and acknowledgement of same as interlocutors, shared management of facilities, etc.

Internationalization of Local Governments

External relations have traditionally been the exclusive preserve of national governments. Nowadays, however, cities need to promote themselves internationally, they tend to joint transnational systems or axes, they form part of regional or world networks or organizations of cities and local authorities, they multiply their bilateral and multilateral relations. It would be paradoxical if the private agents of the city (chambers of commerce, universities, professional and trade union organizations, cultural associations, etc) were to have international projection and presence while local government could not. On the contrary, national governments have the task of facilitating such presence in various ways:

- Political and financial backing for the cities' external promotion work and for work directed at attracting international organization headquarters and public or private events.
- Facilitating the setting up of axes and networks between cities to permit the country's cities to reinforce their positions on the continent and in the world, taking account of the increasing competition between territories.
- Action before inter-governmental bodies (the United Nations, firstly, but also regional and economic organizations and so forth) so that the cities and their organizations are recognized as partners.
- Recognition of the right of local governments to have recourse to international loans and to manage the loans and/or subsidies from international organizations.
- In general, recognition of local government capacity to act as political subjects in international life and before bodies which have until now been exclusively inter-governmental, as long as this concerns matters in their interest or competence (Borja et al, 1990).

CONCLUSION

A strategic plan is the setting out of a city project which unifies diagnoses, specifies public and private measures and establishes a coherent framework of mobilization of and cooperation between the urban social agents.

The participatory process has priority status in the laying down of content, for on this process will depend the viability of the objectives and measures proposed. The result of the strategic plan is not a regulation or government programme (though when taken on by the State or by local government it should also show itself in regulations, investments, administrative measures, political initiatives and the like), but is rather a political contract between the public institutions and civil society. For this reason, the process which follows approval of the plan, the monitoring and implementation of the measures or actions, is as important or more important than the process of consensus-based drawing up and approval.

At a historical moment characterized by globalization of the economy and free market policies, political decentralization, enhancement of local or regional spheres of activity and identity and proliferation of local demands dissatisfied by state responses, the city project (or region project), based on a strategic plan with broad social support, constitutes a great democratic opportunity. It offers, on the one hand, an integrated response from the place in which the problems of a society arise and from which the public and private agents can act in concert, while on the other hand it allows us to rebuild a sense of city and of territory, in an epoch in which the loss of awareness of limits and of dissolution of the ideologies which back collective projects posits the challenge of remaking our systems of peaceful co-existence.

Chapter 6
Urban Policies in Globalization

NEW TERRITORIES AND NEW ECONOMIES

Introduction

Economic globalization posits new challenges for urban policies. On the one hand it generates new opportunities for better positioning in the new international economic relations. Competitiveness no longer depends on natural or energy resources, the traditional industrial base, geographical position, accumulation of capital or the political will of a protective state. The competitiveness of a territory will depend above all on:

- the efficient functioning of the regional-urban system, especially in respect of mobility and basic services;
- membership of global-type communications systems and good information about world processes on the part of the social and economic agents;
- skilled human resources (not just the upper strata);
- public backing for the economic and social agents through 'export protection' policies, favouring synergies and ongoing innovation;
- representative, effective and transparent political institutions which act to set clear and stable rules in their relations with the private agents;
- drawing up of a city (or region) project and marketing of same;
- governability of the territory based on social cohesion and civic participation.

On the other hand, globalization also has destructuring and dualizing effects on the territory and on local societies:

- Broad communication infrastructure schemes and economic promotion work are often approached in function of international competitiveness, leaving whole zones of the regional urban territory on the sidelines.
- Part of the population is left outside the sphere of global communications and competitive activities. In some cases they have been cast out of formal economic activity, while in others they never had any. Here

we find an unclear mix of the structurally unemployed, early retirements, unskilled youth and immigrant ethnic minorities. When this population is concentrated in ghetto areas there arises the vicious circle of marginality.

- The traditional economic activities, the main basis of employment and of fixed-capital investment are entering into crisis, while the activities of the global economy are often random and insecure. Uncertainty limits strong economic initiatives which lend cohesion to the social fabric. Economic globalization stimulates local informality.
- The space of flows, of variable geometry, replaces the visible territory. Identity providing places of reference proliferate or even dissolve. City planning loses its integrating function. The new metropolitan city tends towards discontinuity, the specialization of some zones and the marginalization of others, together with the weakening of multipurpose civic centres of strong symbolic charge.
- The much hailed public–private concerted action, even when expressed in plans or initiatives of global nature (such as a strategic plan or organization of a great event with the attendant list of public works), is often based on agreements between political institutions with oligarchic representation and large economic groups. The social exclusion and marginalization of territorial areas shows itself by omission, though it is none the less manifest for that.
- Promotion of the city is often understood in terms of selling it according to marketing techniques. Part of the city is sold, while the rest is hidden away and abandoned. It is highly instructive to analyse the maps and leaflets issued for tourism or for attracting potential investors. Even public servants have no knowledge of large parts of the city, not to mention the peripheral metropolitan fringes.
- Government of the territory is often understood in terms of protection or repression in the 'in' areas of the city. The public authorities can even abandon de facto control of the rest and relinquish efforts to integrate their populations.

Positive urban policies therefore move between the theoretical requirements of competitiveness and the practical dynamics generated by competition between groups and territories in the era of globalization. There is nonetheless a 'city demand' in response to three types of requirements:

1. for competitiveness: the city as an element which increases density of relations between economic, professional, cultural, educational and research agents. That is, intensification of synergies.
2. for quality of life: the city as diversity of activities and facilities, as an accessible collection of public spaces, as a grouping together of a heterogeneous population, represents a seemingly unlimited range of jobs, services and entertainment.
3. for governability: extension and destructuring of the regional urban space, while they have weakened the nation state and have increased the centrifugal dynamic deriving from globalization, have enhanced the status of the city as a governable territory.

These 'city demands' also express a demand for democratization, for proximity government (or subsidiarity), for decentralization and reduction of bureaucracy, for civic participation and social cooperation.

We can conclude, then, that the main objective of urban policy today is to create a city. This objective finds its clearest concrete and formal expression in the drawing up of large-scale urban projects, as we will see in the next chapter. Creating cities is only possible, however, if the city is provided with an economic development project which combines competitiveness with sustainability in respect of non-renewable resources and the environment, housing, access to services, civic participation and cultural integration. The creation of a city means opting for a concentrated urban environment (to intensify social and economic relations and to encourage cohesion and governability), a dialectic between centralities and mobility (as we will see in the following chapter) and the drawing up by all the urban agents of a city project which impregnates civic culture and manages to achieve broad social consensus (CCE, 1992 and 1994; Storper, 1994; Dupuy et al, 1989; Prud'Homme, 1993; Morandi, 1994; Reich, 1991).

Urban Policies: National Dimension

In the previous chapter we spoke of the important role of local governments in boosting 'promoting' and not simply 'managerial' urban policies. This growing protagonism of local governments would nevertheless not justify denying the role of national governments in drawing up and implementing urban policies. There are three reasons for this.

1. Statutory competence and the main financial resources lie with national governments, eg legislation on expropriation or the promotion of economic activities, or the financing of communications infrastructure. Processes of decentralization towards local and regional powers do not generally transfer all competence nor all the resources required for same.
2. Works and services in the metropolitan cities increasingly relate to plurimunicipal territories. They sometimes affect more than one province or region, and may in some cases be cross-border in character. The participation of national government is then more inevitable still for juridical and political reasons, while it may also be a rationalizing or arbitrating factor.
3. Local governments themselves have an interest in the participation of national governments in the large urban projects, independently of their legal competence. When it comes to negotiating with the large public or private economic agents, to undertaking international promotion or gaining access to loans, collaboration at national level is practically indispensable.

The role of national governments in urban policy tends to change in formal nature. It is marked not so much by its legal competence as by its political initiative and economic weight. Its relationship with local government is more contractual than hierarchical. And, as happens in the relationship of the latter with the private agents, its legitimacy does not derive from its prohibitive or permissive action but rather from its promotional contribution.

In any case, through its action national government must guarantee some basic principles and do what is needed for their application in all areas of the country. It must guarantee some basic minimum levels of equality of all citizens in relation to public services (eg education, health, security, etc). It must likewise protect and reinforce the autonomy of local governments, within a framework of respect for legality and human rights. Through its legislative action and investment measures, it must promote territorial reequilibrium and redistribution of income. And it must regulate clearly and transparently its relations of cooperation with the territorial governments (local and regional).

In their urban policies, national governments must also avoid the risk of dispersion. On the contrary, they must be extremely selective, in accordance with a very strict order of political and legal priorities, in order both to optimize the use of some necessarily limited resources and to avoid hindering the action of other public and private agents closer to the territory.

Within a framework of reflection on globality, and basing ourselves on recent experience of policies agreed between national and local governments (especially in Europe), we propose five main fields of action for national governments:

1. A first priority is opting for reinforcing the system of large cities and cities in general as 'centrality' (nodes of the urban network). Principal Action: communications, external accessibility (ports, airports, railway and motorway networks) and internal accessibility (ring roads, mass intermodal transport system, new centralities). But also integrated logistic activity zones (with new communications technologies) and powerful telecommunications infrastructures (including teleports and other infrastructures linked with the role of cities in the global economy).

2. National governments must consider the question of cities as a 'national source of wealth' and help to boost their competitiveness, especially in terms of support infrastructures for productive activity and commerce and trade in general. It is advisable to stimulate the differential facets of each city and also those infrastructures which position the cities better in their regional and world settings. For example: establishment of a system of trade fairs and exhibitions and facilities for congresses and conventions; headquarters of international organizations and meetings; technological and scientific parks; teleports and other information systems for economic activity (eg for world trade centres); R&D centres to link the universities and the more dynamic and competitive sectors of the economy; city marketing and tourism promotion campaign; design and promotion of large-scale, one-off or periodic events of a cultural or sporting nature.

3. National (or federal) city promotion policy involves capacity and availability for coordinating government departments (almost always more difficult than public–private cooperation). The ideal is to link the integrated view which the cities can provide (or states or regions in some cases), especially if they have a strategic plan, with the (sectoral) plans and investment programmes of the federal government. There are various formulae: consortiums, programme contracts, participation in Strategic Plan bodies, project finance holding companies, etc.

4. The national government must guarantee the existence and sound operation of those infrastructures and basic services which by their cost and nature exceed the (political and financial) resources of local governments: water and sanitation and roadway infrastructure and mass transport systems, together with large-scale environmental operations and operations of a cultural nature. Federal government action in such cases does not necessarily mean direct management or execution (which is generally best implemented by the closest authority), but does involve financial monitoring and participation.

5. Housing and social programmes (education, health, employment, poverty, etc) correspond to the local and state governments. The federal government is restricted to laying down the legal and financial frameworks in order to promote citizen equality. However, critical situations or structural shortfalls call for concerted public policies (exceptional or permanent) which can be promoted by national government (eg plan contracts between the government and cities in France to act in crisis-stricken urban zones). In some cases these programmes can have a concerted collaboration which goes from international bodies to NGOs and neighbourhood associations.

Urban Policy and Economic Base

In the first chapters we outlined the main characteristics of the global economy in the age of information, and the relationship between these characteristics and the urban territorial structures.

The 'natural environment' in which economic activity takes places is today the urban-regional setting, or the metropolitan city. It is here that there can be a greater density of relations, where synergies abound and where there are conditions most favourable for adaptability to various settings and for competitive innovation. The large cities are the multinationals of the twenty-first century. They are a place of encounter and of going beyond state policies and business initiatives. Sound operation of this setting calls for strong public intervention, as we pointed out in the introduction. This intervention involves on the one hand the concerted action of agents (public and private), and on the other hand the laying down of commitments between objectives or dynamics which are, or appear to be, contradictory.

These commitments are of various types:

• Between economic competitiveness and sustainable development.
• Between investment in immediately productive and competitive activities and fixed capital investment in support of activities which are profitable in the longer term or activities of a social nature (housing, collective facilities).
• Between the production of communication and economic infrastructures oriented by globalization and the production of infrastructures for territorial and social cohesion. (This point can be understood as a way of lending specific form to the previous one).
• Between a deregulation which permits more flexible relations between agents and favours private initiatives and the establishment of institutions and clear and respect rules which ensure the achievement of the

objectives of public or collective interest and provide a greater margin of certainty.

- Between the promotion of innovative initiatives and the modern image of the city and city planning work oriented by objectives of redistribution and cohesion of the urban populations as a whole.

We will be elaborating upon these points in this chapter and the next, and especially upon the one which appears to us best to sum up how these commitments can arise: the conception of large-scale urban projects (Chapter 7).

We would now like to call attention to three dimensions of urban policy as economic policy: products, settings and rules. In respect of products, the efficacy of urban economic policy can only be evaluated if it is presented as the maker of specific 'products' whose impact (sale, attraction of investors or visitors, social use, etc) can be measured. Within the framework of globalization, these 'products' can be a response to various objectives:

- Measures aimed a improving the efficacy of the productive processes or the competitiveness of products for the market. One example might be permanent information for the economic agents on the evolution of international markets, on technological innovation or on methods of commercialization. It is essential for competitiveness to opt for differentiation of products, in addition to productivity in their creation.
- Measures destined to provide (or stimulate) an efficient and attractive material base for new economic activities. For example: technological park, logistic activities zone, complex for trade fairs and congresses, area of new centrality which brings together a great diversity of services companies and others, etc. In this case an essential criterion is to check the profitability of the investment in accounting terms of amortization and profit.
- Measures aimed at intervening in the productive base of the city in accordance with 'exports protectionism'. It is not advisable to create a mystery around opening up, nor plump solely for products saleable as of now in outside markets. It is necessary to evaluate the potential offered by the products, skills and resources (material, technical, cultural) of the metropolitan region and to opt for lines of production deemed to be competitive in the medium term. The successful reconversion processes for port and shipyard zones, for textile or tourist zones have almost always rested upon a new approach to the use of existing resources and activities.
- Measures directed at reducing the margins of uncertainty of the private agents. This is today one of the great missions of local or metropolitan government, since globalization increases risk, randomness and precariousness. These measures can also relate to consumption goods (such as telecommunications systems), to demand (for example, a public sector commitment to undertake a series of time-staggered investments or to purchase hundreds of new products, such as electric-powered vehicles) or to financing (such as concessions in duty-free zones, local venture-capital banks, etc). And there are clearly many more fields of action which can reduce uncertainty.

- Promotion and marketing measures. Although city marketing is a relatively new activity, it is nevertheless sufficiently well known to make any detailed outline unnecessary. We might simply emphasize the need to undertake such work through 'products', such as hotel construction programmes, promotion campaigns by means of integrated tourism packages, cultural projects, sale of safe and/or attractive city image, specific campaigns for the attraction of investors, attenders of congresses, etc.

In all such measures it is important to bear in mind always that the medium- and long-term competitiveness of the territory will not depend on immediate successes based on ad hoc competitive advantages which do not generate innovation (such as gaining a place in the global economy in routine mass production links based on low labour costs), but rather on the ability to set up specific differentiated production which is competitive due to its quality rather than its low cost.

The settings are the traditional dimension of urban economic policy. We have already stressed repeatedly the importance of communications infra-structure, sound operation of urban services and the existence of suitable areas for the new productive activities. There are some types of settings whose recent acquisition of importance is worthy of mention: the technolog-ical setting, human resource training, and the environment (which conditions sustainability). These will be dealt with in the coming sections of this chapter. We would now like to mention other types of setting which are not always considered to be decisive for competitive economic activity, but which may nonetheless at times have a decisive influence:

- The social setting. We refer here to the characteristics of urban social life, the weight of poverty and marginalization, sensation of citizen safety, individual and group behaviour in public spaces, the existence and efficacy of personal services, etc. All these aspects are major conditioning or influencing factors on the decisions of the economic agents, on the attractiveness of the city and on the sound running of public services.
- The cultural setting. The cultural range available has an ever greater importance for competitiveness of the city and also for its social cohesion. Investments in cultural infrastructure can be highly competi-tive (although they are at times mere squandering, as occurs in some European countries in which dozens of relatively nearby cities all offer the same range). Cultural infrastructure and activities which must at once serve internal and external demand must also opt for diversity, specific nature and quality.
- The aesthetic setting and the urban environment. By aesthetic setting we refer to the quality of public spaces, of architecture and monuments. And by urban environment we refer to the forms which arise in the city's collective life, the social use of leisure (night life included), etc. This is another dimension of the city, and one which is increasingly highly rated not only by visitors but by the city's habitual users.

These reflections on settings lead us to one conclusion: the importance of public action in the regulation of urban life. This regulation must have the active and voluntary cooperation of the citizens and must therefore form part of civic culture. But it must also be expressed in clear and just rules.

Throughout this chapter and the entire book we have stressed the importance of contractualizing relations between government bodies and the private agents, on the need to reduce uncertainty, on the capacity of adaptation to changing situations, on the synergies which arise in the urban setting. These requirements lead to one conclusion: from the point of view of its economic-social efficacy, the functioning of large cities today calls for the existence of accessible representative institutions which act in accordance with defined programmes, clear rules which ensure public objectivity and responsiveness in public–private relations, and of tacit or implicit conventions (as important or more important than institutions and rules) which permit a certain amount of automatic reaction in relations and behaviour (both public and private). There are, for example, countries and cities in which it is known that administrative procedures are speedy and corruption practically non-existent. This is of itself already a great comparative advantage. In other cases commercial and professional relations operate according to codes which have a long history and which, though of private juridical nature or even just informal, are rarely transgressed. This is another comparative advantage. The greatest obstacle to urban economic development is probably a mixture of bureaucratic complexity, private unpredictability and widespread arbitrariness (Storper, 1994; Prud'Homme, 1993 and 1994; Reich, 1991; Dumont, 1993; Burgel, 1993).

SUSTAINABLE DEVELOPMENT

Sustainable development is one of the greatest challenges facing humanity, though the definition of the concept can be ambiguous. The World Environment and Development Commission popularized the concept in 1987 with the definition: 'sustainable development is development which meets the needs of the present without endangering the ability of future generations to meet their needs'. Sustainable development presents various dimensions which must be taken into account in designing urban development strategies. The sustainable development concept must emphasize development as increase of material wealth, as increased quality of life (variably defined according to culture) and reproduction of the social, material and institutional conditions required for carrying forward this development. Sustainability therefore does not have a single ambient setting, but encompasses an integral view of urban development.

Environmental sustainability is one of the most acute problems of today's world as a consequence of the historical processes of urbanization and development. The problem of sustainability centres upon squandering of resources by the current social organization and over-exploitation of ecosystems. Cities, like human societies, are ecosystems dependent upon interchanges outside the territory which they occupy, requiring for their functioning a guaranteed provision of external supplies, their internal distribution and utilization, and the subsequent expulsion of products and waste.

BOX 6.1 ECONOMIC DEVELOPMENT FOR THE 21ST CENTURY: OSAKA

Osaka's economic development lines lie within the General Development Plan for the 21st Century, approved in 1990 and coordinated by the Osaka 21st Century Association, financed jointly by City Hall, the Prefecture of Osaka and local companies. The plan includes action in various spheres and the implementation of large-scale infrastructure work such as the Kansai International Airport, inaugurated in 1994. Osaka is actively pursuing reinforcement of international economic functions and development of new industries, so that it can become an economic supercity with world-level functions and highly diversified industrial activities. The plan at the same time aims to reform the small and medium companies which have historically been the source of Osaka's economic vitality and creativity.

In order to achieve this primary objective of reinforcing international functions, Osaka has set out four broad lines of action. The first centres on strengthening the functions of international trade on the basis of concrete measures which include the creation of an international trade zone at Osaka airport, around some central activities such as the International Exhibitions Centre and the Trade Centre of Asia and the Pacific. A further aim is to develop support for international trade and investment with the promotion of information systems, the organization of business meetings and trade fairs. Finally, this strategy also takes in the establishment of partnerships with other cities of Asia, the Pacific and the rest of the world in order to promote economic exchange in the private sector with the objective of mutual growth. The second strategic line is directed at reinforcing international financial functions through the establishment of a financial market with the introduction of new financial trading, plus the promotion of new support industries for the financial companies, such as research and information services companies. The third strategy centres on developing new international business centres through urban regeneration of city centre zones and the creation of a new city on 775 hectares of land reclaimed from the sea in Osaka port (Technoport Osaka Project). The fourth economic development strategy is based on promotion of international cooperation to contribute to the economic development of the developing countries through the training of human resources, transfer of technology and management know-how and the promotion of imports.

The concentration of population in the cities and their development over recent years has been implemented on the basis of exploitation of increasingly scarce natural resources without the establishment of appropriate measures to render their recovery nor the availability of functions of regeneration and safeguarding of the natural spaces traditionally involved in life in rural zones. All this has led to over-exploitation of this type of resource and a significant increase in levels of waste, danger of fire, etc, which have

Box 6.2 Pittsburgh: Building a Regional Network for Economic Revitalization

Pittsburgh provides an example of a city that has had relative success in addressing the problems of economic restructuring and industrial decline in the heartland of the old United States steel industry. Despite rapid declines in manufacturing employment and problems associated with increasing global competition, Pittsburgh has been able to develop new and thriving sectors of the economy, combining high technology development and strong growth in education and health services. This has been achieved primarily by building a network of ties between the public, private and non-profit sector which has provided support for new economic innovation, and created new channels for participation in economic development decision-making.

Economic Turnaround

Pittsburgh is still most prominently known for its history as the centre of the United States steel industry. Located at the confluence of the Allegheny and Monongahela Rivers, which form the Ohio River in southwestern Pennsylvania, Pittsburgh developed as the centre of the country's glass-making and ironworks industry. By the late nineteenth century, Pittsburgh produced 75 per cent of the nation's crucible steel, and as late as 1950, a full 25 per cent of the United States steel production was concentrated in Pittsburgh. In the early 1980s, however, the United States domestic steel industry collapsed, and the Pittsburgh region was particularly hard hit. From 1980 to 1985, steel production in Pittsburgh declined by almost a half. Steel plants in mill towns throughout the region closed, and Pittsburgh's entire manufacturing sector was hit hard. Unemployment in 1983 reached 14.7 per cent and many residents moved out of the area seeking opportunities elsewhere.

Pittsburgh managed to avoid the massive urban decline and impoverishment that struck so much else of the 'rust-belt' during this time. Employment in the late 1980s began to climb again and unemployment levels have dropped to 6 per cent. In the past ten years, sectors that have seen the most rapid employment growth include: health care (95 per cent growth), specialized education (91 per cent), high technology (74 per cent) and higher education (50 per cent). Today, Pittsburgh is among the top places in the nation for software; a world-class medical centre; one of the top environmental service providers in the world; a significant advanced manufacturing employer; and is poised to become the robotics development hub of the world. In the past 15 years, the number of high-tech firms has grown by more than 100 per cent, from 1,130 in 1979 to 2,374 in 1993, employing a total of over 84,000 people. According to Corporate Technology Information Services, the State of Pennsylvania has the fifth highest concentration of technology companies (after California, Massachusetts, New York and Texas), with most of it concentrated in the Pittsburgh area. Education has become a significant component of the regional economy. In 1988, for instance, while roughly 11,000 worked for the top seven industrial firms, 37,000 worked for the major universities and colleges. Carnegie Mellon University brought in $29 million in research funds in fiscal year 1979–80, but nearly $121 million in fiscal year 1988–89. In 1985, the university won the national competition for the United States Department of Defense's Software Engineering Institute, a prize worth roughly $100 million of federal funds. In 1994, in the City of Pittsburgh alone, hospitals employed a total of 37,311 people.

Pittsburgh was rated the 'Most Liveable City' in 1985 by Rand-McNally, the second best city for working mothers, by *Working Mother Magazine* in 1990. According to the United States News and World Report it had the fifth best housing market in 1992 (the median housing cost in Pittsburgh was $80,000 in 1994, below the national median of $107,600 in that year), and was rated one of the top 10 places in America to live and work, by the *National Employment Review* in 1991. Pittsburgh remains one of the safest metropolitan areas in the United States among cities with population exceeding one million. The city's murder rate in 1994 translated to 17.8 homicides per 100,000 residents – below the national average of 23.6. Pittsburgh's three rivers offer 70 miles of riverfront in the metro area.

Factors of Success

Pittsburgh's success in dealing with economic restructuring can be traced to essentially three main points: 1. a long history of local government involvement in economic development planning and public-private partnerships 2. strong neighbourhood organizations that have increasingly been able to influence economic development policy; 3. a dense network of non-profit organizations playing a strategic role in economic development throughout the region.

History of Public–Private partnership and Local Government Involvement in Economic Development

Fragmentation of political authority is an unfortunate characteristic of local government in the United States. For example, Pittsburgh itself only accounts for 18 per cent of jobs in the broader metropolitan area. Allegheny County, of which Pittsburgh is the centre, includes 130 different municipalities, plus another 149 special districts or municipal authorities. Thus, because political jurisdictions do not coincide with functional economic regions, economic problems that transcend local political boundaries are difficult to address properly. Thus, for most local governments in the United States prior to the 1980s, local economic development efforts were fragmented and ad hoc. Pittsburgh, however, has had a much longer experience in economic development policy-making. Initially the push for coordination in economic development activity came from the Allegheny Conference on Community Development. Founded in 1946, this organization, representing the major corporations in the area, began to develop partnerships with local and county government to guide economic development in the region. The first stage of revitalization (termed Renaissance I) begun in the late 1940s, involved a $500 million renewal (slum clearance, parks, office buildings, and cultural amenities), and institutional restructuring (municipal service authorities for transit, parking, sanitation, regional industrial development parks, and housing associations). A second major initiative, (termed Renaissance II) occurred in the late 1970s. This $2.4 billion programme revitalized inner city neighbourhoods, developed a light rail transit and subway system and prioritized infrastructure renewal.

The private–public partnerships that were the basis of these economic revitalization initiatives have since become a major trend throughout the United States. They are viewed by many as being a rational, flexible, voluntary and cooperative alternative decision-making structure to augment the local state and the market to 'rehabilitate the civic tradition'. Pittsburgh has a much longer history of these private–public partnerships and has developed a greater expertise. Yet Pittsburgh's experience of restructuring in the 1980s also highlighted the limitations of a partnership with only the private sector. The tensions between corporate strategies of adjusting to global competition and the social costs that this entailed meant that the structure of public–private partnerships couldn't provide the leadership needed for economic restructuring.

Neighbourhood Organizations and Community Organizing
Pittsburgh has 88 neighbourhoods that contain from 400 to 16,000 residents each, are territorially and socially well defined and are recognized by city hall. A well developed sense of place and commitment has supported neighbourhood organizations and networks substantially more than many other United States cities. These neighbourhood organizations became a much more central part of the city's political and policy equation in the late 1970s and 1980s. By the late 1980s, neighbourhoods exercised a real influence on city government, unlike many cities in which downtown interests dictate what is to happen in economic development.

In addition to the long history of neighbourhood identity, the economic decline of the early 1980s stimulated a new round of community organizing. Traditionally, urban movements have concentrated on consumption issues such as rent control, access to housing and social services. Pittsburgh, however presents one of the stronger examples in the United States of labour–community alliances, in which community mobilization increasingly has focused on production issues. There were three major labour–community initiatives in the 1980s that challenged the prerogatives of the corporate elite to determine unilaterally the economic destiny of the Pittsburgh region. The first, the Denominational Ministerial Strategy/Network to Save the Mon-Ohio Valley, was a traditional Saul Alinksy style organization that tried to demand more consideration of worker and community welfare in economic decisions (though it self-destructed from internal tensions in 1985). The second, the Mon Valley Unemployed Committee, was created in 1982 as an outgrowth of initiatives by union locals, and eventually focused on social relief such as mortgage foreclosure relief, job training, food banks and the extension of unemployment benefits. The third, and most important coalition, was the Tri-State Conference on Steel, which was founded in 1979 in response to steel plant closings in the Youngstown area. This coalition was the key force behind the creation of the Steel Valley Authority (SVA) in 1986, which brought together the city of Pittsburgh and nine other municipalities in the area, and included representatives of dislocated workers, religious leaders and local businessmen. SVA's initial activity was focused on preventing the closer of the United States Steel blast furnace at Duquesne by reopening it as a worker owned facility. What makes these initiatives significant was less their accomplishments, but their economic analysis and the fundamental issues they raised about economic decision-making.

Non-Profit Networking in Service Delivery

Pittsburgh has developed a dense network of non-profit agencies that were involved in economic development initiatives on a regional basis. A number of leading analysts point to this network as a leading cause of Pittsburgh's ability to adjust to economic restructuring. Major institutions in the area include:

- The Regional Industrial Development Corporation (RIDC), a non-profit economic development organization that was created in 1954 by the Allegheny Conference on Community Development, focusing initially on redevelopment of the downtown area. In the 1980s, it played a key part in a number of strategic developments. In 1986, in partnership with the City of Pittsburgh's Urban Redevelopment Authority, the University of Pittsburgh and Carnegie Mellon University, it developed the Pittsburgh Technology Center on 50 acres of what previously housed a Jones and Laughlin steel plant, two miles from downtown. In 1988, the RIDC entered into agreement with Allegheny County to coordinate the planning and redevelopment of two closed steel mills in Duquesne and McKeesport (a total of 400 acres of land). About the same time, it also negotiated to buy Westinghouse Electric Corporation's closed plant (4.5 million square feet) in the mill towns of East Pittsburgh and Turtle Creek.
- The Southwestern Pennsylvania Economic Development District (SPEDD) is a non-profit corporation established in 1965 by nine counties in the area, which has been involved in administering a number of low interest loan programmes for small businesses and has provided various types of management assistance to small companies throughout the region. They currently operate 17 small business incubators throughout the region, the largest of which is located in a closed Copperweld Steel facility.
- The Western Pennsylvania Advanced Technology Center, is sponsored by the University of Pittsburgh and Carnegie Mellon University, with funding from the state government. It focuses on technology transfer, and has helped SPEDD's incubator programme.
- The Pittsburgh High Technology Council, established in 1983,

supports high-tech economic development in the region through conferences, educational programmes, publications, and by helping emerging companies with their problems by bringing them in contact with established companies.

• The Mon Valley Initiative is a network of Community Development Corporations (CDCs) in 17 towns throughout the region. They build the capacity of local leadership to undertake economic development projects by offering technical assistance to CDC's in the area.

As Roger Ahlbrandt, Director of the Institute for Industrial Competitiveness at the University of Pittsburgh argues in 1990:

'The Pittsburgh region's economic restructuring in the 1980s has been based on the creation of a diverse delivery system to address its economic development needs... Although the public and private sectors are involved in many of the efforts, the unique element is the important role played by the relatively autonomous non-profits. The region's response grew out of a culture which suppported the creation of non-profit organizations to address newly identified issues and the willingness of all sectors to work together. Therefore, the strong civic tradition in Southwestern Pennylvania provided the foundation upon which development of such a system could occur.'

The extent of community input into the non-profit sector, and particularly into private–public partnerships, remains somewhat contested. Community organizers argue that without significant capacity building, community organizations will inevitably face an uphill battle in having their interests represented in econimic development.

But at the very least, city officials have moved beyond an exclusive focus on supporting and bargaining only with the private sector. As public–private partnerships become ever more fashionable elsewhere, Pittsburgh has already recognized that non-profit organizations are economic engines and thus should receive public sector attention. The non-profit sector, can be as strategic to economic development policy as the private sector. And compared to many United States cities, the level of cooperation and consultation between the private, public and non-profit sector in Pittsburgh is remarkable.

Sources: Advisory Commission on Intergovernmental Relations (1993); Ahlbrandt (1990); Fitzgerald and Simmons (1991); Giarratani and Houston (1989); Hathaway (1993); Jezierski (1990); Sbragia (1990); Schneider (1995); Singh and Borzutsky (1988)

in a way been seen as an independent aspect of urban development. For a while now, as a consequence of a broader view of global development from the viewpoint of sustainability, there has been some attention to the need for political measures to care for our natural setting.

The organization of urban space and of the activities which are undertaken in a city must provide for suitable living conditions for their inhabitants. The maintenance of these conditions must take account of both the temporal dimension – ensuring conditions of living for future generations – and the spatial dimension, without compromising the sustainability of its various spheres of influence, from nearby areas to global aspects, from a viewpoint of aggregate operation of groups of cities.

The world's cities are currently suffering from serious problems of local and global sustainability deriving from the forms of urban organization, unsuitable management and uncontrolled (or controlled by price alone) and unconscious consumption patterns, especially in the areas of greatest wealth, which lead to squandering of resources. The pressure brought to bear upon the environment and upon the global ecosystem by urbanization processes is increasingly great. This leads to a loss of natural capital, without the existence of suitable policies of control, improvement of the existing capital and renewal or replacement of that consumed.

Although the scale and acuteness of the problem seems to show itself most sharply in developing country cities, the urban centres of the northern countries are in fact the ones which have most impact on changes in the world ecosystems. What is more, their policies and technologies impose world standards which reproduce and perpetuate forms of organization and consumption which are scarcely sustainable, in terms of low-density single-family housing, mobility within geometrical growth, motorways, increased waste, higher energy consumption, etc. The reproduction of these models in developing country cities exacerbates the negative consequences due to lack of political democracy, the volume of population excluded, the rates of urbanization and the size of the large metropolises.

Environmental Sustainability

The inhabitability of cities, especially in the districts created over recent decades, is characterized by quite widespread decline of public space, this despite the refurbishment efforts made in many cases. The basic causes lie in defects of design, defects of integration into the districts by means of a more integral planning of more extensive areas, processes of city 'construction' without neighbourhood cooperation, and the growing intrusion of motor vehicles, whether parked or moving.

Despite the considerable amount of work put in by cities to 'urbanize', create or refurbish public spaces, enormous deficiencies are detectable and are basically concentrated in the old quarters and in the working-class residential areas. The expansion of communication infrastructure has given rise to new challenges and problems in the spaces lying between and in contact with other built up zones, and these are added to the shortfalls not yet provided for.

The progressive taking over of public spaces by cars, in addition to giving rise to an incessant transformation of surfaces laid to communication infrastructure – which in the large European cities currently occupy an average of 10 to 15 per cent of the land, and in some cases (Lisbon, Bilbao) as much as 35 per cent – results in processes of expulsion of the weaker and less motorized sections of the population from the public space. Public spaces play an essential role in the construction of a competitive, cohesive and sustainable city. City construction shows itself in its public spaces, which act as places of centrality, as places of creation of district or city identity, and so forth. Public spaces must be accessible and safe, especially for the weaker sections of the population, and must have symbolic features which allow the population to identify with their place of residence. The degradation of public spaces which arises due to lack of conservation, to indiscriminate occupation by cars, to scant integration of the needs of the inhabitants themselves, leads to uprooting from and lack of identification of the residents and users with the territory in which they live, work and consume.

In the current conditions prevailing in cities, the urban environment has suffered marked degradation. This loss of quality of life shows itself in many aspects, amongst which we might note atmospheric pollution, increase of noisy surface area, reduction of climatic comfort, spectacular rises of consumption and waste production, increased insecurity on the streets and greater awareness of the existence of architectural barriers.

Increased Atmospheric Pollution

The quality of cities' air has deteriorated steadily due to increased economic activity and, above all, the rise in vehicle traffic. City traffic is the main source of atmospheric pollution, accounting for 100 per cent of concentrations of carbon monoxide and lead, 60 per cent of nitrogen oxides (which contribute to the formation of acid rains) and 50 per cent of particles. The city's transport sector is, after private transport, the one which consumes most energy and is therefore responsible for the carbon dioxide emissions, which in general in the European Union alone, have shown a spectacular 63 per cent increase since the beginning of the 1970s.

Increase of Noisy Surface Area

Noise, one of the most genuinely urban forms of pollution, also has its roots mainly in motorization. It is estimated that increasingly large sections of population are for this reason daily exposed to sound levels exceeding the 65 decibel limit set by the World Health Organization, with the attendant consequences for health and productivity. The density of cities and the concentration of activities in small spaces contributes to increased levels of environmental noise. In recent years some cities have had to adopt new regulations to limit the use of horns and hooters, penalize excessive motorcycle and car noise and control night noise (bars, discotheques, etc).

Increased Energy and Water Consumption

Increased living standards have gone hand in hand with increased energy and water consumption. In the more developed countries the use of electricity, gas and other petroleum by products has increased enormously, while in the cities of developing countries the use of 'new' forms of energy goes alongside consumption of the more traditional forms of energy (coal, wood, etc).

Reduction of Climatic Comfort and Increase in Temperature, due to Unsuitable Use of Vegetation, Insulation and Ventilation

Urban areas suffer from a process of severe environmental degradation which increasingly reaches beyond the strictly local areas to take on planetary dimensions and places in peril the delicate balance of the biosphere. To take one example, emissions of carbon dioxide and other gases which lead to the 'greenhouse effect' responsible for the Earth's disturbing climatic change, have their main source of emission in the cities as enclaves of demographic and economic concentration. Temperature changes lead to increased energy consumption with the installation of heating and air conditioning systems, etc. Hence an improvement of the environmental conditions of urban spaces is a fundamental prerequisite for safeguarding the planet (Rutelli, 1996; Cohen et al, 1991; Bilbao et al, 1994; Serageldin et al, 1994a and 1994b; Alguacil et al, 1994; Martín, 1995a).

Sustainability and Mobility

The growing importance of mechanized transport flows, which creates pressure on the city centres, is one of the main problems of the urban environment. The large number of movements at rush hours tends periodically to swamp the capacity of existing transport infrastructure and services. This is so even where increased mobility using mechanized means takes place using public transport as well as the private vehicle, the great protagonist of recent decades.

The increased motorization of households and rise in disposable income at a rate much faster than the cost of acquisition and running of automobiles, have led to a steady increase in the use of private vehicles for journeys of all types. The model split between the car and public transport has shown variations in favour of private vehicles in most large cities. And the car's share is still more marked if we consider centre-periphery travel, the immediate consequence being an unprecedented increase in traffic congestion on the main access routes. City centres are therefore suffering from a notable decrease in air quality and increased acoustic pollution, together with a rise in journey times in the city and the attendant loss of competitiveness and quality of life. The reduction of commercial speed and of regularity and reliability of surface public transport leads to a reduction of demand in these networks.

The increase of vehicle traffic is one of the chief barriers to the inhabitability of the cities. In many European cities, the car already accounts for 80 per cent of motorized transport, and the prospects for evolution, according to the recent report 'sustainable European Cities' drawn up by the Experts Group on Urban Environment of the European Community indicates that by the year 2000 'automobility' will rise by 70 per cent in the countries of northern Europe, by 300 to 500 per cent in southern countries and by 1,000 per cent in the eastern countries.

Most of the large, medium and small cities already have traffic saturation and congestion problems due to the avalanche of cars in an urban fabric which has limited spatial and environmental capacity. In spatial terms, for example, automobile traffic takes up 80 per cent of road space, this despite the fact scarcely 20 per cent of the people moving around the city each day use this form of transport. And in terms of energy consumption, it is estimated that the average consumption per person transported at rush hour is as much as six times greater than for public transport.

The conventional policies which have been adopted, bent on adapting the city to the car, and the heavy investment in recent years on roadway infrastructure, although they have helped to relieve traffic congestion, have also encouraged a rise in the number of vehicles on the roads (Wachs and

Crawford, 1992; Ascher, 1995; Figueroa et al, 1995; Ordóñez, 1993; Martin, 1995b).

Social Sustainability: a Global Concept

The evolution of cities differs substantially from one to another. While some cities have made great strides in improving their local sustainability, the large metropolises in developing countries are taking backward steps due to their high growth rates and the inability of their economies and their governments to overcome deficits and meet the new needs. In many cases cities have undertaken environmental protection and recovery policies in an effort to increase internal sustainability, which has improved at the expense of increasing environmental impact in more distant places, or at the cost of an unnecessary destruction of resources in their own areas.

Sustainable development in the urban sphere is a necessity for the survival of societies and involves a global approach to urban development which involves rather more than a 'green' approach. The environmental unsustainability which is reflected in increased emission levels, increased atmospheric pollution, pollution of water and soil, disappearance of natural areas, degradation of urban space and so forth, is only part of the problem. Challenges must be faced such as education of the population, promotion of economies able to create jobs, provision for participation and democratization mechanisms, restructuring of the global society, direct attack on the causes of exclusion of the population, etc. Sustainability is not only environmental, though the quest for new solutions to traditional problems is one of the great challenges. The cutting down of waste, energy consumption reductions and saving, protection of the natural spaces and the struggle against environmental degradation are outstanding subjects which the cities have to confront. These challenges are not merely technical problems, but must instead be met with changes of mentality and habits, thereby including work on education of the population, citizen participation and involvement in defence of the environment, etc.

Sustainability also involves social integration. Large pockets of unemployment and poverty and large masses of excluded population make sustainable urban development impossible due both to the environmental and health risks involved and an inability to offer a peaceful and democratic social environment. Social policies directed at integration of the population through education, employment, access to housing, control of demographic growth, health and so forth, cannot be separated from processes to achieve sustainable development.

The cities of developing countries and developed world cities suffer to a greater or lesser extent from a number of factors of pressure which condition the sustainable development of urban zones. Lack of job opportunities, poverty and poor health are basic aspects of sustainability. Poverty is one of the causes of environmental degradation and deterioration of health. Without income which enables basic needs to be met it is difficult to achieve sustainable development. In developed and developing countries alike, an inability of the economies to provide stable jobs makes it difficult to design a socially sustainable model of urban development. To lack of employment and poverty are added difficulties of access to housing, which must be considered not only as an isolated physical structure but within an urbanized context of public spaces which permit access to urban services and the development of civic life.

There are a number of basic actions which can ensure the sustainability of urban development. These actions have a direct effect upon the factors of pressure mentioned above and, although they find their most severe and sharp expression in the cities of the developing world, they are also applicable to the conurbations of the industrialized world. There are a number of factors directly related to environmental sustainability, which basically include ensuring water supplies, the provision of energy from renewable sources, and waste collection and treatment. Social sustainability means that the inclusion of all population groups in urban society must be ensured through guaranteed access to housing – and access to land – and the right to work, a basic element in achieving improved living conditions for the population.

Economic Sustainability and Competitiveness

Finally, we must not overlook the dimension of sustainability which is linked with competitiveness and quality of life. The new conditions of production, distribution and communication make the quality of urban life into an essential factor of attractiveness for investments and for highly skilled labour. A positive social setting likewise permits increased productivity of human resources, while at the same time helping to develop positive attitudes. Cities play an essential role in ensuring sustainable development. While cities make a large contribution to environmental problems, they are also part of the solution to them.

> 'Human settlements, and particularly the large urban agglomerations, are great contributors towards environmental degradation and consumption of resources. At the same time human settlements, large and small, are little used areas of opportunity: creativity, economic growth, communication, accessibility for the transfer of know-how, and an efficient and effective attack on waste and pollution.
>
> The undesirable implications of the growth of settlements can be confronted and turned around. Human settlements can be managed in an orderly and equitable manner on the basis of participatory management and planning with awareness of the resources used. This skills approach is applied to all urban functions, such as land use, building, water supplies, sanitation, waste management, transport and leisure.
>
> Better management and planning of human settlements, including access to and use of environmentally respectful technologies and reduced demand for mobility and transport can lead to significant energy saving, thus helping to prevent global warming and climatic change.' (UNCHS 1991)

Cities have great capacity for acting in favour of sustainable development, a necessary condition for their survival (*Environment and Urbanization*, 1993; Mitlin and Satterthwaite, 1994; Sachs, 1993 and 1995; Hardoy et al, 1992; Sachs, 1990).

BOX 6.3 ECONOMIC PROMOTION: 'BARCELONA MORE THAN EVER'

Following the 1992 Olympic Games and in a context of generalized economic crisis, the city of Barcelona proposed to maintain and improve the international position achieved on the basis of organization of the Olympic Games. Barcelona's economic promotion world-wide aims to attract people, companies and institutions to visit, set up and invest in the city. There is likewise the aim of improving the international position of the products and services produced by city based people, companies and institutions. Centring on these axes, Barcelona is undertaking specialized international promotion in which certain 'products' strategic for the economic area of Barcelona have been chosen by consensus. The promotion campaigns are approached as sectoral (the promotion and active participation of specific economic sectors) and mixed, that is, based on collaboration between the public and private sectors.

Barcelona, City of Trade Fairs and Congresses

Barcelona wishes to retain its reputation as a 'city of trade fairs and congresses'. For this reason, various institutions and organizations are working to maintain its status and endeavour to become the sixth ranking trade fair and congress city. By 1992, Barcelona had moved up to seventh position in the world ranking of international congress cities. Over 1993 the figures rose, with the first half year showing an increase of nearly 100 per cent, and visitors rising from 41,235 to 82,686 (over half of whom were foreign). The factors which played a part in the process are, on the one hand, the international image and promotion gained by staging of the Olympic Games (creation and improvement of infrastructures for hosting great events and a marked increase of hotel capacity) and, on the other, the work carried out by the Barcelona Convention Bureau and Fira de Barcelona trade fair centre.

Barcelona New Projects

Its objective is to promote in Spain and abroad the city's real-estate range and quality planning, in respect of residential, commercial, office and cultural and leisure facilities. In 1994 the campaign took specific form in two initiatives: the presence of a joint stand at the International Real-Estate Professionals Market (MIPIM) in Cannes, and a Barcelona New Projects Exhibition, which will be travelling to various places in Europe, the United States and Japan.

Barcelona Centro Logístico

The company Barcelona Centro Logístico is now made up of forty Barcelona companies and institutions working to make Barcelona the main logistic centre for merchandise distribution in the south of Europe and the entire Mediterranean. The initiative will centre on actions designed to capture demand and at the same time improve the city's range of services and infrastructures.

Barcelona University Centre

Barcelona's promotion campaign as a university centre is backed by the city's five universities and its city hall in order to attract the largest possible number of foreign students, lecturers and researchers. The aim is also to attract to Barcelona the European-wide research infrastructure to which many of Europe's urban centres aspire.

Consorcio de Turismo de Barcelona

Businessmen in the sector, the Chamber of Commerce and City Hall founded the Corsorcio de Turismo de Barcelona in 1993 to promote the city as a tourist destination by means of setting out Barcelona's tourist products and delimiting their markets.

Barcelona European Financial Centre

At the initiative of the Autonomous Government of Catalonia and Barcelona City Hall, some 40 financial companies formed themselves into a group called the Asociación Barcelona Centro Financiero Europeo. Amongst other activities, the association has contributed towards the great success of the Barcelona Futures and Options Market and the promotion of training in financial subjects and setting up of the University of Chicago in Barcelona. The central objective is to study and define new financial products to permit Barcelona to have a presence in the international financial circuits.

Barcelona Centro Médico

Created by more than twenty private clinics and diagnostic laboratories in the city, Barcelona Centro Médico has for some years now been promoting facilities in order to attract patients from the rest of Spain and from abroad. The campaign, which is beginning to show results, receives support from the Autonomous Government of Catalonia and from Barcelona City Hall, as well as from credit companies and airlines.

Other campaigns being organized

In addition to the above promotions, Barcelona is preparing other campaigns such as Barcelona Diseño, which will boost the various activities which city design can generate in the world. And other promotion work is being planned in specialized sectors such as Barcelona Automóvil and in the pharmaceuticals and foodstuffs sectors.

Source: X Güell and M Ludevid 'La Promoción económica international de la ciudad: Barcelona More Than Ever' in Borja et al (1995)

BOX 6.4 SUSTAINABILITY INDICATORS

Local Agenda 21 United Kingdom

Sustainability Indicators Research Project, The Local Government Management Board 1995

- Resources are used effficiently and waste is minimised by closing cycles.
- Pollution is limited to levels which natural systems can cope with and without damage.
- The diversity of nature is valued and protected.
- Where possible, local needs are met locally.
- Everyone has the opportunity to undertake satisfying work in a diverse economy. The value of unpaid work is recognised, whilst payments for work are fair and fairly distributed.
- People's good health is protected by creating safe, clean, pleasant environments and health services which emphasise prevention of illness as well as proper care for the sick.
- Access to facilities, services, goods and other people is not achieved at the expense of the environment or limited to those with cars.
- People live without fear of personal violence from crime or persecution because of their personal beliefs, race, gender or sexuality.
- Everyone has access to the skills, knowledge and information needed to enable them to play a full part in society.
- All sections of the community are empowered to participate in decision-making.
- Opportunities for culture, leisure and recreation are readly available to all.
- Places, spaces and objects combine meaning and beauty with utility. Settlements are 'human' in scale and form. Diversity and local distinctiveness are valued and protected.

Seattle: Indicators of Sustainable Community June, 1993

Environment

- Wild salmon runs through local streams.
- Biodiversity in the region (specific indicator species to be identified and indicator to be developed).
- Number of good air quality days per year, as reported by the Pollutant Standards Index.
- Amount of topsoil in King County.
- Acres of wetlands in King County.
- Percentage of Seattle streets meeting 'Pedestrian-Friendly' criteria.

Population and Resources

- Total population of King County (with annual growth rate).
- Gallons of water consumed per capita.
- Tons of solid waste generated and recycled per capita per year.
- Vehicle miles travelled per capita and gasoline consumption per capita.
- Renewable and non-renewable energy (in BTUs) consumed per capita.
- Acres of land per capita for a range of land uses (residential, commercial, open space, transportation, wilderness).
- Amount of food grown in Washington, food exports, and food imports.
- Emergency room use for non-emergency purposes.

Economy

- Percentage of employment concentrated in the top ten employers.
- Hours of paid employment at the average wage required to support basic needs.
- Real unemployment, including discouraged workers, with differentiation by ethnicity and gender.
- Distribution of personal income, with differentiation by ethnicity and gender.
- Average savings rate per household.
- Reliance on renewable or local resources in the economy (specific indicator to be developed).
- Percentage of children living in poverty.
- Housing affordability gap.
- Health care expenditures per capita.

Culture and Society
- Percentage of infants born with low birthweight (including disaggregation by ethnicity).
- Ethnic diversity of teaching staff in elementary and secondary schools.
- Number of hours per week devoted to instruction in the arts for elementary and secondary schools.
- Percentage of parent/guardian population that is involved in school activities.
- Juvenile crime rate.
- Percentage of youth participating in some form of community service.
- Percentage of enrolled ninth graders who graduate from high school (by ethnicity, gender, and income level).
- Percentage of population voting in odd-year (local) primary elections.
- Adult literacy rate.

- Average number of neighbours the average citizen reports knowing by name.
- Equitable treatment in the justice system (specific indicator to be developed).
- Ratio of money spent on drug and alcohol prevention and treatment to money spent on incarceration for drug and alcohol related crimes.
- Percentage of population that gardens.
- Usage rates for libraries and community centre.
- Public participation in the arts.
- Percentage of adult population donating time to community service.
- Individual sense of well-being.

Sources: Municipality of Seattle (1993) and LGMB (1995)

HOUSING POLICIES WITHIN THE FRAMEWORK OF GLOBALIZATION

Although this book does not taking housing as its theme, we feel that it is relevant to point to some aspects of housing which are closely related with globalization.

Public Housing Policies and Economic Development

In a context which links economic development with the market it is significant that the countries and cities which have undertaken major housing operations and have provided urban housing for the sectors with low incomes yet integrated into the economy (wage workers and the self-employed) have done so through public enterprise (which can rest partly on a duly oriented market). Nearly all are economically dynamic countries, having been so in the past and remaining so now.

From the point of view of housing production for the working classes, things have changed little. The market does not resolve a problem which is a key factor for economic development (a) due to its contribution to the overall growth of the economy, (b) because it meets a social need which is indispensable if the workforce is to carry out its task, and (c) because if public housing programmes are weak there arise serious dysfunctions of the urban system.

Both in the inter-war period and from the 1950s, the developed countries felt the need to implement ambitious public housing programmes for the working classes. More recently, the 'newly industrialized countries' of South East Asia have done something similar (see Boxes 6.6 and 6.7). With greater or lesser strength, the same political orientation has been posited in other large developing country cities (in Latin America, for example), although with highly insufficient results from the point of view of housing supply and of urban integration. The problem of failure to produce sufficient dwellings is due both to structural factors (lack of public funds, delays in the construction industry, highly unequal income distribution and low solvency of demand

Box 6.5 Integral Social Services Development Plan, Barcelona

Barcelona City Hall and 13 of the city's institutions (government departments, universities, official colleges, trade unions, businessmen and social organizations) promoted the drawing up of a plan to develop the future of the social services, reaching consensus on the social diagnosis of the city and the main lines of action. The plan has been a highly participatory experience in which 125 city entities took part over the course of a year, contributing their knowledge and experience. The final objective formulated was to make a more integrated and integrating city with the active solidarity of the citizens. For this purpose the plan proposes the construction of a social services model in the city based on public responsibility and bringing together public and private cooperation, promoting civic action and optimizing the management of social resources. In this context the public responsibility takes in not only public services but also extends to the overall social services system made up of both public services and private profit-seeking and non-profit services. The role of the public sector basically centres on the planning, coordination, quality control and evaluation of the services, together with linking of public–private cooperation. The private sector (both profit-seeking and non-profit) takes part in the planning and basic running of the services. Within this scenario there emerge a number of strategic lines which anticipate a series of measures.

- The first line of action seeks to boost tendencies towards change which improve social cohesion and equality, with the specific objectives of:
  - providing suitable responses to changes in family and living structures;
  - seeking greater balance in citizen participation and responsibility in public and private spheres;
  - promoting the social insertion of young people, enhancing their potential for solidarity and creativity;
  - positive inclusion of the elderly population;
  - providing an integrating response for immigration;
  - achieving maximum integration of handicapped persons to ensure a city which shows solidarity towards all.
- Improving response capacity in the face of situations of social inequality and exclusion:
  - ensuring protection for children and equality of opportunities in culture and education;
  - facilitating the integration of persons with drug problems in healthy contexts of general living, culture, education and employment;
  - having a positive effect on overcoming situations of poverty;
  - making available housing alternatives to aid the social integration of groups in situations of special need;

— boosting work integration resources for certain groups.
- Promoting the responsible action of citizens and the public and private sectors in the building of solidarity in the city:
  - rationalizing public expenditure on social services in the city;
  - promoting new formulae for private investment in social services and enhancing dissemination thereof;
  - promoting the ongoing training of human resources and the development of new technologies;
  - strengthening citizen solidarity-oriented and participatory behaviour patterns;
  - promoting consolidation and linkage of the associative fabric and the representativeness of the bodies.
- Forming a local publicly run social services system essential for public–private cooperation to optimize the management of social resources:
  - clarification of the sphere of responsibility for running of the public services and the sphere of joint decision-making with private initiative;
  - consolidation and enhancement of service provision by means of private initiative and facilitating the creation of new services companies;
  - ensuring exercise of the functions of planning, coordination, innovation and control of municipal administration over the city's public and private social services as a whole.
- Coordinating social services with the other social welfare systems (health, education, housing, employment, etc):
  - strengthening municipal territorial organization as a basis of the system of coordination of the social services with the various public and private social welfare services, and especially with the education and health system;
  - identification of the coordination requirements in the territory and providing them with a response from the different social welfare policies;
  - establishment of coordination structures with the town halls of the Barcelona conurbation in order to design joint action strategies.

Source: Ajuntament de Barcelona, 1995

to contribute to financing, poor orientation of the financial system, etc) and to a weakness of political will on the part of governments and of social power on the part of homeseekers.

The low level of urban social integration of many housing operations in developed and developing countries alike is mainly due to a disassociation of urban planning and house building schedules. Other factors clearly have an effect (economic ones such as employment, and cultural ones of the type experienced by immigrants), but from the point of view of urban policies the key question is this disassociation. And that is joined by another divide, the one that arises between the administrative work rates and processes and

Box 6.6 Public Housing and Urban Services as the Social Base of Economic Development: Hong Kong and Singapore

The city states of Hong Kong and Singapore are two paradigmatic cases of economic development in the last forty years. Their initial exporting industrial capacity, and their later conversion into advanced services centres of the global economy have allowed them to achieve a per capita income higher than that of Spain and have made them into central nodes of the world economy. Although Singapore is 76 per cent Chinese and Hong Kong 99 per cent Chinese, there are considerable social, political and economic differences between them. Though little remarked upon by international observers, what they both nevertheless have in common is a highly efficient public system of housing and urban services which has been essential for improvement of the living conditions of the population and the training of quality labour.

All land in Hong Kong is public, being rented out by the government according to strategically decided city planning objectives: for example, free land for public housing but very expensive land for large business centres, thereby bringing in funds for the State treasury. In Singapore a strict city planning system controls land use, and the government is the main land operator. Both cities have the world's largest public housing programmes, in terms of the proportion of the population in that type of housing: 47 per cent in Hong Kong and 86 per cent in Singapore. Most of the public housing is organized into self-sufficient suburban nuclei, with provision of schools, health centres, cultural centres, nurseries, social services, collective restaurants, shopping centres and a good public transport system. Overall public services are subsidized. Rents traditionally range around 10 per cent of family income. In Singapore the public programme is being privatized, thus making most of the population into home owners at highly subsidized prices. Calculations made in Hong Kong in the mid-1980s showed that the overall public subsidy to Hong Kong families through housing and urban services was equivalent, on average, to 127 per cent of their wage. This programme of social planning was decisive in many ways for economic development: it permitted the creation of a work-force with good conditions of living, health and education, while at the same time limiting wage rises on account of the major indirect wage taken on by the government; it has made a decisive contribution to social peace, seriously threatened by city and labour unrest in both Hong Kong and Singapore in the 1960s; it has permitted the development of industrial areas with large industrial zones for multinational companies in the case of Singapore, mass-built flats in public housing estates in the case of Hong Kong; it has permitted a very high rate of saving which has largely served to finance development; it has reinforced family stability and social integration amongst populations which were weakly rooted, multi-ethnic (Singapore) or made up of recent rural immigrants (Hong Kong); it has created a sense of belonging

> in internationally isolated city states with uncertain legal statutes; and, in
> the case of Hong Kong, it has permitted the development of a business
> spirit in that the adventure of creating a small business could be under-
> taken with limited risk in a situation of full employment and backed by a
> house and social services ensured for life. It could be said that the benev-
> olent authoritarian states of Hong Kong and Singapore provided the
> local social and spatial base for economic development oriented towards
> the global system. Public housing is the unknown face of the world's
> foremost exporting economies.
>
> Source: Castells, Goh and Kwok (1990)

social group work rates and processes of those 'producing' their houses and
their districts. Both in cases of public house building and the more numerous
cases of independent social initiatives (self-build), the urban integration of
working-class residential groups largely depends on the interactive relationship between the social groups and the public government agents. And
urban integration is an essential factor for the sound operation and, therefore, the productivity of the city.

Housing Programmes and Social Cohesion

The social explosion of the poor and working-class districts in the more
developed countries, first in the United States and then in western Europe
has shown in its full ugliness the social (and economic, cultural and political)
exclusion of major population groups. There arises within them a vicious
circle between this exclusion or social regulation and territorial separation.
These are the ghettos.

The residential ghettos are not exclusive to the working-classes or low
income groups. There is also a proliferation of middle- and upper-class
residential districts which form islands accessible only to those having the
ticket of the pertinent class. The city becomes socially fragmented, dysfunctional and excluding, and socializing public spaces weaken or even
disappear. And this happens both in the cities of the more developed world
and those of the developing world.

Ghettos of the poor groups are often the result of public housing operations which suffer from an error of urban conception due to starting out from
the assumption that producing houses and, at best, ensuring minimum
urbanization and services (transport, school) means producing a piece of
city and conferring citizen status on its inhabitants. The error is threefold:

1. producing single-function and socially homogeneous districts at the
   lower end of the social scale;
2. failing to link this operation with economic and infrastructural dynamics
   which contribute to integration (employment, mobility) of the population
   of these districts;
3. not providing these districts with the urban features which lend them
   some attribute of centrality, of social visibility, of having some of the
   city's monuments.

Box 6.7 Housing as Social Integration Policy in a Multicultural Context: Singapore

Since the end of the 1960s the government of Singapore has implemented a residential racial integration policy as a way of defusing the inter-racial tension which, in its early years, threatened the country's existence. The main ethnic groups are the Chinese (76 per cent), Malays (15 per cent), Indians (6 per cent), most of whom are Tamils, and other ethnic groups (3 per cent). The Malays occupy the bottom of the social scale, with 54 per cent of them working in unskilled and poorly paid jobs. Malay women, moreover, go out to work much less than do Chinese women, thereby reducing family income still further. Urban segregation expressed this social inequality, with the Chinese occupying the city centre while the Malays were concentrated in a district to the east of the city and on the outskirts. The Malays were also the majority inhabitants of the irregular settlements in the city. The party which has monopolized power in Singapore since independence, the PAP, propounded the creation of a multiracial, multireligious and multilinguistic country based on the principles of 'non-communal egalitarianism' and 'multiracial meritocracy'. The strong ethnic tensions between Chinese and Malays, and pressure from the neighbouring republic of Malaysia (with Malay majority) led the government of Singapore to struggle against ghettoization of the Malays, which could have led to exacerbation of tension.

Autonomous political organization of Malays in Singapore was by the same token more difficult. The system of spatial integration was based on voluntary or enforced incorporation of Malays into the public housing system and on refurbishment of the run down areas where the Malays lived. Between 1970 and 1982 the percentage of Malays living in public housing rose from 23 per cent to 77 per cent. Statistical indices show strong desegregation of the ethnic groups in relation to each other (the Malays were dispersed throughout a majority Chinese urban system). Within the public housing estates, however, an ethnic regrouping can be observed: the Malays tend to live in housing at lower height and moreover tend to concentrate in flats in blocks which are almost totally Malay. In 1989, therefore, the government intervened in the sale of privatized public dwellings to avoid Malays – once owners of their homes – regrouping spatially into separate areas. Maximum ethnic limits were thus established for each block: there could be no more than 25 per cent Malays, 87 per cent Chinese or 13 per cent Indians and others in each block. According to a document of the National Development Ministry: 'Living in separate enclaves, community leaders will develop a narrow view of the interests of society. The enclaves would become breeding grounds for communal agitation. All that we have so carefully built up since independence could be thrown away'. In Singapore, the planned city par excellence, the government appears to have discovered that the struggle against urban segregation forms part of the maintenance of order.

Some large cities in developing countries, in Latin America and Asia, repeat the mistakes of the more developed countries. At times with the best of intentions public housing policies with international financing (eg Ciudad Bolívar in Bogotá) reproduce in extended form the present-day ghettos into which many 'grands ensembles' (France) and similar districts in other countries have turned. Instead of mixing groups of different social levels and activities and services both local and central, the policy option has been for mass production of housing for the lower income groups, without paying them any heed and fragmenting demand. The result is districts in which the rule of law plays no part or is soon watered down, in which the employed and cultural integrated members gradually give their places up to more marginalized groups, so that, instead of forming an integral part of the city such districts become the 'other city', the one on which the formal city turns its back. However unwished it may be, there is clearly a relationship between the effects of these housing policies and the excluding and dualizing dynamics which derive from globalization.

Public Policies and People's Self-Building

The bulk of housing production in the developing countries is not done by the market or by the government. It is done by the people. Houses and districts have historically been more of a social construction than a government action or an economic operation. The most common processes involved historically included:

- Tolerance or 'laissez-faire'. An 'illegal' or 'alegal' city is added to the legal city. This consolidated city subsists today in many cities of the developing countries. And it is increasing in the sphere of the Metropolitan Region;
- Repression. Authoritarian emptying of central areas or ones incorporated into the dynamic urban fabric which had previous been occupied by self-building. The phenomenon simply arises farther away;
- Public social housing programmes. Always very much less than the expressed needs of the populations of the self-built districts, they often give rise to the same problem, this time in a vertical direction.

Later, and especially over the last twenty years, more flexible policies have been tried based on cooperation between a large number of agents (government bodies, employers, social groups interested as builder-inhabitants, etc). This type of action allows the specific needs of the population (economic, cultural, family) to be catered for, promoting their cooperation and the use of suitable technologies, materials and designs. It likewise permits the implementation of operations of a different nature such as the creation of urbanized refuge structures or the refurbishment of self-built or run down districts.

In the context of the economic, social and cultural dynamics linked with globalization, however, these specialized policies have very limited efficacy, and they run the risk of merely making exclusion more tolerable. For this reason there is today a tendency to implement more integral strategies which include education and socio-cultural programmes, job creation initiatives, support for community self-organization, attraction of economic activities and cultural facilities, etc. That is, a strategy based on the non-acceptance of the concept of marginality.

Innovative Urban Projects and Housing Programmes

In the next chapter we will discuss the great urban projects in today's city. We would like here to point to the importance of linking the most important projects for the change of scale of the city and the housing programmes. We will mention only two types of projects.

Old and New Centres
The old centres swing between social decline and tertiary congestion. There have in some cases, been misguided policies directed at eradicating economic activity or residence, while in other cases the market, accelerated by global economic opening, has hyper-specialized some zones and abandoned others. The old centres are nevertheless accorded greater value in that they combine some policies (improved urbanization and basic services, quality cultural facilities, security and new public spaces, reconversion of centrally located enclaves such as ports or stations, etc) with urban socio-cultural processes such as tourism or gentrification. It has in some cases proved possible to add to these policies and processes a component of housing policy based on urban 'acupuncture', either by improvement of existing facilities or by a multiplication of small-scale new operations. These policies, based on public–private cooperation under a variety of juridical and financial arrangements, can generally permit the maintenance of social heterogeneity in the central areas.

The new centralities are often posited as tertiary, infrastructural operations par excellence. But only when they are linked with housing programmes can they generally achieve a sufficient level of economic profitability and, above all, become city-constructing operations.

Large Infrastructures and Facilities Operations
These are the operations inherent to competent cities characteristic of globalization. Such operations may nevertheless form part of a disintegrating and dualizing dynamic in respect of the urban–regional fabric if they created specialized spaces (communications nodes, logistic activity zones, technological parks, trade fair or congress centres, and the like) – that is, places which are not multi-purpose. At the extreme, these spaces can be well linked with the world and forming a set of ghettos in the city. The incorporation into such large projects of ambitious socially heterogeneous housing programmes is the best guarantee of their urban integration, and often too of the economic profitability of the operation in the medium term. Examples here might be the experiences of reconversion of port or railway station areas (or the new areas created by high speed train stations, as in Lille, France). On the other hand, housing operations which do not have the attraction of strong infrastructural features, big facilities and skilled tertiary sector areas can lose much of their potential as creators of the city (here we might compare the various cases of Olympic villages).

Housing Programmes and Universal Models

The need for mass construction of housing due to accelerated urbanization, the financial and technical importance acquired by certain international organizations (UN, World Bank and Regional Development Banks, supra-state unions), ease of communication between civil servants and experts in the information age, and the interests of the construction sector, have led to the drawing up and execution of standard models of mass housing construction. This standardization shows itself in various ways:

- The utilization of the same socio-economic indicators in regions which differ widely in terms of family structure, income type (cash or other), relationship with the environment, etc.
- Design of dwellings without regard to the aspirations and specific needs of the population and the inherent cultural forms of the human group and of the city.
- Financing in accordance with international models which do not mobilize truly available resources in each city and in each district and lead, on the contrary, to the squandering (by the weight of bureaucracy and corruption).
- Production of housing without regard to the setting, services and employment.
- Social homogeneity of the residents, which facilitates 'ghettoization' of the district and hinders the installations of facilities and activities which integrate it into the city.

We believe that housing programmes must opt:

- for adaptation to the social groups at which they are directed, to their demands, resources and inherent living rates;
- for formal difference, by the utilization of specific materials and technologies, by a capacity for generating identity and being seen and appreciated from the outside;
- for the social and cultural heterogeneity of the people who will be living in each area or district of the city.

If these requirements are met, two positive effects are achieved: the efficacy of each operation is maximized from both the economic and social points of view, and operations are undertaken which counteract the marginalizing or dualizing dynamics at work, that is, operations which create a city (Caldeira, 1996; Jacquier, 1992; Percq, 1994; Leal and Cortés, 1995; Polèse and Wolfe, 1995; Ascher et al, 1995; Topalov, 1987; Délégation interministérielle à la ville, 1995).

Chapter 7
Strategic Plans and Metropolitan Projects

STRATEGIC PLANS: FROM THE TERRITORIAL PLAN TO URBAN PROJECTS

Crisis of Planning, Ambiguity of Projects

Criticism of urban territorial planning (or general plans) has been common-place since the 1970s. The relative inoperativeness of these plans is generally accepted where they do not rest upon economic and social dynamics which permit their implementation in the form of projects. Charges nevertheless appear to be highly exaggerated, especially in view of the fact that much greater disasters have been perpetrated without plans or overviews of the city's future. Perhaps it would be better to think of Brecht's reflection: 'If horrible cities have been made following a plan, that was because the plan was horrible, not because there was a plan'.

Historical experience reveals the importance of plans, rules and general conceptions about the relationship between buildings, activities and public spaces in the production of the city. This is true both for homogeneous cities resulting from a prior approach such as the grid or a roadway and building model (Edinburgh, Pombal's Lisbon or Haussman's Paris) and the more successful implementations of 'new towns' or 'villes nouvelles'. Even those 'urban products' which strike us as apparently more chaotic or spontaneous (lively squares and promenades, markets and cultural areas, etc.) owe much to government planning and by-laws.

There is today a renewed trend towards recognition of the regulating and promoting role of government in the drawing up and setting under way of large-scale projects, although the partnership of the private agents is almost always required for their execution and management. The ideological inertia of the 1980s is nevertheless leading many governments to renounce that role and to place blind faith in private initiatives. Criticism of projects undertaken solely with a view to short-term private wealth (eg the London Docklands) should lead to a resumption of public responsibilities. There is nevertheless a certain ambiguity about the concept of the 'large-scale project' as a driving force behind, and guidance for, urban development.

Firstly, it is forgotten that behind a large-scale project there is always, explicitly or implicitly, an overall city plan or schema. The plan or schema may have various juridical foundations, enjoy greater or less social consensus or opt for balanced or heavily unbalanced development, but there is a political will which is expressed by deed or omission. The orientations may nevertheless be very different, as in the urban projects of Barcelona and London in the 1980s.

Secondly, these large-scale projects quite often relate to initiatives promoted by agents who have an interest in remaining outside any coercive overall framework. These may be private economic groups, but also public agents, especially those with well-positioned land holdings (port authorities, railway companies, etc). Nor can we overlook the particular 'author' culture of the designers of urban projects, who may plump for formal singularity instead of linkage with the hinterland.

Thirdly, ad hoc projects, even where they are, or are supposed to be, complex operations, must in so far as they are promoted by government bodies adapt to the sectoral or one-dimensional character of those operations. That is, the promoting government body tends to consider just one function (eg roadways or housing) to the detriment of the project's complexity, a factor essential for it to be a 'producer of city'.

For all these reasons, we feel that we must be on our guard against mythologizing the large-scale projects in themselves, against supposing that flexibility or deregulation (with respect to general plans or regulations) automatically resolve their viability and their suitability within the setting and that partnership ensures the potential complexity. The exhaustion of classic territorial planning and the ambiguity of the supposedly isolated large-scale project oblige us to propose planning suited to the nature of works on new metropolitan or urban-regional spaces (Ascher, 1995; Borja et al, 1995; Bohigas, 1985; Bohigas et al, 1994).

Scales of Intervention and the Pertinence of Strategic Planning

The diffuse city (or the new urban–regional spaces) call for large-scale work to link up the territory. Such work is often understood as specialized, functional operations, almost always linked with communications or with activities connected with the 'globalized' economy (teleports, World Trade Centres, trade fair and congress precincts, technological parks, logistic activities zones, etc). This approach reinforces the damaging territorial effects of globalization, since it accentuates inequalities and fragments and segregates both the activity areas (de facto zoning) and the social groups (generalized ghettoization).

It is useful to distinguish between work in terms of its scale (large, intermediate, minor) and its relations with planning which links economic-social strategies with actions in the territory. The large scale of a project starts in recent years from a strategic view of the territory. It is not so much a matter of undertaking projects which are multidimensional from the outset as of ensuring that three conditions are met:

1. that the work relates to a scenario with future and economic, social and cultural objectives;
2. that the work has coherence with other projects and dynamics undertaken in other parts of the territory;
3. that the work has metastatic effects on its hinterland, that is, effects which generate initiatives which boost its linkage potential.

That is, it is a question of projects complex in their conception, multifunctional in their dynamics and generating urban–regional centralities or centralities of the new metropolitan urban system, situated at the regional or macro-regional scale.

The intermediate scale is that which takes place in the existing city, this being taken to mean the conurbation, or the city centre and its close lying periphery. This is the scale which includes city centre renewal work, promotion of new development axes and new centralities. Such operations sometimes focus on regeneration of potent yet obsolete zones (ports, stations, barracks, factories, etc), at other times on infrastructural work to improve the hinterland and provide attractive centrality features (such as combination of a quality road or axis and investment in 'excellent-quality tertiary' activities). Where the work is not in response to a strategic vision of urban development (or is an erroneous vision not relating to any real dynamics), then it becomes mere inoffensive work, with no effect other than a change of use or form in a city zone. Its strategic value will be provided by:

• the coherence of the project with other parallel or complementary projects which condition major aspects of its viability (accessibility, public decisions of a fiscal or investment nature, traffic or environmental measures, etc);
• the quality of execution of the project, both in terms of physical aspects and of facilities, services, image promotion, etc;
• the capacity to mobilize public and private initiatives and funds and to generate the social uses required by the work.

The minor scale of work is that which relates to ad hoc projects, projects which in spite of their relatively small scale also have a strategic function in urban development. We refer here to work distinguished by:

• an integrated character, that is, one whose conception brings together a certain diversity of uses and certain formal qualities;
• providing a response to challenges or shortfalls which condition city development or which decisively reinforce existing dynamics;
• constituting in themselves features which enhance certain areas of the city.

Such work is highly diverse in nature and can relate to monument building, building of business facilities or premises (hotels, shopping centres, leisure centres, etc), refurbishment of streets or groups of buildings which can be revalued due to their position or symbolic character, creation of a point of high visibility and accessibility, etc. But their strategic value does not lie so much in the specific function or form of the work as in its effect on the urban dynamic.

Strategic Planning

We have referred in other chapters to strategic planning (see especially Chapter 5), but it would be useful to specify its basic elements and the ways in which it differs from conventional territorial planning (which we shall term 'master plan').

Strategic planning is a way of directing change based on participatory analysis of a situation and its possible evolution and on drawing up of an investment strategy for the scarce resources available at the critical points.

The diagnosis takes into consideration the settings (globalization), the territory (in its various dimensions) and government (or system of public agents). Special consideration is given to dynamics and work under way, social demands, critical points, obstacles or bottlenecks and potential.

The diagnosis is used to determine the foreseeable situation, possible scenarios and the desirable situation, which is taken as the starting point for laying down projects to attain it. The work includes objectives, lines or strategies to be implemented and specific projects which can be got under way in the short term (physical projects, economic or social programmes, government measures, civic campaigns, etc).

Strategic plans generally include measures relating to:

- accessibility and mobility;
- social balance;
- human resources;
- information and telecommunications;
- services to production;
- quality of government;
- quality of public services;
- culture;
- economic infrastructure.

The commonly cited benefits of territorial strategic planning are:

- short-term action;
- helping to identify the most effective use of resources;
- positioning the city to take advantage of opportunities;
- identifying and developing 'champion projects';
- future vision;
- concentration of energy;
- gaining perspective;
- objectivity;
- separating reality from fiction;
- collaboration between public and private sectors;
- awareness of city and building of consensus;
- doing the important things.

The final objective is the dissemination of strategic thought, the process being more important than the results themselves.

The risks of the strategic plan result from insufficient social participation and consensus, incorrect definition of objectives and selection of projects or from an inability to set up effective monitoring and promotion of the projects. The following are cited as the most common errors:

- generating expectations greater than the final perception of the work;
- over-generic objectives;
- little executive commitment by the agents;
- an exclusively political perception of the plan;
- failure to execute the plan.

Similarities between the strategic plan and territorial master plan (or general plan) include:

- planning over a long time-scale;
- city scenario or model as starting point;
- similar importance of subjects relating to economic development, environmental quality and social equilibrium;
- considerable importance of diagnostic and prognostic studies;
- the projects adopted involve immediate action which affects the future;
- they provide perspective and future vision of the city;
- they redefine the role of the city and its relations with the immediate hinterland;
- rejection of improvisation.

Box 7.1 highlights the differences between strategic plans and master plans.
    The participation of the public and private agents is an indispensable condition of a strategic plan and distinguishes it from other forms of planning. The main characteristics of this participation are as follows:

- It takes place at all phases of the planning, from drawing up of the diagnosis through to monitoring of the projects.
- It should ideally include all the public and private agents. Contrary to what might appear to be logical, the most difficult aspect is nearly always that of achieving the participation of government departments (except those leading the plan).
- Part of the population has low levels of organization, leadership and social visibility. It would nevertheless nearly always be over-hasty to conclude that they do not count when it comes to bringing them into the structure of the strategic plan.
- Communication aimed at the citizens and marketing aimed at the exterior form part of the very process of strategic planning.
- Negotiated agreement on strategic work, both between the agents responsible for carrying it out and between those who must promote the work or monitor it, together with social consensus about the work, constitute the essential factors of the participatory process.

Banalization is probably the greatest risk today besetting strategic planning. Precisely because it involves a flexible structure, a relatively open process and a global agreement which has the force of a 'political contract' but not a legally binding one, it calls for very strong management will. But it also lends itself to becoming 'woolly thought' and pseudo-legitimization for a number of measures and projects connected only on paper.

Box 7.1 Differences between Strategic Plan and Master Plans

Territorial Strategic Plan	Master Plan
Integral plan with some territoriazable objectives.	Ordering of urban space.
Accords priority to projects but does not necessarily locate them in space.	Determines land uses as a whole and locates with precision the general systems and broad public works.
Based on consensus and participation in all its phases.	Design is responsibility of government, with 'a posteriori' participation.
Utilization of qualitative analyses and critical factors.	Utilization of territorial and physical-medium studies.
Plan of commitments and agreements between agents for immediate or short-term action.	Regulatory plan to regulate potential future private action.
An action plan.	A plan to regulate action.

Monitoring of projects, promotion of same by ad hoc participatory committees, commitment of the participating agents responsible for each of them, degree of fulfilment of the objectives and evaluation of their impact will permit the efficacy of a strategic plan to be measured. A strategic plan is justified by its results, and these must be perceived in the short term (within two to five years following approval) (Busquets, 1992; Castro, 1994; Henry, 1992; De Forn et al, 1991).

From Strategic Plans to Large-Scale Urban Projects

The hierarchical or organization-chart relationship of strategic planning is increasingly called into question. And something similar can be said of strategic plans. The projects are not the last by-product of a process working down logically from the desirable scenario, with the objectives next, the strategies or lines of action following them, and finally the works, projects or measures. The more modern strategic plans tend to establish a dialectic relationship between the basic elements of diagnosis and broad objectives noted right from the first phase of drawing up and the large-scale projects which are on the tables of the main public and private urban agents. As the plan progresses it will tend to establish priorities and relationships between projects, though these projects will in turn make a decisive contribution to setting the objectives and lines of action of the plan.

Before moving on to analyse the main features of large-scale urban projects, we will outline briefly the contribution a strategic plan makes to large-scale projects and the process of definition thereof within the sphere of the plan. The strategic plan becomes a process which legitimizes the large-scale urban projects. It must lend territorial and economic coherence to the main projects and ensure that they serve to link the urban-regional space as a whole. The impact of or effects deriving from these projects must maintain a compromise between economic competitiveness, environmental sustainability and social cohesion. The participatory nature of the strategic plan must help to integrate these dimensions into the large-scale projects. The plan will therefore explain to authors in charge of large-scale projects the requirement to ensure their multidimensionality (not only their immediate functionality and maximum profitability), and will create the conditions of obligatoriness to make this possible. When it comes to specifying content, forms and times of projects, the plan sphere must permit a certain rebalancing of the negotiations between the strongest agents (government departments, economic groups, etc) and the weaker agents (citizen groups, research centres, etc). The inclusion of large-scale projects in the strategic plan, in so far as the plan is a large communicative operation and normally obtains broad social consensus, transfers these qualities to the large-scale projects (often accused of being wasteful, even anti-social). The reverse may nevertheless happen, that is, that popular ad hoc projects help to legitimize and disseminate the plan and its proposals. The strategic plan/large-scale projects dialectic can thus become a process of civic mobilization and education. The projects gain in content, transparency (corruption is more difficult) and dynamic impact. For its part, the plan reveals its efficacy and its credibility and dissemination increase. Although it can occur in relatively short periods of time (between two and five years), the complexity of this process normally comes into contradiction with political, electoral or government times. For this reason, a plan and large-scale projects must have their own timing, independent of the political and administrative cycles of institutions.

The large-scale project definition process, in the framework of strategic planning, is not a mere result of the will of the agents who take part in its drawing up. The following aspects, at least, have to be taken into account:

- The existence of a national or regional plan, of an Act of Parliament or government programme which lends it a political or legal base.
- The possibility of arriving at a decision on the priority nature of the work shared between the main agents (public and private) responsible for its approval and execution.
- Opportunities of a financial (international loan, for example), political (large event in preparation) and physical (such as land recoverable due to obsolescence of present installations) nature.
- The existence of a promoter or operator to lead the project.
- Social consensus, to include acceptance by public opinion and by the media.

These conditions do not have to all exist at the same time, though the lack of any of them must be considered as an obstacle to be overcome.

In strategic planning in practice, the defining process generally goes through a number of different phases. In the initial 'pre-diagnostic' phase some projects which are already 'mature' may arise, either because the agents responsible already planned to implement them or because well-informed urban sectors are calling out for them strongly and they have already gained social acceptance. The pro-active diagnosis stage allows the plan commissions, of broad and plural composition, to identify some actions which are symbolic of the proposed objectives. On the basis of this the management bodies can then begin to encourage definition and promotion of some large-scale projects, in parallel to the drawing up of the plan. Once the desirable scenario, the objectives and the lines of action have been chosen, the commissions draw up a list of projects. The commissions at this stage are not the same as those in the previous phase, but are made up of public and private representatives of those institutions and organizations oriented towards promoting a particular strategic line. The central bodies of the plan (political and technical) redraw and select these lists in order to achieve the maximum possible coherence and in order to establish an order of priorities which facilitates execution of the plan. On the basis of the approved list of projects small groups or committees are created with the mission of drawing up (or having drawn up) a basic design for each one of these (this design must include bodies or agents in charge, financing, timing, etc). The project groups or committees have few members and a predominantly political (decision-makers, promoters) and technical (experts) character. The projects pre-designed (basic design) and approved by the central plan bodies (this being the last phase of drawing up and approval of the plan) are then taken up by ad-hoc commissions entrusted with project monitoring, promotion and, where appropriate, implementation. This is the final stage of implementation of the plan. Those projects which have not been implemented within two to four years of approval of the plan and show no signs of being implemented within a short time-scale should be considered as unviable for the time being (Godet, 1991; De Forn et al, 1991; De Forn and Pascual, 1995).

LARGE-SCALE METROPOLITAN PROJECTS

The Metropolitan City: Its system and Urban Projects

The metropolitan city in our time is an economic, social and functional reality in the making. The complexity of metropolitan realities, including the complexity in institutions, is such that the new city – an urban–regional space – is fashioned through large-scale projects rather than through institutional organization and service management. The present-day metropolitan city is no longer merely a juxtaposition of densified centres, districts, socially or functionally specialized areas and successive peripheries. That metropolitan city exists, and obviously requires institutional coordination (it is pluri-municipal, and involves action by all the public authorities at once) and joint management for some services (water, waste disposal, transport etc). But there is another metropolitan city, on a larger scale. The new metropolitan city is best understood as a system or network, with variable geometry, articulated by nodes, strong central points, defined by their accessibility. Quality in this new urban–regional reality will depend on the intensity of relations between these nodes, on the multifunctionality of the nodal centres, and their capacity to integrate the whole of their population and their territory through a suitable system ensuring mobility.

The new metropolitan city is best understood as the result of three processes, or three distinct yet interrelated dynamics: globalization, concentration and communication. Globalization requires of large cities – of metropolitan cities – that they provide competitive platforms for their economic activities, skills for their human resources, a good exchange system for ever broader spheres (including the continent- and world-wide spheres), promote their international image and function internally in an efficient way with clear, stable rules and conventions. However, in the short- or long-term, globalization has territorial repercussions that amount to a challenge for the cohesion of the whole. Globalization fragments the urban–regional territory into areas and groups that are 'in' or 'out', while at the same time 'universalizing' the products and messages of the metropolitan city.

The concentration of activities and function, though not necessarily of the population, means that the metropolitan territory becomes the natural medium for economic activity, characterized by its articulation with markets of variable geometry and by the synergies arising between the interdependent agents involved (institutional, company representatives, professionals, etc). This concentration has its strong points, in material and symbolic terms, in the communication nodes – ie urban centres, or places having versatility. However, these nodes are often monofunctional, and they express the need for bringing cohesion to the territory and the population rather than the afore-mentioned fragmenting dynamic.

Communication is at once the main characteristic feature and challenge of metropolitan cities. Competitiveness in globalization requires the full development of communications with the world outside (ports and airports, telecommunications, new road and rail infrastructure, conference and congress centres, trade fairs and exhibitions, etc), as well as internally, in so far as the metropolitan city is a system of urban centres. Optimum communication is the prerequisite for the functioning of the new metropolis, as indeed it was previously, though now on a much grander scale, both in terms of relations with the hinterland (which may be national or continental) and with its own metropolitan territory (discontinuous, variable and featuring dynamics that fragment and marginalize).

It is in this framework of new challenges that the issues of metropolitan action arise. Metropolitan action must respond to three requirements that are at once both complementary in their goals and contradictory in their sectorial or practical execution: competitiveness, integration and sustainability. Metropolitan areas are subject to two types of large-scale action, those deriving from public-sector planning, expressed in documents such as regional development schemes and sector-based schemes (for transport, access, coastal development, miscellaneous facilities, etc), and those deriving from one-off decisions, taken by both public and private agents, and often without regard to planning (such as access works and link roads, the creation of a shopping centre, etc)

In recent years an intermediate path has been developed: strategic plans. Strategic planning is based on three principles:

1. defining urban goals on the basis of current dynamics;
2. the permanent dialectic of goals–projects–repercussions;
3. public and private agents acting in concert at all the stages of preparation and implementation.

The metropolitan space in its urban–regional sense – ie discontinuous, functional, and subject to forward-looking action – is thus the strategic space par excellence – strategic space in the sense of economic space. The urban–regional sphere is nowadays the 'natural framework' for economic activity, rather than the company, which is ever more dependent on its environments and their synergies, and rather than the nation state, which cannot cope with globalization processes and which is less well suited to working with the wide range of private economic and social agents. The metropolitan strategic space is also the new space for socio-cultural integration. The formation of urbanized areas in which the city runs the risk of becoming diluted, the inequalities and marginalisation affecting social groups and territories, and the complexity of the institutional structure that makes that structure less readily visible, are all challenges that the city must rise to if it is to avoid having the processes of socio-cultural disintegration prevailing over those of economic and functional integration.

Can the new metropolitan city form once more, on a larger scale, the model of the city of the past? First we must ask ourselves what the defining features of that model are. Throughout the twentieth century, in both European and American culture, there is agreement on pointing to at least seven factors:

1. the concentration of population and activities (industrial and service activities);
2. the density of social relations deriving from the heterogeneous and complementary nature of social groups;
3. diversity in functions;
4. centrality with respect to a hinterland;
5. socio-cultural cohesion expressed in civic culture;
6. the existence of political institutions and capacity for self-government;
7. image or visibility as seen from outside the city.

Do these features, which are still regarded even today as positive or desirable by many, exist, or are they viable, in the new metropolitan city? In the metropolitan city there are two contradictory dynamics that underlie two opposing visions of the city. These two visions (which are sometimes simplified as the American model and the European model) are equally part of reality, as are the dynamics on which they rest, and often coexist in urban schemes and projects. For one thing we find the urbanization that is the result of the space of flows, the variable geometry territory, mono-functional nodes that lead to 'weak spots'. Taking things to extremes, we could speak of urbanization without a city. For another we come up against the will (political, intellectual, social, professional) to produce the city, as a space that optimizes synergies, as a territory of cohesion and governability, as a set of 'strong points' that generate cultural identity. In both cases a key issue is the mobility–accessibility that ensures the articulation of the urban system. And another key issue is the notion of centralities, in the true sense of functional nodes, seen either as functional nodes or as multipurpose places, that lend cohesion to the territory so that it may function as a whole.

The main goals of large-scale strategic action programmes are those enabling a qualitative leap to be made as regards the accessibility and mobility of the urban–regional space and the generation and reconversion of centralities in the urban–regional territory as a whole. Internal accessibility and mobility are prerequisites for the competitiveness of the city as an 'economic medium' and for the city to perform its social integration function. That is why most large-scale strategic processes are linked to operations involving mass roadway and transport operations, logistic activity zones, communications infrastructure creation or reconversion (stations, ports) etc. On this basis infrastructural and promotional operations of an economic nature are implemented: technology parks, trade fair and conference sites, areas for companies providing services to other companies, etc. Nowadays there is also a tendency to view cultural and tourism related facilities as economic infrastructure too, and also to integrate those two uses in the same areas of the territory.

However, building the metropolitan city requires adding further centralities on top of mobility. The present-day dynamic nearly always leads to the congestion of strong, multipurpose and integrating central areas on the one hand, and on the other to the diffusion of an anomic urbanization in which the vices of public zoning multiply the ill effects stemming from sectorial initiatives taken by the administration and those stemming from the mercantilist stance of each private agent. The creation and/or reconversion of urban centres presupposes a potent public initiative (recovering obsolete areas, infrastructural work for accessibility, expropriations, attractive or prestige-giving public amenities, etc) to encourage private investment. The generation of centralities not only meets the objective of multiplying the existing, congested centres or recovering former centres that have deteriorated for certain central functions; it is also seen as an operation intended to change the scale of the city, to articulate and upgrade urban peripheries and to lend a strong image of modernity to the territory. Public spaces are thus a key goal in building the metropolitan city, in so far as they help in creating centrality and giving a boost to integrating mobility. Infrastructure and transport systems do not guarantee mobility, essential though they are. The creation of a conglomeration of skilled tertiary activities does not automatically lead to centrality. Only the existence of public spaces and facilities that are accessible, safe, versatile and possessing aesthetic quality and a symbolic import – ie culturally significant – creates centrality. Because urban centrality, in the sense of a condensation of the city, is not so much the node bringing together the flows of the metropolitan space as the place for meetings and identities, the expression of civic sense and the substrata of the city's marketing and patriotism (Ministère de l'Équipement, 1994; Arquitectura de la Ciudad, 1992; Borja et al, 1995; Busquets, 1992; Castro, 1994; Henry, 1992; Delarue, 1991; Figueroa et al, 1995; Meyer et al, 1995; Ghorra-Gobin, 1994; Secchi, 1989; Virilio, 1994; de Queiroz, 1994; Eurocities, 1994; Délégation Interministérielle à la ville, 1995).

Urban Projects: The Structuring of the Metropolitan City

Large-scale urban projects are today what defines the building of the metropolitan city. The efficacy of infrastructural projects linked to mobility,
multiplying accessibilities in effect and generating centralities, depends on
their integral nature, ie their versatility, their capacity to be of use over and
above their specific or sectorial function. These projects need to be part of
an articulated process in which activities of one kind (eg physical infrastructure for mobility) are conceived as elements of a system, and articulated with
activities of other kinds – or even helping to generate them (eg new areas of
urban development with elements of centrality, physical and symbolic identity
related elements, and public spaces and amenities as factors for social redistribution, job creation, etc). Lastly, large-scale projects have strategic value
depending on their capacity to foster transformations of the regional–urban
medium that enhance its attractiveness and cohesion. There are a number
of criteria which, in our view, enable the viability and the urban effect of
large-scale strategic projects of an infrastructural nature to be assessed:

- Forming part of a city project. It could be a strategic plan, or a development or regional development plan, or a municipal action plan
  backed by broad consensus, or a coherent package of projects negotiated with the national government. Another possibility is a general
  framework with a global city planning approach for public works
  connected with some major event or with the reconversion of a set of
  strategic areas (port, railway stations, etc) or obsolete industrial areas,
  or implementing an ambitious programme involving access routes and
  links, etc. The key issue is that a binding relationship be established in
  all cases between the global project (more or less explicit, though it
  must be fully endorsed by the political leadership and enjoy popular
  support) and the physical projects, duly planned and financed.
- Opportunity. The opportunity for taking action may be ready-made or it
  may be 'invented'. In large cities the various authorities take day to day
  decisions which are potentially strategic, leading to events which, if they
  are planned in advance and promoted, may serve as levers for transformation; and some private agents (or public companies) set out
  strategies and prepare initiatives that can generate future repercussions
  without negotiating beforehand the way they fit into the whole. An
  obsolescent zone is an opportunity, even for centrality. An operation
  that was initially 'specialized' (eg a ring road or an area for logistic
  activities) can give rise to an urban development project on a higher
  level. A major international event (a world fair, Olympic Games etc)
  can transform a city (eg Barcelona) or merely leave some infrastructure
  in an underused condition afterwards (Seville).

    Taking advantage of 'opportunities' is an excellent test to check on
  a local government's potential for promotional leadership – or that of
  the public or public–private agent presented with the opportunity. The
  need or the setting of a time horizon (predetermined by an event such
  as the Olympic Games or some external agenda, such as a decision on
  the headquarters for an international body, or one set by a plan (eg

BOX 7.2 FOR FELICITOUS URBAN DEVELOPMENT

(A draft decalogue for the use of urban-development managers)

1. Cities have streets, not roads. The city is a public space.

   Making a city involves building places for people, for walking through and meeting up. It is making shops, squares, restaurants and cinemas. Thoroughfares are only meant for vehicles in a secondary way; groups of people are more important. Private uses are the least important considerations. The city is, first and foremost, a set of public spaces surrounded by buildings and trees.

2. Public works begin and end.

   Works are finished properly. Mistakes are somebody's responsibility, and that somebody must be held to account. Non-fulfilment must be penalized and any harm done punished. Anyone making money through assaults on the city must go to prison. Local authority staff will only have credibility if they stand up to economic groups acting with apparent impunity.

3. Urban development materializes in a programme of public works, yet it only builds the future city if it comes in response to a global project that is known, balanced and desired.

   It can be termed the strategic plan. Centralities must be defined – main development axes, access points and strong features in the districts. Urban development must ensure mobility for all, and consequently it must deconcentrate it. Citizens need to visualize the city, to see their neighbourhood, to understand its routes and to identify with its centres.

4. Urban development operations are integrated, strategic actions.

   Each operation must have its complement/continuity in facilities, design, social and cultural action, environmental improvement, public safety and job creation. The city is not a set of compartments, and urban policy cannot be just a string of sector programmes. The city is a mix, and urban policy an intelligent, sensitive combination.

5. In the city, the shortest way between any two points is the most beautiful one.

   Urban aesthetics make the city visible. Each project must have its own architectural justification, its cultural significance and its gratifying perception. Inhospitable thoroughfares and public spaces are a needless aggression for all and, above all, for those who most need the city – the ordinary people, women, old people and children. The vast majority.

6. A democratic city is a visible city, with physical and symbolic references that let its people know where they are.

   Centres must be accessible and multipurpose, in terms of urban uses and cultural meanings. The most used routes transmit the image of the city to the majority: if they are not pleasant, people will not be pleasant with the city, with others or with themselves. Districts, all of them, need identity and social value – they must have their own significant buildings and build their own attractions. Urban development policy must light up real and metaphorical lights in each and every part of the city.

7. Building the city of the future is a task for all. Yet there is no creation without a project, and the project must be integrated, global.

It is our political and professional duty to create and to make accessible the means whereby the project may take in the needs and wishes of the majorities. These means must be in line with the cultural mechanisms of the people: models and exhibitions in the districts, multimedia presentations, explanatory and promotional campaigns. The citizens exist, but often those who monopolize power and knowledge prefer to ignore them.

8. Progress in the city is measured by progress in the quantity and quality of its public spaces.

It is a matter of priority to be acquainted with them: the ones that exist legally and materially, and the ones that could. Public spaces must be conquered from other state authorities (barracks; port, railway and airport areas; Ministries and autonomous bodies that have obsolete buildings or underused spaces). Also to be conquered are the private ones, institutional ones (like the Church) or business ones (partially abandoned factories or blocks – the speculators are hovering). The walls that prevent the majorities from seeing and using the city must be knocked down.

9. There is no positive urban development without a capacity to invent and plan.

The underground space must be conquered: for service galleries, for car parks, to ensure more intensive usage possibilities for the city. Points of convergence of routes and transport lines are privileged elements for urban development: public spaces and facilities must endow them with centrality features. Future centralities must be invented on the basis of strong public action in the present: administrative or cultural operations, skilled tertiary sector fields, transport terminals. The city of tomorrow is built by reinventing the past of the city, and city designing at the frontiers of the present-day city.

10. The quality of urban development depends on the socialization of architectural culture and on the aesthetics of public spaces, yet it also depends on the penetration of civic culture in bureaucratic bodies and professional corporations, on the integration of social demands, and on collective obsessions.

Nobody has a monopoly on urban knowledge, but everyone has fragments needed to build the city. It is not a matter of putting one fragment alongside another, but rather of combining them in accordance with the possibilities of the day and the space. Only in that way will a city be built with places (of significance) instead of territories (administrative in nature), a city for living to the full at all times and in all places, and not one to endure as one makes one's way around amid congestion and ugliness.

> To transform the city one must know it. You get to know cities with your feet. Before proposing thoroughfare schemes and transport systems, one must walk around the city and mix in with its people. The urban planner works not so much in a laboratory as out in the street, not going everywhere by car but rather hopping from one mode of transport to another; he or she does not only talk to colleagues or to professionals, but rather with the variety of people that live in the city. At some time or other, each district and each works site needs walking round, going into the houses and talking with the people. Transforming the city entails a lifestyle.
>
> *Exhibition by J Borja at the Bogotá Urban Development Institute, Colombia, 1995*

Strategic Plan 2000 or 2010), creates favourable conditions for linking up the global plan and the package of large-scale projects, for the purpose of getting the public agents to agree among themselves (which is often the hardest part) the details of the cooperation between the public and private concerns, and of encouraging a favourable, participatory social atmosphere.

- The blend: plurifunctional or versatile conception in large-scale urban projects. Any large-scale urban project, however 'specialized' it may be and however 'marginal' it may seem with respect to centralities, can be made to foster diversified urban development, to improve accessibility and mobility in the metropolitan area, to create public spaces and to lend a 'sense of place' to the territory. The will to blend uses and activities, to bring diverse populations together and to articulate specialized operations with global development processes must be present from the outset in any operation. Even when implementation starts with sector specific action, the conception must be global. Versatility will be possible if it is inherent to the plans, and it will subsequently determine the capacity for evolution and adaptation of the urban fabrics. The obsolescence which in our times hovers over ambitious projects must be borne in mind – a teleport, and communications node or a technology park, for example.

Three complementary functions strike us as being of particular importance:
- the generation of public spaces, collective amenities and monuments that reinforce symbolic identity;
- the impact on employment;
- the urban development of the surroundings, bearing in mind the possibility of generating centralities, the impact in terms of redistribution (housing and services), environmental sustainability, formal or aesthetic quality, and using urban development to finance the operation.

Recent experience in undertaking infrastructural projects for mobility provides positive and negative examples, even within the same city (eg Rio: the red line implemented in 1992 as compared with the current approach to routes for 2004).

- Integrating and transforming the urban fabric. In many cases it is important to preserve or to produce formal continuity between the new operation and the pre-existing fabric, especially if it is a good quality fabric (eg Puerto Madero – Buenos Aires – the initial strategic plan). In other cases it is advisable to implement a strong, wrenching and prestige-bringing operation precisely to make that continuity possible (eg Balmaseda – Santiago de Chile, or Villa Olímpica – Barcelona). In some case undertaking a fundamentally symbolic project may turn out to be highly effective (eg Arche de la Défense – Paris) in establishing continuity. In other cases the operation requires the strong action of a formal break with the immediate surroundings, eg downgraded areas, precisely in order to establish the physical, social and symbolic relation with the city and its centralities, for example good cultural facilities in a downgraded historic area (Ciutat Vella in Barcelona). In all these cases it is advisable to distinguish and to foster three different urban processes:
  - integration with the immediate environment, yet also the effects of transforming spill-over, either in fostering other strong action projects, or through urban 'metastasis' (often not so much the result of strong initial action as of urban 'acupuncture' actions);
  - the balance between the change of activities, uses and populations and the maintenance, even if only partial, of the area's own fabrics and social groups;
  - the dynamizing effect on part (or all) of the city, physically, economically and culturally.
- The change of scale in the urban structure: new centralities. Not all large-scale urban projects are of the kind that can generate new centralities. Moreover, new centralities are not the result of just one project, but rather of a set of multiple action projects (though there can be a basic urban design project and an implementation schedule for the main works). However, all large-scale projects must indeed have some relation or articulation with old or new centralities, ie have favourable repercussions. Furthermore, in most cases, they should generate some elements of centrality. For example, it would not seem to be a sound approach to make an operation like Rio Centro (with the name Centre included!) so marginal with respect to the urban structure. On the other hand a specialized operation like siting some of the main Olympic activities on the island of Fundão is approached as making it an area with elements and articulations that will give it a relatively strong centrality (Rio 2004 project).

  The new centralities are characterized by the following features:
  - they are a highly complementary set of actions and concentrated in a few areas defined as priority and viable areas, nearly always in frontier zones between central areas and peripheries;
  - actions under way or planned are at once infrastructure and communication nodes, attractive areas for skilled tertiary sector people and emblematic or monumental projects;
  - articulated or concerted actions involving private and public agents are already present, or can be encouraged with relative ease;

  The results of the new centralities are:

Box 7.3 The Transport Logistics Platform at the Llobregat Delta

In the metropolitan region of the city, the most complex restructuring and transport infrastructure building operation in Spain is being implemented. It involves extending and reorganizing the port and airport of Barcelona and its road and rail access routes, in order to arrive at the transport logistics platform for the north east of the country, and perhaps the most important one in the south of Europe. The proximity of the port and the airport, and their location so close to Barcelona, has meant that the entire operation is approached using a single territorial unit: the Delta at the mouth of the Llobregat river, in a space belonging to the municipalities of Prat and Barcelona. This fact, together with the ecological wealth of the Delta, turn the project into something much more ambitious than merely articulating a transport logistics platform. That is why the objectives of the programme also contain a broad environmental programme, which involves building the biggest waste-water purifying complex in the metropolitan area, diverting and channelling the mouth of the river Llobregat, recovering and stabilizing the beach line, and other measures for protecting and remodelling the wetlands and lagoons of the Delta. The scale of this activity, the territorial and environmental impact of the infrastructure planned and the protection requirements of an ecologically complex zone have prompted the need for setting up a coordinating committee for all the authorities involved. These come from three institutional levels: state, regional and municipal. However, nearly a dozen public institutional agencies and metropolitan bodies are also involved.

Such an ambitious coordination experiment is new in Spain, and amounts to an exercise whose working rules will serve to lay down future methods for territorial action. The commission, with representatives from forty institutions and directorates general, has an executive committee comprising four members, representing the state, regional, metropolitan and municipal authorities. The primary function of this executive committee is to examine the plans and projects coming from each body, and the contradictions with all the other aspects of the matter. From its work comes the definition of planning guidelines that take in the spatial and functional limits of each project, and the definition of the corrective measures to be incorporated in them. From the commission's work come partial agreements, in the form of territory planning criteria and agreements between the levels of the administration that are involved in each subject. The planning and execution of the agreements is kept in the sphere of authority of each administrative level involved, the monitoring of the agreements passed being the responsibility of the standing committee.

The main operations scheduled can be analysed from functional and territorial standpoints, the same ones as are analysed by the monitoring commission. The functional standpoint is the basis for the port–airport unit, the coast improvement work involving water purification and beach regeneration, the urban reordering of the urban front of the Prat municipality affected by the road and rail access routes to the port and airport, and the protection programme for the coastal wetland in connection with changing the course of the river. The territorial standpoint is the basis for differentiating the coastal area, with planning problems deriving from the need to extend the port and the airport, the urban area of El Prat, through which all the access routes come, and which also looks onto the river Llobregat, the remodelling of the urban front of the port and the river in the city of Barcelona, and the planning of the road and rail infrastructure routes taking advantage of the course of the river Llobregat and its penetration in the delta, affecting a dozen different metropolitan municipalities. From the strict standpoint of each of these operations, the main objectives can be summarized in the following parameters:

- The Port: Major restructuring work is going ahead to the port of Barcelona, entailing its transformation in terms of logistics and a redefining of its infrastructure on the basis of this objective alone. A zone for transport logistics activities is being built, covering nearly 300 hectares, designed to attract the world's main goods forwarding operators. This operation, which has turned it into the main receiver of containers on the Mediterranean, means extending it southwards, towards the river Llobregat, and this has made it possible to liberate the old port of the city, converting it into a large urban area for leisure and business pursuits.

- The Airport: Barcelona airport fully modernized all its territorial and control installations for the occasion of the Olympic Games. However, it continues to function with two runways that cross each other, which limits its capacity to just over its annual figure of 11 million passengers. Furthermore, its contribution to goods traffic is on the low side. The extension operations scheduled entail building a third runway, parallel to the main one, and a large territorial zone for goods with facilities for airways maintenance companies and other sector specific operators.

- The Railways: The operations for enlarging, reforming and integrating the port and the airport also involve restructuring their rail access routes. Getting the railway to reach the port with the standard European gauge (the Spanish railway network uses a different gauge) is an important part of reinforcing the transport platform, and is a chance to restructure the regional railway network, which currently mixes passengers and goods together along its access routes to the metropolitan area, to the detriment of mass public transport. Furthermore, there are plans for the high speed train to reach Barcelona, from Madrid and from France, it running along the same corridor, which could be used to have a terminal at the airport.

- The Road Network: In addition to the enlargement of, and modifications to, the access routes to the port and the airport, it must be stressed that the building of the huge urban ring road called the Ronda de Dalt also impinges on this territory, this being a stretch that was left pending execution at the time of the Olympics. This planned system is complex, with a new motorway penetrating the metropolitan area along the right bank of the river Llobregat, the completion of the Ronda de Dalt, and alterations to the access routes to the airport and the port; in all there will be over 60 kilometres of fast roads, the building of which also involves altering some of the large junctions in the basic metropolitan network.

- The Baix-Llobregat Purifying Station: Planned for siting at the mouth of the river Llobregat, in an area of 45 hectares, is the building of the largest waste water purifying station in Catalonia, which is to treat the waste water of 40 per cent of the metropolitan population, with treatment flows of 260 cubic hectometres (Hm) a year. The project is one of great technical complexity, on account of its location and scale, and it includes major works such as a sea effluent point, for sludge treatment and tertiary treatment facilities for part of the water, it being proposed to reuse it for agricultural purposes and for feeding the coastal wetlands.

- Channelling the River Llobregat: Channelling the river and diverting it at its mouth are needs that arise from enlarging the port and building its access corridors. Given that the river runs between agricultural and urban fronts, and ends in a coastal space of ecological interest, the planning must take account of a sizeable set of variables; among the more important of these are the environmental aspects affecting matters such as possible changes in the feeder networks for the river's subvalving, reserves of drinking water for Barcelona, cleaning up industrial deposits in the former riverbed now to be occupied, altering the refilling of the wetlands, and the repercussions on the coastal morphology.

- The Coastal Zone and the Wetlands: At the end of the Llobregat Delta are the wetlands of La Ricarda and El Remolar, which are major lacustrine spaces, with nesting birds, protected by the Plan for Spaces of Natural Interest of Catalonia and its European CEPAL status. They are spaces that are affected by all the action plans described, it being planned to use those action plans to increase their existence and protection circumstances, and to consider public management of them as natural parks. These spaces are also located in a four kilometre long dune front, currently affected by strong erosion due to the influence of the dyke in the port of Barcelona; the project envisages the consolidation of the coast and its regeneration as a sea/natural-space contact zone, balancing awkwardly with the use of the adjoining beaches for metropolitan leisure.

The operations as a whole have a public budget put at four thousand million dollars, for an operation that in principle had a schedule of up to fifteen years. The need not to miss economic opportunities stemming from competition between European spaces meant that the most costly operations are now being subjected to great pressures for immediate execution.

Source: Personal Communication from Manuel Herce, Member of the Management Committee for the Llobregat Delta Plan, Barcelona

- a change of scale in the city, ie the structured territory in the urban–regional sphere is extended;
- a greater number of city residents and users can enjoy access to the areas that are highly rated because of the range of services they have and their symbolic character. In quite a few cases the new centrality enables sectors that are poorly integrated into the city to gain access to a higher level of urban quality;
- more sustainable development conditions are created in so far as the new centralities enable the congestion, costs and waste of existing centralities to be reduced.

• Urban design (in formal terms) is an ingredient of the material content and the economic viability of metropolitan projects. As they say in Italy, first the drawing, the model, the video ... and then the rules, the programme, the plan. That is what they call 'the preliminary project'. Operations seeking to restructure a central area in a city or to create a city in no man's land must first be visualized. If that is not done, it is unlikely that public and private agents will make a full commitment to a complex, long-term project. And it will be still more difficult to obtain support from institutions, society and the media. Design entails defining a set of forms that ensures versatility and accessibility, that encourages a wide range of uses and the evolution of those uses, and that lends a mark of quality to the whole. The aesthetics of an operation are part of its economic viability and part of the community's quality of life.

• The management model for large-scale projects is defined from the outset of the operation. A large-scale project (sum of projects) entails complex management, taking in at least the following:
  - scheduling the operations;
  - designing the projects;
  - financing the actions;
  - coordinating the agents;
  - implementing the works;
  - marketing the products;
  - maintaining the whole.

The main content of each of these needs to be established from the start in order for them to be structurally related. For example, the financing is dependent on the timing of the scheduling; the design of the architectural projects and the urban development of the surrounding area enables gains to be worked out, and they can be oriented towards financing; the marketing of the products is linked to the design and to the participation of all the agents; the cost and obligations of maintenance must be established at the start, since they influence the efficiency of the operation; and so on. It is on the basis of defining this complex management model that public–private cooperation can be regulated. Large-scale urban projects require an initial leader, usually some public authority. This leader entrusts overseeing the management to a managerial structure. As the project progresses, coordinating the main agents and the relative autonomy each has in developing their projects takes on greater importance. However, the coordinator is the guarantor of the coherence of the whole – or should be, at any rate.

BOX 7.4 COLOGNE: THE REGIONAL FREIGHT TRANSPORTATION PLAN

Cologne (Köln) is located at the heart of Europe, with the benefit of a dense network of communications infrastructures. Since the early 1990s, the city of Cologne has been drawing up a regional freight transportation plan whose aim is 'intermodality'. This programme seeks to reconcile the range of strategies developed. The development of the plan was based on a series of consultations with the main representatives of the sector, some of their customers and the public administration. The plan sets out to develop a large number of projects, some of which were very soon implemented. The most spectacular case was the starting up of the intermodal terminal and the 'urban logistics' terminal. The Cologne-Eifeltor intermodal terminal is a strategic point for the whole Rhine region. Having been opened in 1967, it is now undergoing reconstruction and expansion. This project has brought the city of Cologne and the Deutsche Bahn (the railway company) into association in developing a highly technological base, through close negotiations and cooperation. The railway company and the mail will have their distribution platforms, a European-dimension infrastructure being consolidated, since the mail service is already cooperating with four other mail administrations in Europe and one in Australia. Alongside these logistics terminals are a number of commercial premises for transport companies, as well as companies in technical, social, business and other services. An urban logistics terminal will also be set up and reserved for regional companies devoted to transport activities, complete with all necessary spaces and services. These logistical platforms will be fully connected internally and externally with the German motorway system.

The organization of the projects shows the will to develop the least environmentally aggressive transport systems, giving the whole plan a highly ecological nature. Thus it is sought to transfer a major share of the road traffic onto rail through improving the services of the rail freight agency, of which the city of Cologne is the majority shareholder.

The regional plan also analyses relations between territorial planning and heavy goods vehicle traffic, which is expected to increase a great deal over the next few years owing to the greater preponderance of small and medium-sized companies and the proliferation of industrial parks in the urban periphery. It must also be borne in mind that, on account of its geographical location lying between three large European ports and central Europe, Cologne is on the routes of a large volume of trucks. Of the 110,000 trucks that are on the move every day in the region, some 25,000 are passing through. To counter the increase in traffic – and in pollution and noise – and also to improve the loading and unloading systems that hold up the traffic, Cologne has drawn up two cooperation schemes:

1. Cooperation between transport companies with comparable production levels: they share trucks for transportation assignments to customers they have in common.

2. Installing an urban logistics terminal where all goods for distribution in a particular region of the city are deposited; later, those goods are distributed in smaller trucks. The extra cost generated by this step has provoked a number of adverse reactions.

In December 1995, the Rhineland-Westphalia Land declared Cologne a model city for urban logistics. Worthy of highlighting in that process is the intense partnership between the administration and the industrial sector, which has enabled efficient transport-organization actions to be carried out. Alongside that, also worthy of note is the will to reconcile overall strategies on the basis of highly operational specific projects, this having made efficient policy management possible in the long term.

Source: Cologne City Hall, published in Eurocities (1995), Working Document, Brussels, 'Best Practices'

Public–private cooperation today does not follow the traditional two-stage scheme – first public action for the non-profitable part of the operation (how could it finance it?) followed by private agents promoting the development of the lucrative activities. Public–private financing must be planned from the start, either on the basis of subsequent income (beware: the toll-city cannot systematically be opted for), or by recovering capital gains and complementary urban developments (*Urbanisme*, 1995; Nello, 1995; Herce, 1983, 1993, 1995a, 1995b; Esteban and Ferrer, 1995; Busquets, 1988, 1989, 1991, 1995; Acebillo, 1995; Garcia and Villalante, 1995; Koolhaus, 1995; Mignaqui, 1995; Fernández, 1995; Fernández De Luco, 1995; Leira, 1987, 1990, 1991, 1992, 1995, 1996; Portas, 1985; *Alfoz*, 1985; AU, 1991; Maragall et al, 1995; Barcelona Metrópolis Mediterránea, 1990; *Rassegna*, 1989; Solà Morales, 1988, 1993; de Cáceres et al, 1992; Dupuy et al, 1994; *Monde des Debats*, 1994; Singer et al, 1993).

CONCLUSION

Throughout this text we have tried to emphasize certain key ideas:

- The main goal of urban policy today is creating a sense of city.
- The government of the city is embodied today in those institutions, groups or individuals that are capable of generating leadership in promoting such as to define or take on a project for the city.
- This project translates mainly into a set of large-scale projects that are at first sight sectorial or specialized but which are or seek to be versatile, transforming and articulated in a coherent whole – ie strategic.

BOX 7.5 ROTTERDAM: THE RIJNMOND ROM PROJECT

Rotterdam, with the biggest port in the world, is a complex, dynamic city. For many years great efforts have been made for the benefit of the environment, yet as a whole the results have left a lot to be desired on account of the heavy traffic and the weight of industry. In view of the environmental problems, the wish to improve the quality of living and the need to restructure the great port to keep the city competitive, the national, regional and local authorities, in conjunction with the industrial and commercial sector, decided to work together to offer the people a great industrial complex that would enable jobs to be created and the conditions needed to improve the environment and the social climate to be met, with their sights set on the year 2010. The aim of the project is reinforcing the city's port activities while also providing the means to improve living and housing conditions in the Rijnmond area. Most of the action plans incorporate some component benefiting the environment and the fight against the current pollution problems, showing that economic promotion actions – rehabilitating the port – can be carried out in line with sustainable development – protecting the environment, improving the quality of life and so on.

The Rijnmond plan drew up a working methodology that under-pinned its success. Firstly it must be mentioned that the approach is integral as regards subjects – it includes social and economic elements, transport, housing, etc – and as regards promotion – public and private sectors are to participate. The assessment is also integral, bringing in all the partners involved in the process. The approach is also modulated and evolutive. It is controlled and assessed constantly, fitting in with the changing circumstances of the context, always in a jointly agreed way highlighting the democratic approach of the process. The approved plan sets the development strategy for the port, taking in the aims to be achieved as regards the environmental goals cited in the national plan. The development of those plans stressed the priority actions: enlarging the port; improving access to the port and the industrial zone; develop-ing public transport, freight transportation by rail, boat or oil pipelines; improving the environment with measures aimed at controlling current problems; consolidating the urban space; expanding the natural spaces and leisure areas; and encouraging cooperation between agents to achieve the objectives. These objectives have been specified in the form of 47 different projects.

Despite the criticisms made and the uncontrollable parameters at local level, in implementing those projects a structure was set up that coordinates and adjusts the various projects in hand. In financial terms, the total bill for the operation amounts to five thousand million dollars, a fifth of which is devoted to the 1993–97 period and the remainder to be spent in the period up to 2010. Private contributions may amount to some fifteen thousand million dollars by the year 2000. First indications show that the plan is having very positive effects on the area: the creation of 15,000 jobs by the port activity; an increase of 1,200 hectares of industrial land; the creation of 1,750 hectares of green and leisure spaces; and also the considerable decrease in the number of people affected by industrial pollution and the attenuation of the risks associated with living near a port like Rotterdam.

Source: Rotterdam City Hall, published in Eurocities (1995), Working Document, Brussels, 'Best Practices'

The idea of creating a sense of city nowadays poses a critical question that large-scale urban projects must answer: the dialect between centrality and mobility. Or how to optimize the assets of the metropolis city through restructuring projects (reconversion or starting from scratch) making possible the extended reproduction of the city as fixed capital, human capital and symbolic capital. These physical projects are the materialization of processes and initiatives whose character is economic, social, cultural, political and image related. The physical project is a compromise reached between political decision-makers, professional company executives, cultural agents and social representatives. The government of the city faces a paradox. On the one hand, globalization enhances the role of local governments (the principle of proximity), and large, complex action programmes that are also highly localized require precisely institutions and political bodies that keep very close to their territories. On the other hand, local governments have little or no international presence; they are subject to legislation, and depend for their resources on national governments (and sometimes regional governments too); they have a relatively weak position with respect to public or private economic groups; large-scale strategic action plans are not in their field of responsibility (or are only partially so); and furthermore they correspond to a metropolitan city that is fragmented in institutional terms.

Under these circumstances the creation of leadership in promotion depends more on political initiative than on any legal settling of fields of authority. This initiative will take the form of a set of large-scale strategic projects, corresponding to a concerted global project, that must have a logical, viable model for setting priorities, that must be legitimate and visible for the society, and that thus create a favourable framework for negotiating and reaching agreement with the higher levels of the State and with the economic agents. Large-scale strategic actions cannot be one dimensional, ie they are at the service of one goal and in contradiction with others. If we accept that the goals of the policy of creating a sense of city are economic competitiveness, social integration and sustainability, then these dimensions must be present, to a greater or lesser extent, in all large-scale urban projects. Thus, for example, when certain infrastructural operations or even some strategic plans are criticized for responding solely to goals of competitiveness, then either the criticism is valid – in which case those operations or plans are not – or it is not valid – ie it stems more from ideological prejudices than from acquaintance with the project. Large-scale infrastructural work, such as a ring road or reconverting a railway or manufacturing area, can also be income

Box 7.6 Buenos Aires – Puerto Madero

The project for rearranging the Puerto Madero port reflects the wish to transform and recover an area of great historical and strategic value for Buenos Aires. Puerto Madero, located between the River Plate and the traditional centre of the city, is a relatively large area (130 hectares of land and 40 hectares of water divided up into four docks) with great potential for centrality. The Puerto Madero Plan sets out as the main objectives the recovery of the port for commercial, residential and civic uses. In this sense the intention to remodel the old port into a fundamental urban element with a river front in the service of citizens is noteworthy. It entails incorporating the creation of a large green leisure space into the work, with good links with the rest of the city design. The Puerto Madero space, on account of its centrality, is to be incorporated as an area of new centrality in order to contribute to the economic lift-off of Buenos Aires, offering tertiary and residential spaces. Puerto Madero can provide a chance to break the dynamic of exclusive uses of the land, fostering new patterns of residential quality by including green zones along with architectural designs.

Developing all these courses of action requires defining a powerful accessibility system in order to integrate the Puerto Madero space coherently with the structural system of Buenos Aires. Laying down two large entry gateways to the north and south of Puerto Madero enables them to be connected up to the regional system. Similarly, the existence of public transport routes is to be provided for. Special care is to be taken as regards not breaking or separating the old centre and the new centre with large infrastructural works (the La Plata-Buenos Aires dual carriageway or motorway).

Development of the Puerto Madero Plan began with the formation of a public company, the *Corporación de Puerto Madero* (national government/municipality), which commissioned a master plan from a mixed team of experts (the Planning Office of the Buenos Aires City Council directed by Alfredo Garay, and the Barcelona consultancy firm *Consultores Europeos Asociados* directed by Joan Busquets and Joan Alemany). On this basis (see the *Plan Estratégico Antiguo Puerto Madero*, 1990) a tender was arranged involving local professionals for the development of the plan. The execution of the plan by the corporation was based on synthesizing the top-ranking proposals, covering on the one hand the basic urbanization works and offering the development of individual units (beginning with the pre-existing sheds) to private enterprise.

Outlined below are the specific objectives of the Puerto Madero Plan as set out in the 1991 Strategic Plan:

Specific Objectives of the Plan

Puerto Madero, the City's River Façade
An attempt to establish a new relationship between the city and river, through a port that had become lost to the city over previous decades.

The transformation of the old obsolete port into an urban component of the city is to enable a new front to be established, one that Puerto Madero itself had hindered. The extraordinary feature of the stretches of water of the docks as well defined units offered a unique situation that few cities enjoy in the historical and nerve-system centre. The new urban uses maintain the existence of the docks, though now refurbished for civic and citizen activities.

The Costanera, the City's Main Green Space Once Again
The opportunity afforded by this transformation will enable the Costanera (jetties) definitively to become a structural component in the urban green system. For that purpose it will have to be clearly linked to the pre-existing urban pattern – the tree zone, the open air cafes and restaurants, the games areas (cycling, skating) – in short a free space for the port dweller as it was in former decades. Enhancing the Costanera will also bring greater visual and pedestrian attractiveness for the ecological zone, which is to be regarded as an existing reservation set apart for the intensive use of the Costanera itself.

Puerto Madero as an Opportunity for a New Model for the Centre
The privileged position of Puerto Madero could provide modernization for the centre of the capital city by incorporating new central activities that will be needed in the immediate future. This could help the economic lift-off of the city and boost its role with respect to the international system of capital cities. It could also indirectly avoid the negative transformation of the traditional centre of Buenos Aires, whereby the free-competition/office and traditional square block/tower block changes in activity and morphology were arising without offering a coherent image in the sector.

New Central Residence Options
With this new centre model, the option of a central housing unit of the apartment type depending on community services and spaces arranged by square blocks could amount to a major qualitative leap, giving an alternative to the only current model (the peripheral house with garden) for sectors working in the centre. Its priority location opening onto the Costanera also results in having a population group that will make continuous use of this large open space.

New Tertiary Space Options
This is no doubt one of the strongest potential requirements in city centres over the next decade. The new forms of work tend to seek forms of organization in groups of a certain size, larger than the batch of Buenos Aires square blocks. To achieve that, new spaces and aggregation forms that are coherent with this new requirement will have to be defined. The first eastern band of the docks offers an excellent opportunity as a new centre reference, and nearby the existing institutional axis opposite the jetties along the avenue.

Re-use of the Jetties and the Architectural Heritage

The privileged position of the Puerto Madero jetties and their good location with regard to the docks makes them particularly appropriate for housing civic and citizen amenity uses. The excellent build quality enables them to be re-used in a contemporary way, so becoming an urban attraction point and a motor for the collective life of the sector.

Likewise some silos in the port sector can become architectural landmarks in the whole, and house special activities within the development proposed. Certain cranes, the bollards, stone pavings and the existing vegetation can all serve to provide continuity of atmosphere and interest in the new proposed uses of this emblematic space.

New Intermediate Density Residential Area Options

The scale of the action could allow for the development of a residential area of intermediate density, meeting the demand for larger housing with notable quality in the surroundings. Small gardens lined up with the building work will increase the sense of residential space. Their location at the join between the tertiary strip and the central residence could confer the role of joining area for the dominating activities on it.

Own Access System

Developing a unit on this scale demands defining a powerful accessibility system to be arranged coherently with the structural system of Buenos Aires. Defining the two entrance gateways to the north and south of Puerto Madero allows them to be connected up to the regional system. The passageways in the central docks assists with connecting them up to the existing urban grid. The underground transport system can be extended into this sector, and the overland transport system can use the main circuits. In any event, it is important to achieve continuity of access with the existing city, paying special attention to the routing of the La Plata–Buenos Aires dual carriageway or motorway – between the city and the jetties – to avoid it becoming a break between the existing centre and the new centre. International experience shows that this component could be critical for the proper development of the sector.

The Main Axis: 'Historical Centre–Ecological Reservation–River'

The main reference point between the two centres and the river must be the main green spine which, along with the guideline of the Avenida de Mayo, defines a representative space of the first order. This axis will now link the political centre with the new Puerto Madero centre, and suggests a possible canal in the ecological reservation enabling the presence of the river to be perceived from the Parque Colón esplanade. The significance of this axis, orthogonal to the city façade, maintains by analogy both the importance of this foundational space and the constant sense of river as previously established by the customs and the first bridge – in the form of a pier or landing jetty.

Absorption of the Scale of the Transformation
The scope of this transformation means it must be approached in such a way that, without relinquishing the advantages in terms of image and innovation afforded by its large size, it may involve units that are controllable is scale and size, to avoid speculative mechanisms on the one hand, which might otherwise get out of hand, and architectural misfits on the other, which would lead to a situation of urban chaos. For that purpose, it is important to define a process with a global image that can be developed part by part, ensuring a certain liberty at that level so that the promotion can develop its own specific programme, provided that this programme is in harmony with the general structure of the sector, in order that the sector can aspire to being a real urban unit. Similarly, on the intermediate scale of the real development, some room for manoeuvre must be allowed for responding to executive projects.

Public Initiative Plus Development with Private Investment
The transformation of Puerto Madero, as with the recycling of so many obsolete zones in major cities in Europe and America, must be approached with an urban definition stemming from public initiative, yet with development being implemented in concert with private investment. In this sense the transformation can ensure the reappraisal of a central zone, and also achieve the proper urbanization of other components for open, intensive use by citizens.

Puerto Madero, a Significant Urban Entity in Buenos Aires
In short, the aforementioned objectives bring together the will to transform in a coherent way an urban component of the city that is significant on account of its historical role in the formation of the modern Buenos Aires and on account of the strategic value of this central land. On top of its location attributes are its feature of having areas of water and prior elements that lend it unique properties. Moreover, this urban unit has extra value deriving from the single title to the land, which facilitates maximum advantage being taken of this opportunity. It is therefore logical that the management mechanisms tend to assure an optimum urban planning result. Fostering a public initiative corporation seems to be the best way to channel a transformation that is ambitious in citizen terms and realistic in terms of the investors who are to be responsible for giving it content and use in the medium term.

Source: Busquets et al, 1990

redistributing operations if they ensure the creation of centralities that are accessible to the people in general and improve the amenities and services of the surrounding area. To take another example: when it is held that rehabilitation work on a downgraded peripheral area is spending money to the detriment of productive investments, no account is being taken of the fact that if the operation is properly approached it can lead to major savings under

Box 7.7 Melbourne South Bank: Remodelling an Obsolete Industrial Area

The central objective in remodelling the South Bank, an old industrial area affected by the recession and by the abandonment of industries, and poorly connected to the centre, was the creation of a new centrality zone. The project included a very wide range of action enabling the South Bank to be integrated into the centre of the city of Melbourne. From among these courses of action we may highlight the following:

- improving road access by building large avenues that form two large-scale east-west communication axes in the city;
- converting the streets adjoining the river into pedestrian walks with direct access paths to the main thoroughfares and the central district;
- building housing units in order to achieve mixed use of the land;
- building business, commercial and leisure complexes, the axes of the new centrality;
- developing commercial infrastructures;
- developing large open spaces.

It is important to stress that this rearrangement of the South Bank was carried out as a concerted effort on the part of various social and economic agents. The federal government and the state government took part, the latter being the owner of most of the land and responsible for planning and investing in the infrastructures. Alongside them, the local authorities played an essential role in developing the housing, while most of the investment was handled by private agents. The implementation of the remodelling of the South Bank included some aspects that it is worth dwelling on. Firstly, there is the absence of a special administrative authority for the development of the project. Mechanisms of concertation and coordination were developed enabling the project to be carried out through ordinary administrative procedures. Flexibility is another essential feature of this action. The plans were adapted to changing economic and social conditions, without abandoning the agreed strategic guidelines. Lastly, citizen support must be highlighted, for without it many of the projects developed would not have met with the success they have enjoyed.

Source: Mireia Bell (1996) Working Document, Barcelona

other headings: safety, water pollution, etc. And it is also an action programme that adds skills to human resources. And to take one further example: the range of cultural facilities. This is an investment that contributes both to social integration and to competitiveness. And to the extent that it develops civic culture, it has a positive impact on sustainability.

We could go on citing more and more examples. In any case, here is our challenge: our bet is that in any large-scale urban operation it will always be possible to trace the presence of these positive dimensions; if it is not, we would argue that it was possible for them to be there, and that if they are not then criticism is very much in order. Last but not least, whether or not large-scale urban projects have this multidimensional nature depends on the efficacy of the democratic system based on the decentralization of the State and local autonomy, representativeness and transparency in the government of the city, and the multiplication of mechanisms for participation and communication.

Chapter 8

Metropolitan City Government

METROPOLITAN CITIES TODAY

Urban agglomerations are the result of the economic and demographic growth process that has led the population to gather together where activity and expectations are the greatest, ie in cities, and particularly in large cities, thus creating serious problems of territorial and social imbalance. In advanced countries, where demographic growth has levelled out, the problems are no less serious since the demands made on large cities are still growing owing to their being the nerve centres for their country's development.

Urban agglomerations or metropolises have become a state-wide issue. In them are concentrated both the greatest growth potential and the most pressing social problems. In them the most dynamic and innovative activities are pursued, and there too are to be found the greatest marginalization problems, with wealth and well-being existing side by side with the greatest inequalities and imbalances.

The social, economic and cultural reality extends well beyond the city taken as a municipality, and occasionally even spills over broader boundaries – the county, state etc – becoming a territorial reality not catered for in the legal system. The central city's decisions affect the inhabitants of the peripheries, and the latter use the central city without being represented on its decision-making bodies.

This real city lacking any representative structure is also the city that is projected out to the world outside, whence it is perceived as a single unit, and it also establishes relations as a single unit with other agglomerations, with which it spins a network of cooperative actions and competencies at the world level.

Universal though they are as a phenomenon, urban or metropolitan agglomerations do not lend themselves to uniform treatment since their reality is multiple and complex. The very physical reality of the agglomeration is difficult to take in. European cities, for instance, cannot be spoken of through reference to global city models such as New York or Tokyo. In Europe one must speak rather of an urban system comprising some 40 large systems and a large number of very dynamic intermediate cities with major centrality functions, among which there are relations not only of competence but also of complementarity. The large cities of developing countries, with their rapid, unchecked growth, cannot readily be compared with the previous ones either. The legacy of history, cultural traditions and forms of social and political organization differ greatly from place to place across the planet, as do the levels of social and economic development achieved, all of which puts constraints on developments and on solutions adopted aiming at institutionalizing the metropolitan phenomenon.

When seeking to analyse the problem, a distinction could be made between agglomerations that have some type of metropolitan government, those that have none but are nonetheless coordinated from a higher level, and those that have no kind of coordination at all. Two types of agglomeration can be distinguished from among those with a metropolitan government. The first is the metropolitan structure that is fashioned by law on top of pre-existing municipal governments, obliging the latter to act jointly in a number of predefined functions. This is the kind of organization encountered, for example, in the large cities of Brazil and Canada, or in French Urban Communities, and it is usually the result of the growth of the agglomeration beyond the administrative limits of the central unit. This same type of growth has come about in what could be called 'metropolitan municipalities', though in these there is no administratively differentiated central unit. Metropolitan municipalities may in some cases have been formed from a clear historical nucleus, though in other cases they are the result of the parallel growth of different cities. In both cases the resulting conurbation is transformed by law into a metropolitan municipality. This type of solution is commonly found on the Asian continent and, with the exception of Tokyo, mainly in developing countries with little in the way of democratic tradition, where rapid, uncontrolled urban growth has led to the setting up of special bodies for this urban reality. They are usually agglomerations which are or were state capitals, and which are in any event the main centres for economic, political, social and cultural development in their respective countries, which is why they often have special administrative treatment. As examples of this kind, we could point to Ankara, Istanbul, Bombay, Karachi, Peking and Shanghai. Cities with special statutes, such as city states or federal districts, function in the same way: Hong Kong, Singapore, Seoul, Vienna, Brasilia.

The government structure usually has two levels, the metropolitan level covering the entire agglomeration, and the district or smaller-unit level. Since these are local governments in their own right, many of these metropolitan municipalities have legislative competencies that are specified in fiscal, urban planning, economic and social measures, in addition to the usual competencies or areas of authority of metropolitan structures. Where no metropolitan authority exists, one form of institutionalization of the urban agglomeration consists of adapting it to the organizational structure of the state, taking advantage of pre-existing administrative units at higher levels such as the province or region. In these cases, areas of authority are shared out among the municipalities of the agglomeration and one or more higher administrative levels, which often involves the superposition of several administrative levels having competencies over one and the same territory. This solution in fact amounts to a 'regionalization' of the metropolitan issue in that it attributes the functions of coordinating and managing the agglomeration to a higher administrative level. Some examples are the Ile de France

Region, the Autonomous Community of Madrid, American cities such as Los Angeles or Miami, and North African cities such as Rabat or Casablanca. This kind of solution is prone to give rise to conflicts in competencies owing to the superposition of action programmes and financing, and the lack of representativeness of the municipalities which make up the agglomeration.

Another kind of coordination is functional coordination, ie the establishment of mechanisms or institutions for providing services or specific functions in territories specially defined for the case in hand. This solution, which is very common, is the one that has been adopted in cases of metropolitan governments that have been abolished, such as London and Barcelona. We also encounter it in Australian cities such as Brisbane, Perth or Sydney, where coordination arises at state level owing to the poor recognition of local governments or, as in New York or Chicago, when the agglomeration spreads far beyond the administrative limits of the state or county.

Finally, there are agglomerations with no kind of supramunicipal coordination. In such cases cooperation mechanisms may be established between municipalities, with global or specific aims. This kind of cooperation is found everywhere in the world, and among examples of it would be Amsterdam, Washington or Montevideo. It is interesting to note that, as happens with functional coordination, it also appears when metropolitan bodies disappear (London, Barcelona).

The organizational structure adopted by the metropolitan area is one of the many factors than influence the distribution of competencies among the various administrative levels that come together in it. Generally speaking, metropolitan areas with a well defined system of competencies and sufficient resources to pursue them are few in number.

Despite the diversity in organizational forms, a constant feature is the exercise by the higher levels of global and strategic planning functions and the performing of services needing a large area, whether for reasons of efficiency or on account of their repercussions: transport, housing, the environment, waste disposal, and water supplies and treatment. The lower administrative levels exercise functions of a more local kind, ie those requiring greater proximity to the citizens. Even so, the sharing out of competencies among the various bodies that come together in the metropolitan area is a complex matter that depends as much on the type of metropolitan organization adopted as it does on, among other things, the general structure of the state, relations between administrative levels, the degree of autonomy of the local authorities, etc.

In broad terms, a distinction can be made between those cases in which the administrative level of the metropolitan area is part and parcel of the global structure of the country, and those in which there are specific metropolitan bodies, whether governing or coordinating. When the administrative level of the metropolitan area is part of the general organizational structure of the country, its competencies, defined by law, are those associated with the administrative unit involved: a region (Ile de France), a county (Los Angeles), an Autonomous Community (Madrid) or some other one. How these competencies differ from those of local bodies operating in the metropolitan territory is clear in principal, though this does not mean that no conflicts arise. For example, there have been disputes in Paris between the region and the state for control of transport policy.

When a metropolitan government or structure exists, it is generally rare for its competencies to be clearly defined and its resources adequate. In general, the competencies of metropolitan bodies are not exclusive, they being shared with state and local bodies, thus generally giving rise to conflicts between the various administrations acting in the same territory. The complexity increases when, as very often happens, there are specialized bodies for performing certain services, or bodies dependent on central government. Moreover, the importance of large cities for the development of a country tends to encourage state intervention in a good deal of their spheres of action, such as in large-scale projects of national interest requiring sizeable investments, and this occurs, moreover, in a context in which we find a widespread tendency – and one that could be regarded as running counter to this – towards the decentralizing of functions by the central state in favour of the regions.

Lastly, the matter of competencies cannot be disassociated from financing, since those competencies obviously cannot be properly pursued if they are not backed by adequate financial resources. Metropolitan income comes basically from the traditional sources: local taxes, charges for services, and transfers and subsidies from other state or local bodies. Modes of financing found comprise a wide variety of combinations of these sources. There are cases in which state transfers make up most of the income (Brazil), others in which a good deal of it comes from charging for a service (transport in Copenhagen), others in which municipal taxes account for the bulk of the income (Montreal), and a range of other combinations. As regards funds stemming from taxes, this source may consist of a share in the tax revenue of metropolitan municipalities, as in Canada or in the counties of England, though there are also cases of direct revenue for the metropolitan body, as in the French Urban Communities.

In any event, metropolitan financing possibilities depend on the local financing system in each country, and it is the case that while needs in large cities are increasing – and financing requirements along with them – governments are increasingly reluctant to transfer resources and financial capacity, owing mainly to restrictions on public spending. Furthermore, state transfers are increasingly geared to specific ends. As a result of all this, there is a widespread tendency for large agglomerations to try out new forms of management and financing, ones that were traditionally regarded as being private sector methods, particularly the participation of private capital through the forming of mixed companies. In some cases, public services have been directly privatized, as in London, though the privatization may also be linked to the granting of international aid payments, which directly or indirectly impose certain forms of organization. In general terms, metropolitan bodies face serious financial limitations. They have insufficient autonomy and revenue collecting power, they are dependent both on central or regional governments and on the municipalities that make up the metropolis, and the resources they have are inadequate for the competencies assigned to them.

We thus encounter a phenomenon that is common to nearly every country, one that is vital both for the development of those countries and also on account of the serious problems it poses, and yet one for which there do not appear to be any sufficiently satisfactory solutions. This is not surprising given the magnitude and complexity of the problem and the many forms of resistance that its institutionalization entails. Among the most frequent problems that emerge when analysing metropolitan areas we find the following:

- The reluctance of the municipalities making up the urban agglomeration to lose their autonomy in favour of a higher level. Their resistance is understandable, and is encountered everywhere. It would also appear to be difficult to avoid, though the best solution is undoubtedly a strong, democratic metropolitan authority.
- The resistance of higher levels of the administration to the existence of a metropolitan body with a broad, regional mission, it being seen as a rival power by those higher levels, particularly when the relevant authorities belong to different political camps. This was clearly the case with two metropolitan governments that were abolished, the London one by its central government and the Barcelona one by its regional government.
- The proliferation of administrative bodies is perceived – and rightly so – as meaning more bureaucracy and more public expenditure. The good management of services entails, among other things, clarity and transparency in allocating resources and competencies. That is why it is important to avoid as far as possible the creation of new structures taking advantage of pre-existing ones, an option that has been adopted in Italy with the new legislation on metropolitan areas.
- The democratic deficit. There is no pressure from the citizens for solving metropolitan problems as such. Supra-municipal bodies, in so far as they are not directly elected, are perceived by the citizens as remote and beyond their control.
- Defining an appropriate metropolitan sphere. This point should not give rise to conflict if it is taken into account along with the natural competencies or functions of each sphere. Generally there are two spheres that are complementary: a broad or regional sphere, appropriate for strategic and territorial planning and for coordination with higher levels (either the state or a regional government); and a restricted sphere, agglomeration or urban continuum that is appropriate for intermunicipal cooperation and the provision of certain services.
- Reconciling the principles of efficiency in service management and performing them at the closest possible level to the citizen.
- The need to reconcile the interests of the many public and private agents that play their parts in the metropolitan territory. A strong metropolitan authority is a necessary condition but not sufficient in itself. It is needed in order to act efficiently to achieve the greatest consensus and participation, and that participation should be a continuous process independent of electoral swings, and so there should be suitable meeting ground mechanisms.
- The inadequacy of financial resources. This is another of the problems affecting most metropolitan bodies, and one of the factors which, as previously noted, induces them to try out new forms of management and financing.

Despite the difficulties, it cannot be doubted that large cities need a suitable framework for them to be well governed and operative. We live in a time of accelerated changes and of growing competitiveness, and in an increasingly interrelated world in which municipal networks for cooperation and exchange are proliferating. Metropolitan authorities must be strong and well legitimated agents, capable of negotiating, and possessing a brand value that makes them more competitive vis-à-vis the world outside. The dimensions of the international market impose new conditions on those competing in them. Confrontation no longer arises only between individual companies, however large; it also arises between productive systems that may find themselves backed up or weakened in a decisive way by the quality of the territorial and organizational system within which they find themselves – quality in services and facilities, the environment, services to companies, communications systems, etc. All without detriment to the 'internal' function of the metropolis, ie its role in integrating the inhabitants that make it.

Beyond the Metropolitan City

In the 1960s the term megalopolis became popular in connection with highly urbanized areas containing a number of urban centres. The model was the north-east of the United States. In Europe the drive to plan urban territories that went beyond the agglomeration lead to the concept of 'region-city'. However, these concepts were rarely translated into institutional form even though they were viewed as spheres lending themselves to territorial planning. The metropolitan city has nearly always developed in successive crowns. While the first one has the features of the periphery and has generally been the sphere for metropolitan institutionalization at a minimum level concerned with urban planning and service management (water and sewage, transport, waste disposal, police, housing schemes etc), the second crown took pre-existing urban nuclei as its basis. It is precisely then that the paradox of metropolitan government emerges: the strength of the central city comes up against that of the local authorities of the second crown. That confrontation hinders the creation of government structures just when they are most needed to lend coherence to a wide range of initiatives promoted by a number of public and private agents.

In the 1980s, the combined effects of global economic competition and progress in communications media defined new urban-regional territories, with variable geometry and great institutional complexity. This has led to a new institutional definition of the metropolitan city tending to identify its sphere with that of intermediate entities (provinces, departments or the like). That is what is behind certain current reform schemes in some European countries, such as Italy and the Netherlands. However, the new economic territorial realities go beyond this, spilling over regional and national borders. New strategic spaces emerge – the macro-regions and the urban axes.

Macro-regions are multipolar urban systems whose strong points are the metropolitan cities that articulate them. Though there is nearly always a stronger city, some balance is present between the centres of the macro-regional urban systems. In a higher territorial sphere we find the urban axes or macro-systems, in which a greater density of relations is present and in which, in some cases, common goals are defined. In Europe the 'banana' has become popular – the main axis of the urban economy running from London to northern Italy. Another complementary 'banana' is the European 'sunbelt', linking Barcelona (north-east Spain) with the southern end of the other banana. Other axes, already consolidated in some cases (such as the Rhône-Rhine axis) or now forming (such as the European Atlantic arch) are already showing a certain capacity for fostering common projects. In all these cases, governability does not depend on whether or not a new institution is created, which would be practically impossible within current state frameworks – and anyway the resultant institution would be very precarious on account of the dynamic, variable geometry of the urban-regional areas. Governability depends rather on the capacity to define and execute large-scale projects designed to turn those areas into a competitive and cohesive territory. That is the challenge of what has recently been called the Metapolis (Ascher, 1995; Pumain et al, 1991; Delfau, 1994; Berry, 1976; Belil, 1988; Chesire, 1994; Sallez, 1993; Hall, 1993; Lawton, 1989; Martinotti, 1993; Lenoir, 1992; Consoni et al, 1995; Ajuntament de Barcelona, 1991; Ascher et al, 1992; Borja and De Forn, 1991; Borja, 1988; Alemany and Borja, 1986).

GOVERNING THE CITY

The governability of the regional-urban territory thus involves three different levels:

1. The strategic level: the level at which public and private agents come together for carrying out and managing large-scale work in infrastructure and facilities. It is the large city's new hinterland, but it is often a regional polycentric space too.
2. The metropolitan level: the level of institutional cooperation to guarantee both the management and the promotion of the real city or the sphere of daily life of the active population. It tends to be a decentralized supermunicipality.
3. The city-municipality level or central city of the metropolitan region. It is the political sphere in the strict sense both because it is governed by a representative institution (directly elected in general) possessing broad powers and because it attributes brand value to the territory as a whole. This level is the political test par excellence of governability in the city of today, even if that seems to contradict what was said about the importance of the regional-urban space. In the central city are concentrated the contradictions and the main areas of potential of the metropolitan territory. It has a strong government, close to the social and economic agents, and has the capacity to negotiate with other public administrations. It has almost universal competencies and is expected to take the lead. Its initiative, or lack of it, marks the metropolitan territory as a whole, and structures – or fails to structure – the strategic space. It is not so much a matter of providing a theory for the domination of the central city over its hinterland as for the central city's responsibility to promote, to manage and to integrate, as previously analysed. However, this is an appropriate point for turning to the matter of which political forms can best enable it to fulfil that responsibility.

The City as a Political Opportunity

Our era, so very media-based, personalizes political representation. Mayors tend to be directly elected (or else at least to be the front-running candidate from the winning party). In large cities, decentralization in districts can be honed through the direct election of the president (who is sometimes a member of the group of councillors). Experiments are run on open candidate list formulae, or electing some of the councillors by districts, through a mixed system in which the city lists to which proportionality is applied would compensate the representational distortion of the majority system. In general, legislation on elections should be restricted to certain basic principles (universal suffrage, frequency etc), recognizing each municipality's right to innovate and to try out various formulae depending on its particular features and the political wishes of its citizens (the electoral system for each municipality would be the object of consultation with the electorate).

The political parties that run in national elections are not necessarily the same ones as those that should run in local elections. City politics is not a scaled-down carbon copy of national political patterns or even of the traditional culture of parties. In some countries (eg the United States – in California and other states – or Canada), political parties, by law and by custom, merely express their support for lists of candidates or for certain individual candidates. In municipal elections, only groups of electors and individual candidates should run, they possibly receiving the support of one or more parties and also of bodies and groups of all kinds.

Voting is obligatory, programme-based and universal. Citizens have political duties as well as rights. They can return blank or spoilt ballot papers, but they cannot refuse to vote and then insist on their legitimate rights vis-à-vis the municipal government. Candidates must commit themselves to a programme, and failing to carry it out, as denounced by a certain minimum number of electors, could entail being disbarred from running in the following elections (if so decided by an ad hoc tribunal comprising representatives from the judiciary, the municipal council and civil society). All citizens who can prove that they have lived in the municipality for one year, whatever their nationality, would be electors, and two years' residence would give foreigners the right to run as candidates.

The message of participation is common to all, and at election times all candidacies pay lip-service to it. However, we believe that for most citizens it is a matter of priority to facilitate their everyday relations with public authorities. We propose that town councils (or in large cities the districts and neighbourhood offices) should jointly provide a single reception desk and/or telephone for the administration as a whole. Under no circumstances could an authority ask the citizen for documents or data which are on record in another department or even in a separate public administration. In many cases oral statements could be accepted as being as valid as an official document on public record. The municipal administration should also become a duty solicitor for the citizens in their dealings with other public administrations and service providing companies. To defend the citizens, arrangements should be made for the creation or approval of arbitration and reconciliation tribunals, fiscal councils, user information and defence offices, charters of rights regarding privacy, the environment, employment in proximity services and urban maintenance, housing for young people, etc – and all without detriment to the creation of municipal justice (on the basis of justices of the peace by districts, who could also be directly elected) to settle disputes between neighbours, to impose penalties on petty urban delinquency, offences against the environment and public spaces and amenities, to protect in a subsidiary way the rights of the citizens, and entitled to act in other cases, with the consent of those involved, through reconciliatory arbitration proceedings.

Although the practice of communicating with the administration by telephone has spread, it should be the rule rather than the exception. It is absurd that a town hall cannot do what any local shop can. Yet that is not enough. Citizens are entitled to interactive communication with their administration, which is theoretically nearer to them. Nowadays it is a duty of local governments to ensure that the city is cabled and to facilitate its interactivity. It also seems essential to democratize the audiovisual panorama by authorizing and encouraging town councils to back local television and radio stations run by social groups and professionals – though without neglecting parallel material backing for associations, for consultations and referendums prompted by the people and for the development of a range of formulae for public–private cooperation in managing urban facilities and proximity services.

The Decentralization of the City

The political and administrative decentralization of large cities and the organization of the metropolitan area – particularly the agglomeration, urban continuum or 'real city' – are two inextricably linked processes, or ones which are dialectically related – ie the greater the 'metropolitanization' the greater the 'decentralization', and vice versa. Decentralization should be based on units or territorial zones (districts) which possess historical geographical and/or socio-cultural characteristics, ie of a kind making the existence or construction of a collective identity possible. They should also have as clear a physical image as possible (it is better if major arteries define districts, uniting rather than separating them), and it is desirable that they be or can become multipurpose in social and functional terms. Districts need to be big enough (by inhabitants and area) to make the exercise or management of functions and services possible.

District government could fall to a city-elected representative (councillor) acting as the direct delegate of the mayor and directing, with a technical political team, the executive administration of the district. The direct election of the president, either by designation by an elected district council or by the majority holding political group in the area (which breaks with the principle of unity in municipal government) is easier if functions are attributed to the district that are deconcentrated, strictly regulated and open to citizen participation, or if citizen decentralization is set within the more global process of the aforementioned 'metropolitanization' process. In the early stages perhaps the simplest solution is to have a district or neighbourhood executive in line with the governing majority in the city.

The district council takes over functions of stimulating, monitoring and control, information, consultation and proposal, though in general it has few powers of decision (except if there is a metropolitan government). It could be interesting to experiment with direct election to the district council, under formulae enabling neighbourhood candidates, individual candidates etc to run as well as party candidates. For instance: each elector votes for names amounting to two thirds of the total number of seats to be filled in order to ensure the presence of minorities. The possibility of forming the council on the basis of all the bodies and groups existing in the district should not be ruled out either, though then it would have a more corporate character and could end up being less representative of the population as a whole unless at the same the residents are encouraged to join together in associations.

The deconcentration of competencies, functions and services is a relatively complex process in technical and political terms, and it cannot be left to improvisation. The implementation of each 'package' of competence transfers must be painstakingly studied and applied so as not to send costs and disfunctions spiralling upwards. Among other things, the following must be borne in mind:

- The match between functions and services transferred and the technical, financial, material and staffing resources needed to execute them.
- The articulation between these decentralized and/or deconcentrated functions and services and the central bodies who are to look after the basic rules, the programming of the whole, the coordination of execution or management, technical back up and assessing the results.
- Administrative restructuring and the introduction of new management systems and technologies, since the new administration cannot simply be a reproduction of the previous one.

From what we have said it can be deduced that we are not concerned about focusing on the debate between decentralization and deconcentration. Evidently, a major deconcentration of functions and services is being proposed, but in so far as those functions and services are integrated in territorial terms into a political leadership structure, subject to control by a representative assembly and open to broad participation involving the people, we believe that we should be talking about decentralization.

Involving the People

The participation of civil society in the government and management of the city is once more on the agenda today. In addition to the general reasons for it, those that are common to other times in history (political democratization, the social demands of the sectors that are sacrificed in the name of urban development and the demand for collective identities), there are now other more contemporary reasons for it, such as:

- The growth of the city and of its activities multiplies the quality of life problems and increases the city residents and users' demands for social well-being. The problem issues are ever more specific in what they cover and the demands come from heterogeneous groups. Public provisions must be differentiated and they need the demands to be clearly expressed in order to adapt to them. Regulatory provisions for those demands, which can be contradictory in many respects, require a range of mechanisms for participation, both in the planning and study phases and in the execution and management ones. The involvement of the people is nowadays an essential requirement of local democracy.

- The range and diversity of the functions and services covered by the administration give rise to costs that are ever more difficult to meet, and tend to generate bureaucratic structures that are ever less efficient in economic and social terms. Cooperation between public and private groups in its many forms and scales (ranging from the participation of major economic and social agents in a strategic plan to cooperation involving grassroots groups or individuals – whether voluntarily or paid – in performing social services such as caring for old people) is now an essential mechanism in public management. Participatory management is a functional necessity.

- The palpable crisis of representative democracy can be offset, at least in part, at the local level, at which there is a direct and ongoing relationship between elector and elected, between governor and governed – ie the personalization, communication and control of political representation.

- The marginalization and exclusion processes that are always arising in our societies – often more visibly, closer to us and more seriously in large cities – can be countered more effectively in local territorial spheres, where it is possible to combine integral action, social proximity and immediate solidarity.

All these reasons lead us to address the urgent need for political and legal development work enhancing the involvement of people, which is a precondition for general efficiency. The juridical nature of that participation brings obligations for the strong and backing for the weak. Involving the people often poses problems that are difficult to solve if what is entailed is guaranteeing or assessing the representative status of the groups or associations that have dealings with the government and municipal administration. In some cases thoroughgoing regulation is called for – for example in the number of members or of signatures needed for prompting a poll. In other cases the action must be as pragmatic and as well adapted to the particular situation as possible – for example the monitoring commission for a special plan or social programme. Those actively involved in those cases are decided upon in terms of their being those directly interested or in terms of their capacity to play a part. Participation, whether in neighbourhoods or in the municipal sphere, needs sector specific bodies to be set up, for example economic and social affairs councils, welfare councils, public safety councils, transport and traffic councils etc. The representative status of the bodies taking part in these organisms is determined as much or more by the initiative they display than by the number of people associated with them.

The main goals of participation are:

- Developing participation in defining programmes and projects, in carrying out work and in managing municipal services: public hearings on four year plans, facilitating polling by districts or neighbourhoods, trying out new forms of sectorial involvement for the citizens in large-scale services and municipal companies, and above all increasing the number of channels of communication with the people by making full use of new technologies – for example, running trials on telematic consultation in the districts.

- Fostering initiative and voluntary work through special campaigns and programmes that stimulate and direct social energy towards targets of collective interest debated in public.
- Reinforcing the web of associations through a policy of supporting bodies so as to enable them to improve their technical and administrative capacity and to make them competitive when it comes to expressing opinions, carrying out activities or managing services of a general nature or services for their members (Borja et al, 1990; Ajuntament de Barcelona, 1990; Roncaylo, 1990; Curti and Diappi, 1992; Vourg'h and Marcus, 1993; Charte Européenne de femmes dans la Cité, 1994; Alape, 1995; Ventura, 1995; Polèse and Wolfe, 1995; Consejo Territorial de Planeación Santafé de Bogotá, 1995; Ziccardi, 1995; Carrión, 1994; Concha et al, 1994; Sivaramakrishnan, 1996; Ducci, 1995; *International Social Science Journal*, 1996; Rodríguez and Winchester, 1996; Borja, 1996c, 1987; Sachs, 1996; Alemany and Borja, 1986; Castillo et al, 1996; *Inchieste*, 1994).

CONCLUSION

By way of a conclusion, seven principles are put forward for bringing local democracy and citizens' rights up to date, principles which form part of a document drawn up by the author in response to a commission by the Spanish delegation to the Habitat II Conference (Borja, 1995). The evolution of the rights of cities and citizens goes hand in hand with globalization processes worldwide and with urbanization nationally and regionally.

1. The right to take part in international life. Local governments are nowadays in fact agents in international life on account of the importance of economic and cultural relations between sub-state territories, on account of the role they have (or endure) with regard to migratory processes, on account of the global need for them to share in the responsibilities of compromises made between economic growth and environmental sustainability, and on account of their real and potential function in socio-cultural integration and political participation. It is therefore necessary to acknowledge the right of cities, their governments and their civil society to establish relations, to set up networks and to take part in international associations without central governments acting as intermediaries, and also to participate in the United Nations system through their representative organizations.
2. The right to political innovation, including involvement in defining electoral and organizational systems, in service management modes and in financing mechanisms, within a framework of basic principles (eg universal suffrage).

BOX 8.1 CITIZEN PARTICIPATION: CITIZENS' RIGHTS AND INSTRUMENTS FOR PARTICIPATION

Below is a summary of the main mechanisms for participation set out in the context of the project for a charter or special statute for Barcelona (Proyecto de Carta Municipal, 1991). Rights that are recognized by basic legislation and that are anyway inherent to being a citizen are taken in and developed. Furthermore, attention must be drawn to the innovation entailed in recognizing a number of urban social rights, closely linked with quality of living, whose aim is defending the citizen with respect to the new kind of problems that stem from urban development, or ones which have not so far been given full consideration from the local point of view. Privacy, public safety, and vulnerability vis-à-vis large service companies are matters that it is wished to broach in the charter, out of a conviction that the local administration, together with the citizens, whether organized or not, is the best framework for their specific treatment, though without losing sight of an overall vision of urban problems.

Communication and Information

In order to make the citizens' right to receive the greatest amount of information on municipal activities possible, the charter establishes that state administrations shall grant municipalities all such authorizations or concessions that are necessary for municipal radio and television stations to be set up, these then being able to carry out any activities allowed by their resources. The right of citizens to use these media is also envisaged.

Individualized Public Information

Taking advantage of similar experiments previously carried out by the city council, the formula of individualized public information is also envisaged. Through this system, and without detriment to the use of the official public information channels, it is intended that the citizens in general or the groups concerned may be informed of municipal action while at the same time expressing their agreement or disagreement, along with any suggestions they may have. Individualized public information is therefore an institute enabling individual or collective participation to be achieved, either through informal groups or through structured associations:

- Individualized, through bulletins sent to the entire population or to specific groups, and the creation of the open telephone and mail box.
- Collective, through surveys sent to groups with particular identity features or distinct interests of their own (informal groups).
- Associated groups, through participation councils.
- Territorialized, to ascertain differences of opinion and demands in various districts.

Citizen Consultation

Recognizing the right of every citizen to be consulted, the charter envisages the capacity to arrange that kind of consultation. As the most significant progress in this respect over current regulations, under which this formula has already been tried out, it is proposed that the plenary council should regulate both modes, and that, in the case of consultations that are district-wide in scope, consultations can be called for at the prompting of 1 per cent of the district's residents.

Rights for Suggesting, Requesting and Complaining

These rights are already recognized and exercised (there is a book for the purpose in each district), and they are backed by the Municipal Charter, adding the right for them to be made widely know through the communications media available to the city council.

Public Hearing

The city council undertakes to arrange a public hearing every year on the Action Programme or its review, the municipal budget and the tax ordinances, though the possibility is envisaged of it being at the request of citizens individually (by signature sheets) or collectively (bodies or groups of bodies proving that they have a certain minimum number of members) on any matter of municipal competence.

Citizen Initiative

The citizen initiative is maintained as a form of contributing economic resources, goods, rights or personal work for carrying out activities of municipal interest, for which purpose the districts will have to allocate funds from their budgets each year.

Regulation Initiative

The notion of citizen initiative is extended to cover the capacity to propose the passing of regulations, through district or sectorial councils, or at the initiative of a promoting group having the backing of 1 per cent of the people over 16 years of age that are on the electoral roll.

Civic Management of Infrastructure and Facilities

While citizen initiative is intended for courses of action not envisaged in the Municipal Action Plan, civic management is created as a new form of citizen intervention in municipal management. In recent years, experiments have been made with encouraging results in direct management by the citizens of facilities that fall under municipal competence. This formula has been developed particularly in the cases of civic centres, sports facilities and youth centres. Now the aim is to further the city's role, and the Municipal Charter proposes that organizations and bodies of a civic nature should be able to take part in the management of services, facilities and infrastructures owned by other public administrations as well (eg the port and airport), to which organizations such as trade unions, the Chamber of Commerce and users' associations can contribute greater dynamism and initiative, and in which the city, through the city council and these bodies, must take a more prominent role.

Citizen Campaigns and Municipal Cooperation

The response to major social problems (drugs, public safety, marginalization etc), the capacity to take measures to improve (or to halt the deterioration of) the quality of city life (traffic, the environment, the architectural heritage, hygiene and cleanliness, etc), and the social and cultural promotion of the citizenry (in general or by broad groups), all require campaigns to be carried through enabling citizen cooperation to be articulated through a range of formulae – eg public support for individual initiatives ('Barcelona ponte guapa', for improving the appearance of the city), or collaboration organized in mixed structures (citizen security councils organized by districts) or by contracting services of a social nature out to private groups (home-help cooperatives), or promotional campaigns connected with improving services and facilities (sports promotions, providing access to and cleaning the beaches, organizing visits to museums or works in the city, etc). These campaigns enable innovations to be made in the mechanisms of communication, cooperation and support for citizen initiatives.

Consultation and Participation Bodies

In order that they may be consulted by municipal bodies, proposing joint solutions to the problems concerned, the territorial consultative councils (covering the city or a district) and the sector councils are confirmed in the Municipal Charter. At present, in addition to the councils of district bodies, other sector councils are already taking a hand in municipal management, such as the councils on social welfare, youth, schoolchildren, sports, etc. Moreover, it is possible to create consultative councils on an ad hoc basis. That was the case with the drawing up of the strategic plan and the debate on the Municipal Charter itself. In both cases, bodies or individual citizens directly related to the sector concerned can now be represented. We outline below the main features of three recently formed councils that strike us as particularly innovatory: Municipal Justice, Taxation, and Social Welfare.

The Right to Privacy

There are two sides to information. Just as we went into the citizens' right to be informed, so we must not forget that the authorities, in pursuing their mission, are gathering more and more information on the citizens. In the charter, the Barcelona City Council undertakes to guarantee the privacy of citizens by issuing regulations for the use of registers, residence records and other public instruments, and takes this into account before implementing each new technology in municipal management.

Citizen Access to the Administration and the Transparency of the Administrative Process

In order to achieve greater transparency and accessibility with regard to the administration, significant improvements have already been made to citizen–administration relations, and some innovatory provisions have been introduced in the charter project. In this context, it is laid down that the city council shall not demand data from citizens when those data are already on record in the administration itself; verbal statements on personal circumstances are accepted without further proof; and the 'single reception point' is to be made the rule as regards authorizations and applications for services, as is now happening with water, gas and electricity. In addition to the proposals set down in the Municipal Charter, services already in existence are being improved, such as '010, Barcelona Información' or the District information Offices, and new experiments are being tried out, such as the 'Teléfono 900' for dealing with certain administrative affairs.

Environmental Rights Charter

Barcelona, like any large city, is a complex system with a multitude of interrelations. The systems – and the city is no exception – cause disfunctions. Thus some matter and energy becomes waste and pollution of the environment, transport causes noise pollution, many forms of advertising lead to visual pollution, etc. These disfunctions taken together become assaults on the urban environment. Hence the Municipal Charter binds the administration to draw up a Charter on Environmental Rights to set out and guarantee those rights for all the citizens of Barcelona. It is this charter that takes account of environmental factors in planning strategies; that ensures the prudent, rational use of raw materials; that can be a major tool in preserving, protecting and improving the quality of the environment; that, by drawing on the experience of the ordinances on environmental protection and the quality of life, may serve to protect citizens from the assaults occurring around them, whether in the form of atmospheric pollution, noise pollution or water pollution; and in short one that protects the urban environment, guaranteeing the ecological and environmental sensitivity of all action taken in the city. In addition to this, the city council is entitled to set up systems for collaboration and agreement with public and private bodies and with individual citizens to ensure that environmental policies are in line with the city's needs. This collaboration may have economic components and/or effects on the individual totals for rates and duties, so that actions affecting the environment can be punished or rewarded.

Defending Users and Consumers

Another new feature is the recognition of the municipal authorities' capacity to defend the interests of the citizens vis-à-vis large companies, whether public or private, that perform public services. The charter also recognizes the general defence of the citizen as a consumer, taking over competencies in inspection and imposing penalties as regards pricing, labelling, advertising etc, and fostering collaboration among the sector's bodies and entities. The city council will deal with the protection of the citizens with respect to building and public service companies, and will participate in the governing bodies of companies holding concessions for public services (water, gas, electricity, telecommunications). One of the instruments for developing these functions is the Consumer Arbitration Tribunal, as provided for in the General Statute on the Defence of Consumers and Users. This is designed as an arbitration body for settling – ex-officio or at the instigation of a party – any claims and complaints made concerning products and services. The arbitration system is based on voluntary submission by consumers and companies to arbitration for settling conflicts, applying criteria of equity and reconciliation. Representatives of consumers and companies will be present in it. The arbitration awards are executable straight away, there being no higher body under this procedure.

The Municipal Justice Council

We have already referred to the sector councils in local management, and yet, on account of their specific character and their innovatory implications, we must make special mention in this section of the Municipal Justice Council, whose main aim is to supervise the functioning of the tribunal and the municipal courts. In this context, the council will provide a prior report on, among other things, the appointment of and changes to the body of municipal magistrates. It will also draw up an annual report on its own functioning and that of the municipal tribunal for the city council and for the General Council of the Judiciary. The charter provides that the Municipal Justice Council be presided over by the Mayor, and that it be made up of, among others, the President of the Higher Court of Justice of Catalonia, the Director of Public Prosecution of the Higher Court of Justice of Catalonia, the President of the Municipal Tribunal, one representative each from the General Council of the Judiciary, the Public Security of the State and the Generalitat, the trade unions, neighbourhood organizations and professional associations.

Public Safety

For the purpose of consolidating a model for public safety for citizens entailing action not only in terms of repression but also in prevention and in fostering citizen participation and solidarity, the charter envisages the founding of the Municipal Council for Public Safety and the Prevention of Delinquency, presided over by the Mayor, as the body for participation in this sphere. This Council for Public Safety and the Prevention of Delinquency will be of mixed composition, as in the case of the Municipal Justice Council previously mentioned, and they may even be merged in the future. In the present-day council there is already participation by organizations of trade unions and employers, guilds, and neighbourhood and professional associations, along with representatives from the city council and the provincial government office, the police and the judiciary. This Council may be metropolitan in scope if so agreed by the town and city councils involved and the supramunicipal bodies of the conurbation. The Local Security Board, the presidency of which is allocated to the Mayor as already laid down in the national legislation, is the coordinating body for the various branches of the policeforce at work in the municipality. This Board will be complemented by the Tables for District Police Coordination, presided over by the President-Councillor thereof, and these have already begun to operate in our city.

The Taxation Council

The Taxation Council is a specialized body attached to the Department of Finance. It is made up of experts of acknowledged technical competence in tax matters. Among its functions is that of providing proposed settlements for appeals and complaints lodged by citizens in connection with taxation. The council has the power to draw up a settlement proposal which, though not binding, may be allowed by the city council's decision-making bodies, as has regularly happened since it began its work.

The Strategic Plan

The integral vision of the city offered by the charter, as a reference framework for solutions to the problems of the large city, broaches new aspects as regards the management of the territory. The approach to strategic planning is accepted as the reference system for defining which elements are to be sited in the territory and as a formula for drawing up forecasts regarding the type and levels of activity that are desirable in the city, and their distribution – without contradicting the aim of territorial planning as an instrument for the physical siting of elements making up the structure of the systems and for urban planning, closely related to their economic and social function. Strategic planning systems are in addition a highly valid instrument for coordinating and setting priorities for activities on the territory of other administrations, and also for establishing the bases for public–private cooperation in joint action programmes. The framework of a strategic plan likewise ensures transparency and public debate in defining and setting priorities for large urban projects.

Public Participation in Municipal Urban Provisions

Public information on planning instruments must be arranged in such a way as to ensure the fullest possible acquaintance of their content on the part of the citizens, through publicity mechanisms already provided for or through newly launched means (exhibitions, lectures etc), bearing in mind their necessary decentralization. By extending the previously mentioned mechanisms, articulating the notion of the monitoring commission will be arranged where necessary. the urban report is also indispensable in town planning and works projects, specifying the uses and needs for these plans and projects, and it will be produced jointly with residents through participatory instruments. Use will be made both of the most communicative classical media (such as models) and of new technological possibilities (video, cable).

Social Services

The municipality organizes the range of social services on the basis of the principle of viewing this service as a right for all the citizens, from the standpoint of promoting equality of opportunity and improving the economic and social security of the citizens. Within the framework of this political stance, and in order to insure that minimum social goals are achieved, the city council has developed positive action towards less favoured individuals and groups, though steering clear of a culture of dependence, developing whatever resources the individuals and groups possess and fostering their participation in the active life of the municipality. In order for this participation to come about, it is necessary:

- that the services be territorialized, both primary and specialized services, and closely linked to other personal services in order to achieve integral service for the individual, group or community;
- to achieve a coordinated network, both for quality in the rendering of the service and for the necessary public-private cooperation, which is very important in this sphere.

Population Sectors for Special Social Attention

There are population groups that, on account of their personal and social characteristics, encounter particular difficulty in maintaining normal levels of interrelation and integration in city life. These groups are users or potential users of the specialized programmes and community programmes that make up the network of municipal social services, and need special social attention.

Ethnic Minorities, Foreigners, Immigrants and Refugees

The presence of foreigners must not be regarded as negative, as a threat or as a source of social tension, but rather as a real possibility for dialogue, an expression of international cooperation and social and cultural enrichment for the city itself. In order to ensure respect for and the defence of the rights of foreign immigrants and ethnic minorities, without discrimination of any kind, the city council intends to do all it can to respect and ensure respect for those rights. Consequently, the Municipal Charter, in line with the work of the Research Commission on Racism and Xenophobia of the European Parliament and also the Foreigners and Refugees Working Group of the Municipal Council for Social Welfare, has laid down the right for all foreigners registered as residents in the pertinent register to vote in municipal elections. Until such time as this right can be made effective, fulfilling the conditions set by the Spanish Constitution, the city council itself undertakes in the Charter to make provisions for some procedure by which foreigners may be represented in the participatory bodies. In addition to the social policies pursued by the City Council for the benefit of foreign immigrants and ethnic minorities, the real right to suffrage as consecrated in the charter is the greatest guarantee of integration in a society which is taking on a multiracial and multicultural form.

The Travelling or Nomadic Population

The existence of a sector of the population with a nomadic lifestyle is not a new phenomenon. Lately, however, it is acquiring growing importance throughout Europe. Ways of attending to this social sector are already up and running. Thus in France (where the nomadic population is put at 250,000 people), a ministerial order obliges all towns of over 5,000 inhabitants to set aside specially prepared places for them. In Spain, Seville has already begun work on a space of that kind. The charter, even though this phenomenon is not a major one today in Barcelona, makes provisions for it. Thus, getting round the chronic lack of space in the city, the charter envisages reserving municipally owned land, provided that this does not impede the execution of plans, for people on the move, the city council deciding on the temporary and usage arrangements.

Severe Poverty

The charter, in the social services section, takes as its starting point the principle of equality, with a view to preventing and eliminating, among other things, the various forms of social and economic marginalization. Severe poverty is basically a big city phenomenon, and in some cases (such as the homeless of New York) amounts to a social epidemic. It is on account of its being a large city issue that the charter, as in many other fields of social services, envisages broad acceptance of powers – in this specific case, with the aim of taking part in the social rehabilitation processes which, without creating welfare dependency, may serve to set those concerned on an outgoing, dynamic course in this world.

Related Note
There are other sectors of the population which are particularly vulnerable and/or liable to suffer discrimination of all kinds: senior citizens and children, the long-term unemployed, dependent women, handicapped persons, drug addicts etc. These groups, whose importance can be ascertained just by listing them (together they amount to the majority of the population) are or should be the main 'clientele' of the general participation mechanisms, though they also need specific mechanisms linked to the public programmes affecting them.

Source: Borja et al, 1991

Box 8.2 The Right to Vote for Foreigners

Foreigners' voting rights are very much an issue today. Keeping a significant section of the population, one that lives and works in the city, without political rights is proving increasingly repugnant to democratic consciences, and it also hinders the already difficult process of the socio-cultural integration of immigrants who, whatever the reasons they had for leaving their country (politics, socio-economic reasons, religious reasons) may be, find themselves marginalized. On the other hand, granting local political and social rights comes up against major political and legal obstacles, and can provoke adverse social reactions that can end up leading to effects that are the opposite of what was intended. Furthermore, unilateral policies can also lead to major differences between cities and aggravate the problems of those which make the strongest commitment to integration policies. Despite all this, we believe that formulas must be found for ensuring the social and political participation of foreigners who have been living in the city for a year or more, including the right to vote in local elections. Immigrant integration policies must be approached at the global level, since it is a problem that is common to all cities rather than specific to one. However, it is advisable to study various formulae that have been applied in various countries or cities:

- Some countries recognize the right of resident foreigners to vote without waiting for reciprocity or for such recognition to become the general rule in the political and economic area to which they belong (eg various Latin-American countries).
- In other cases it is the cities that innovate, encouraging the election of representatives of foreign origin who are integrated (even if formally without voting rights) in the municipal representative bodies.
- More recent is the case of supporting association forming among foreign or ethnic communities, and making provisions for their participation in bodies of a social, educational or cultural nature.

However, these very diverse situations and global solutions can be approached on a national or regional (continental) level, but not at a world-wide level. There is a huge difference between the problems of multicultural cities in the most highly developed world, in which a democratic deficit arises that seems increasingly anachronistic, and the problems of urban areas in scantily developed regions, in which the rule of law and socio-economic integration are weak, and in which there coexist compartmentalized yet stable populations and others that result from massive population flows sparked off by wars or catastrophes (half the population moving between cities is currently in Africa).

3. The right to take over competencies traditionally associated with the central administration or the private sector – in urban safety and justice, economic promotion and work creation, and especially in the development of new means and technologies for communication.
4. Local governments, for their part, must guarantee political and legal equality for all the citizens, whatever their national or ethnic origin.
5. Equality of the sexes should also be fostered at all levels in local government and association movements.
6. Local governments should foster collective life and association forming among all social groups, particularly those that need greater public attention on account of their poor urban social integration.
7. Finally, the large city, its government and civil society, must accept their centrality function in regional and national spheres both as a right to receive special treatment from national and international bodies and as a duty to guarantee the use of the city by the towns in the region and by the nation (the entire population's right to the metropolis).

More than the market or the administration, it is the people that make the city.

Chapter 9
Cities in the World Scenario

THE INTERNATIONALIZATION OF CITIES: URBAN SYSTEMS, FLOWS AND NETWORKS

The 1980s produced a new situation in the world based on new equilibriums and flows. One of the most notable features was the increasing internationalization of the economy and, in parallel to this the internationalization of culture, information, fashions and behavioural habits. That internationalization was possible thanks to the development and dissemination of communication systems which permitted permanent and speedy relations with any territory. Telephones, fax machines, airplanes, etc became the world space in a space of single relation. But this space has centred increasingly upon the urban areas. Flows have a source and a destination, and those are the places where population, activities and power concentrate: the cities. Increasing internationalization brings new territories into the consolidated economic and political systems while at the same time generating new processes of imbalance between those parts of the territory which receive these flows and those which do not.

The increasing internationalization of political, social and cultural life has also affected cities, the principle nodes of relationship, production and interchange. The processes of globalization do not arise at the fringes of cities, but cities play an active part in them at the same time as they are affected by them. The traditional urban systems based on national hierarchy – capital, regional centres, country centres – lose their rationale with the development of mechanisms of insertion of the urban nuclei into world production, communication and exchange systems. The cities become part of urban systems which do not follow a rationale of territorial continuity but are instead structured in function of nodes (the urban centres) and axes (flows of merchandise, people, capital and information) between them. Territory tends to become itself as a network of interconnected spaces having their strong points in the urban nodes, departing from the traditional urban hierarchy running from the national capital to the provincial capitals.

The need to operate in an internationalized and globalized context necessarily leads to the establishment of relations with other urban centres, to allow operation in broader frameworks. Increasing interdependence and complementariness between medium-sized urban centres is reflected in the fact that city–region relations appear to lose intensity in relation to the importance of links between the different urban nuclei of a single region or of different regions. The structuring of city networks is a basic requirement for completing a more solid and balanced spatial structure at national level and for achieving well-rooted and complementary centralities of its territorial setting.

Internationalization has led to a change of scale of the action framework. In this context, cities need to have conditions of production, relationship and residence which allow them to consolidate themselves as attractive and competitive within a space larger than the traditional regional or state framework. The attraction of cities is based on a combination of factors, which include the quality of their human resources and their innovation capacity (vocational training and technological and business modernization), infrastructural provision (accessibility, communications, industrial land, office space, etc), environmental and social quality (location, housing, social climate, culture, etc). The new setting of action is characterized by:

- The generalized process of internationalization of all aspects of life and the clear globalization of production.
- At the same time, and with roots in the economic crisis of the 1970s, the city has taken on a new role in global development, becoming one of the essential actors in the economic recovery of the territory.
- To these two features should be added the importance of information as a key element in the taking of decisions and in positioning at international level.
- Finally, though none the less important for that, and to some extent as a consequence of the factors outlined above, competition between territories, and especially between cities, has increased enormously in recent years.

The increasing internationalization of economic, political, social and cultural life constituted the spark for the development of mechanisms of cooperation between territories which intermingle with the processes of competition. Cities take part in the globalization of the economy and of communication. Internationalization brings with it increased competition between territories which develop in parallel with the increase of cooperation between cities. The twin concept of cooperation–competition is one of the factors marking relations in the world urban system. Cooperation, necessary for membership of an international system, has as its ultimate objective an improvement in competitiveness. One cooperates the better to compete. This involves an interplay of equilibriums in which cooperation arises when the gains in competitiveness are greater than the possible losses of existing comparative advantages, and when there occurs change of scale of action which means that cooperation becomes an instrument for consolidation on that level. Competition between urban areas is generally established in terms of specialization or of geographical proximity. Cities tend to encourage one or more of the specialities in which they seem to have a comparative advantage, and they implement an exterior promotion policy based on that speciality. Thus cities such as Paris and Frankfurt compete with London and between each other to consolidate themselves as the financial market of Europe, while others such as Strasbourg, Luxembourg and Brussels compete to be the seat of the European Parliament.

Geographical proximity brings another type of competition between cities. The cities form as central points of increasingly large areas of influence. Nearby cities compete to consolidate themselves as centres of economic, cultural and political attraction for the macro-region. This competition can change into cooperation when nearby cities agree to implement certain projects which can be beneficial for the region as a whole. There are examples of European cities which have undertaken joint projects to defend their interests in the face of other territories. The dynamics of competition play an important role in consolidation of the world urban system. Public measures in support of greater re-equilibrium in an effort to achieve a multi-nodal distribution of economic development will continue with a view to consolidating a spatial model of the economy which is more diverse rather than more concentrated.

The internationalization of cities is clearly reflected in institutional terms in the active participation of urban governments and of the main development agents in international life, basically through three mechanisms: participation in associations of cities, membership of networks and the development of city marketing and active presence at international events (Belil et al, 1992; Veltz, 1995; Ascher, 1995; Borja, 1996b; Belil and Borja, 1988; Soldatos, 1995; Campagni, 1993; Savitch, 1996; Hall, 1996; La Terra, 1995).

The Development of City Networks

City networks have experienced an enormous upsurge since 1985, having become consolidated in the 1990s as an almost inescapable strategy of the majority of large- and medium-sized cities. The main objectives of city networks revolve around the need to:

- create a lobby system to face up to third parties;
- consolidate minimum territorial, economic, political and demographic spaces to permit the generation and utilization of economies of scale and agglomeration, plus the implementation of leading-edge infrastructures and activities;
- find a place in an international system which permits access to and utilization of a growing volume of information and the exchange of experiences and technologies;
- achieve leadership functions;
- find the cities a place, through the networks, in larger spheres of action.

The interest and commitment shown by some international organizations in the networks of cities, regions, companies and other types of bodies has also consolidated utilization of networks as instruments for joining international financing systems. In short, city networks become instruments and mechanisms of promotion of urban centres by bringing them into broader and denser areas of relationship. City and region networks have been classified in very diverse ways, using as main criteria the sphere of cooperation and spatial sphere of action, the lobby function, transfer of technology and positive experiences, catalysing function in the development of the local economies and the generation of international economic cooperation, the origin of networks built around existing informal relations, networks built on complementary interests, by external agents (the EU) or at the initiative of the members themselves, the characteristics of their members, and so forth.

Strengths and Weaknesses of Networks

Participation in networks is for cities an aspect of their strategy for membership of an international setting and a strategy for improving their competitiveness. But no advantage or drawback is absolute and valid for all networks or all their members. The main positive features of city networks are:

- They allow their members to join in a system of higher relations.
- They permit access to large volumes of information.
- They become consolidated as mechanisms for the implementation of the exterior policy, promotion and image of the city.
- The leadership and image functions find an excellent ally in the networks strategy.
- They can serve at the same time as a stimulus for the internal development of quality of life and competitiveness.
- In a world subject to a fast rate of change, the networks permit a certain permanence of a line of work in time, since the existence of outside commitments permits ad hoc contingencies to be overcome.

Networks break with the rigid model of regional and state aid, emerging into a sphere of acknowledgement of particular interests in various regional spheres and identification of cities and regions as active players in the construction of an internationalized space, accepting the logic of the network instead of the pyramid. At territorial level, networks open up the possibility of a new form of territorial organization which constitutes the fragmentation of a hierarchy essentially based on urban functions (of management, commercial, political, etc) by establishing new organizational criteria. Thus are built up areas of relationship and regional spaces defined by the urban nuclei which make them up and not administrative boundaries. The superimposition of networks, and therefore of spaces of relation, adds a further element of complexity to these new organizational trends. The newly emerging territorial organization is based on flows and is defined by actors – in this case, the cities.

City networks are consolidated as systems for direct participation of the cities in the building of a world in which the traditional systems of international regulation tend to be incomplete. Networks are also consolidated as a complementary system of international solidarity and application of redistributive policies (though this works only to a scant extent in practice) in that they give rise to dissemination effects for aid, best practice and technologies from the most dynamic and advanced urban centres towards those with development problems or economic and social crises.

Alongside these clear advantages of participation in networks, we should also note by way of example some of the problems or difficulties deriving from this mode of operating. The great diversity of situations, types of organization and so forth of the various cities sometimes gives rise to conflicts of interest which jeopardize the continuity and results of cooperation between cities. The ad hoc difficulties of various scenarios slow down the implementation of common projects. This framework, of itself full of contradictions, suggests that the main beneficiaries of networks are basically their most active and powerful members, which can lead to distortions of internal relations. In short, networks have a role to play in improving the competitiveness of member cities, providing a system of relations between the main elements or agents which constitute that space. They are, in fact, the most suitable instrument for joining a system which as a whole tends itself to function entirely as a network.

Networks in the Face of Formalized Bodies of Representation

City networks appear as instruments of representation complementary and alternative to the formal bodies of representation already existing at international level. But they are neither a substitute nor a competing system. They differ in many ways from the formal representative institutions. Box 9.1 below expresses succinctly and in a simplified manner some of these differences.

The consolidation of some city and/or region networks as active and powerful groups has led to friction with some consolidated formal organizations. A framework must be developed in which the formalized bodies manage to incorporate a networks representation system which allows them to be coordinated and represented by the established democratic channels (Buursink, 1994; Dunford and Kafkalas, 1992; Dupuy, 1991; Camangi and Gibelli, 1994; Cohen et al, 1991; Cohen, 1996a, 1996b; Belil et al, 1992; Morandi, 1994; de Queriroz, 1994; Curti and Diappi, 1992; L'Événement Européen, 1993; Landáburu, 1993; Neuschwader, 1993; Cohen, Ruble, Tulchin and Garland, 1996).

BOX 9.1 CITY NETWORKS AND FORMAL BODIES

Formal Bodies	Networks
Organic structure	Associative structure
Territorial base	Actor/agent base
State representation base	Plurinational. No State base
Global vision	Specific objectives
Representation	Presence
Bureaucratic organization	Ad-hocratic org. (greater flexibility)
Homogeneous members	Heterogeneous members
Stable/not very adaptable	Changing/adaptable
Low mortality	High instability
Hierarchy (2nd/3rd level)	Network

UNITED CITIES AND UNITED NATIONS

Introduction

Economic globalization, the multiplicity of agents operating due to the possibilities of new information technologies, and the large number of interdependencies at world scale call for a political leap in order to create regulatory mechanisms to provide a response to this new situation. The United Nations system and the large number of international conferences (political military; on states, peoples and frontiers; or economic in nature, especially for regulating trade) do not constitute sufficient mechanisms for ordering the contradictory dynamics of economic competitiveness, sustainable development, quality of life and governability of territories. One of the great challenges which the international community currently has to resolve is that of bringing local and regional governments (that is, the political institutions of proximity) and civil society organizations into the continental and world systems of regulation. And especially into that of the United Nations which, despite its name and its declaration of principles (which makes reference to the union of peoples), is due to its strictly governmental composition grossly insufficient for laying down the regulatory mechanisms required by the new economic, social and cultural relations.

United Nations Conferences and Globalization

United Nations conferences since the Rio 1992 Conference on the Environment and Development, have permitted a statement of the problems facing humanity as a whole. This has been possible because three factors have come together:

1. Globalization of the economy, due above all to the telecommunications revolution. The local and national economies have opened up, and every region of the world – whether by deed or omission – is interdependent in relation to the rest. Problems cannot be resolved in isolation, or by sectoral aspects (eg the environment alone) or regional aspects (eg the Mediterranean alone).
2. The end of the cold war and of the power blocks policy have rendered possible a new relationship between states. If on the one hand globalization has weakened the role of national governments, it has on the other hand made them into the great protagonists of the problems of economic and political regulation on a world scale (peace conferences, GATT, etc). Governments are the representatives of human groups on the international bodies and at international conferences.
3. The much acclaimed 'global village' of information has created conditions more favourable to the development of universalist values. Human rights, protection of the environment, the struggle against poverty and the rejection of violence are today widely shared values. It is no longer enough to 'think globally and act locally'. We might note the international importance acquired by NGOs such as Amnesty International, Greenpeace, Doctors and others 'without frontiers', Habitat International Coalition and a number of NGOs working in the

Box 9.2 Urban Information: City Rankings

The city is the centre of social attention. News and opinion about the urban world proliferate in newspapers, magazines, congresses, television reports and radio debates. In the framework of this attention to urban matters and to the cities, the drawing up of city rankings has become fashionable. Research centres of recognized prestige and high circulation magazines compete in information gathering and production on the cities in comparative terms with the objective of arriving at evaluative hierarchies of cities. Long lists of urban centres are drawn up, with some being chided and others praised on the basis of indicators, calculations and arguments of the most diverse types.

The importance of urban information for global planning of growth and development appears to be increasingly unquestionable. At the same time, however, the shortcomings of current urban information processing is also increasingly clear. The quantity of urban information available, but above all its quality and comparability, reveal a serious delay in development of a fundamental instrument for planning and running of the basic organizational mode of present-day society: the city. Within this framework, city rankings constitute an instrument which endeavours to make up for this lack of information, but does so in way which (apparently inevitably) falls into banalities and stereotypes. It should not be forgotten that some of these rankings are presented as valid instruments for decision-making in investment processes, location of activities, assessment of city centres, etc. Most of the rankings set out to offer a classification of cities by order, based on quality of life and capacity to sustain development processes in the new socioeconomic order, thereby supposedly facilitating decisions about which city centre offers the most potential. Despite differences in method and sphere of study, all the rankings aims to set out a sufficient number of evaluation factors to permit condemnation of the poorly classified cities and an invitation to glorify those that head the list. This urban trial entrusted to journalists and researchers is implemented on the basis of indicators (social, economic, cultural, etc) measuring the goodness or badness of the city or urban area in question.

Given the great diversity between cities in respect of location, natural setting, historical tradition, economic development and social, administrative and political organization, the sphere of study must first be set and limited according to a common characteristic which becomes the main value on which the strength or weakness of an urban area depends in the end. Imagination here goes little beyond what apparently defines a city most generically: population concentration. Mostly, though not entirely, the first indicator which establishes a definitive cut off point between cities is size in terms of population (more than 100,000, 200,000, 500,000 inhabitants, etc), on the basis of which a number of indicators are drawn up and from these are derived the level and quality of life of a specific urban centre.

Most of the rankings currently appearing are devoted to study of four broad themes: the relative importance of the cities (in general in terms of wealth, growth and job-creation capacity), quality of life, degree of internationalism and the attractiveness of the urban nucleus, measured in terms of economic dynamism.

The Rankings Analysed: Summary of Categories

Ranking of importance	Quality of life	Internationalism	Attractiveness
Wealth	Economic dynamism	Setting – geographic – human, cultural and recreational – educational – sociopolitical – economic	Quality of life – geographical situation – demographic dynamic – transport costs
Growth	Level of life	International – international function – interchanges – cosmopolitanism – reception services	Image of the city
Job-creation capacity	Setting	Socioeconomic support – new technologies – research (partnerships) – communications	Institutional incentives
	Social aspects	Demographic behaviour	Economic setting – business dynamism/ company creation – employment – age of economic fabric – labour costs – labour relations – upper tertiary – work productivity – quality of labour
	Transport Culture and education Security		

One way or another, the various classifications tend to centre their assessments on the economic setting and quality of life, choosing different indicators for each of these aspects.

The Rankings: City Marketing Operations

The cities enter the world of marketing fully in order to attract companies, investments and all types of cultural and sports activities and the like. There are several city promotion instruments: communication or marketing directly or through large-scale events, the creation of public, mixed or private bodies, the creation and development of technopolises, financial aid to companies, etc. Rankings are one more instrument of external promotion of a city. They generally help to define the competitiveness of an urban area in the international market in comparison with other cities. The rankings permit not only highlighting of the attractions of the city in question, but also downgrading of its potential competitors. The indicators and variables used in a ranking are totally arbitrary, as are the scales used to evaluate the various indicators and the universe of urban areas taken for building up the classification. The attractiveness of a city can be measured in different ways depending on the objective of the sale. If the idea is to sell the city as a tourist centre, then stress will be laid on its good climate if it is in the south, its museums and attractions if it cannot claim much sun, etc. Classifications of urban areas help to show the unity and also the complementary nature of these regions. Thus, they can show the homogeneousness of different cities within a single region by comparisons based on certain chosen indicators. At the same time, other indicators may help to boost the image of complementariness which can be built up on the basis of some specific characteristics. The rankings show various facts of importance for cities. Through analysis and assessment thereof, we have observed that it is essential nowadays to undertake lengthy work to arrive at urban indicators capable of pinpointing the main problems of cities at the end of the twentieth century and help with the implementation of policies and solutions.

Despite the fact that much of the world population will be living in cities by the year 2000, there does not yet exist a clear and comparable system of urban information. The rankings are an instrument for information gathering about cities, but their promotion and marketing component makes them into instruments too arbitrary to be considered valid for comparative analysis and the laying down of policies and solutions. Furthermore, the urban indicators are in themselves confused and full of cultural deviations. Each of the themes or phenomena which occur in the urban setting could be reported, assessed and quantified using different indicators, none of them definitive, global and universally valid. To this should be added the fact that evaluation of each of these measurements is clearly influenced by the dominant urban ideology. By the end of 1990, for example, quality of life evaluated in terms of open spaces, air quality, noise, etc, had become an important indicator of level of development. In other periods and in other societies the proportion of industrial activity or ownership of private cars can be consolidated as one of the chief development values. Despite their arbitrary features and ideological and cultural deviations, rankings are nevertheless instruments which spur information gathering about cities and parallel phenomena.

spheres of housing and the city, alternative telecommunications networks as Internet was initially, networks of groups promoting local development and job creation initiatives (the other face of economic globalization), etc. The more traditional agents of civil society likewise tend to act in the international field: chambers of commerce, professional associations, etc. Due to their very nature in some cases (eg the internationally oriented NGOs), or due to the public nature of their activities (eg world congresses of professional associations, such as the International Union of Architects and its 1996 Congress on the City), the international activity of civil society is a fundamental factor in the building of an internationally minded awareness.

As a result of these three process based factors, United Nations conferences such as Rio 1992 (Environment and Development), Vienna 1993 (Human Rights), Copenhagen 1995 (Social Development), Beijing 1995 (Women) and Istanbul 1995 (Habitat, Cities), have despite their specialized nature tended to take an integral approach to the problems of humanity. Similarly, such formally intergovernmental conferences have gone well beyond that intergovernmental character in their preparation processes, during the events themselves and in their subsequent implementation (in, for example, the much publicized Agenda 21). On the one hand, the intervention of non-governmental organizations, in the broadest sense, has been increasingly important, with participation on the preparation committees, national committees and delegations, alternative forums, monitoring committees and conferences, etc; and, on the other hand, United Nations conferences have become big media events, with an enormous impact on public opinion, and therefore with considerable power of dissemination and legitimization of the problems, proposals and accords.

Glocalization
The global approach to problems, the integral or interdependent character of the proposals and the universalist vocation of values calls for a runway to land on, or, as in the large airports, at least two runways. One runway is clearly made up of the states or nations represented by their states. They constitute the main framework of public policies, as well as being the only agents which can reach general agreements in international relations. But this is not enough. The United Nations conferences and the experience of world and regional international organizations (World Bank, European Union, etc) have accorded new value to the local dimension in two main aspects: as the sphere of application of the integral policies (eg environment, economic promotion and social integration); and as a framework for concerted action by government bodies and private agents. Great value has been attached to the principle of subsidiarity or proximity of public administration and to the participation or cooperation of civil society.

This local dimension is today very closely linked with urbanization. Not only does most of the population live in cities, but in various regions of the world (Europe especially, but also America and part of Asia) urbanization characterizes both the ways of life and of settlement of almost the entire population. As a result, United Nations conferences, and especially the Agenda 21 for implementation of their agreements, assign a major role to

Box 9.3 City Networks: Critical Factors of Network Operation

Not all networks function, or have potential for success. A number of critical factors permit them to be successful and maximize their benefits and advantages. Amongst these critical factors we might stress:

1. Leadership: as a complex organization, the network needs leadership capable of:
   – organizing complex projects;
   – managing conflicts and anomalies;
   – processing and disseminating information world-wide.
2. Profitability: the network has many possibilities of success when the cost-profit ratio of the product or service obtained by the network is better with collective action than with individual action. Where the cost-profit ratio in the network is not better than that of individual action, then any difficulty can jeopardize the very reason for existence of that network. The added value for the cities participating in the network must be clearly apparent.
3. Common project: networks must be formed based on the existence of a desire for common project, and not the reverse. This common project must not be detrimental to the diversity and specific nature of each city. It must for this reason be clear from the outset that networks do not provide global solutions for specific problems.
4. An objective and a clear product/service: the network must have a clear objective shared by all the cities which form part of it and made specific in the form of a product or service desired by all members. The final product – whether tangible or intangible – must be structured right from the outset. Ambiguity of objectives and/or products gives rise to conflict of interests and reduces networks to an attempt to become part of European financing systems or mere pressure groups.
5. Specificity: the survival of most networks involves a process of specialization which takes form in setting out the role to be played in the European urban system. Generality and globality usually lead to dispersion.
6. Dimension: networks cannot be universal. The need to share a common objective necessarily limits the size of the networks. Limited experience in international work means that dimensions must be manageable and controllable. The optimum size of the network will be determined by the product and its cost-profit curve.
7. Control systems: the diversity of members, work methods, etc, means that a clear and strict methodology shared by all and guaranteed by the leader must be imposed upon operation of the network, so that progress of the work, relations and costs can be known at all times.

8. Evaluation: networks are not only forums for discussion between different cities. Evaluation mechanisms for partial and final results must therefore be set out to allow analysis of the level of success of the work, satisfaction of the needs or expectations of the various members and the participants' commitment to the experience.

9. Political presence: the involvement of the political elements/agents with decision-making powers in each city is necessary to ensure that the cities' needs are met, that the political will exists and that continuity is ensured.

10. The rules of the international game: local organizations have the local space as their usual framework of action. International action involves a change of scale of action and also new outlooks. Little experience of international work in a setting of diversity of organizational and working cultures can lead to much conflict. Networks must take as an operational basis the resolution of conflicts by way of consensus of all their members.

11. Guaranteeing the transfer process, at political and technical levels, towards one's own organization and towards the other city agents. The success of a network largely depends on the capacity of its participants for organization, planning and management. We will briefly outline here some factors which permit network operation to be rationalized. First, however, we must make a few observations:
   – Networks are not a universal solution to all problems and aspects of regional development and territorial imbalance. For some products or services bilateral cooperation can be a much more effective solution (eg for technological transfer).
   – The inherent logic of services production conditions the organization and structure of networks.
   – Networks can scarcely give rise to clear and economically viable results over the short term.
   – A necessary but insufficient condition for participation in networks is the existence of a surplus of human, economic and/or technical resources in the city.

local government, and particularly to policies which can be implemented in urban spheres. This is what has come to be known as glocalization, that is, links between the global and the local. This notion is today applied both to the economy (the city as a good economic medium for optimization of synergies) and to culture (local identities and their dialectic relationship with media based universalism of information). Here, glocalization means placing emphasis on the urban setting and the management–coordination–promotion role of local governments in the implementation of policies which take account of and adopt stances with respect to global terms of reference. In short, globalization plus proximity.

But there arise here some paradoxes which hinder the progress of glocalization. Firstly, United Nations Conferences are intergovernmental. The local authorities are absent or have a merely testimonial presence on some delegations and at certain 'special' events. They also have, naturally enough,

Box 9.4 Telematics and Cities Networks in Europe

Telecommunications infrastructure is an essential factor for cities' productivity and competitiveness in the new global economy. Frequently, however, telecommunications have been used as a factor to attract companies to a city, in an attempt to take investments away from other cities. Evaluation of the results of teleports in various contexts nevertheless shows that the largest budgets spent have hardly shown any significant effect on company location decisions. If a city is attractive for investment, the telecommunications operators will take it upon themselves to find the market. On the other hand, the use of telecommunications in combination with computer systems and data bases is showings itself to be important for cooperation between cities networks, and is a practice implemented particularly in Western Europe. Intercity networks, backed by telematics infrastructure, serve three main functions: as a method of exchange of information on municipal management problems and policies; as a means of cultural and economic cooperation between cities; and as a way of influencing national governments and the European Union to obtain funding for cities. French cities pioneered such experiments during the 1980s, backed by the central government and the telephone company. One of the first projects was the 'Reseau Villes Moyennes', based on Minitel databases and services. Other cities used fibre-optics to connect the city centre via a teleport to surrounding localities – as in the case of Roubaix, connected with Lille and the industrial zone of Wallonia, and of Montpellier around its 'technopole'. In the United Kingdom, Glasgow and Edinburgh have set up a common telematics system, and Manchester, London and Huddersfield have created an information exchange network through interconnected 'host' computers open to other potential municipal users. Telematics is also becoming a powerful instrument for the development of intermunicipal cooperation initiatives in Europe. The Eurocities network, for example, with 60 members, has set up a group of 'telecities' (headed by Amberes, Barcelona, Bologna, The Hague and Nice) which have created a real-time connection system for intermunicipal cooperation strategies, called Geonet.

Another example of computerized intermunicipal cooperation is the 'European Urban Observatory', which disseminates information on municipal management methods which have shown their effectiveness in certain contexts. A third example of this movement towards the use of technology in cooperation between local authorities is the 'European Regions' Network for the Application of Communications Technology', in which several regions of the United Kingdom, Ireland, Denmark, Holland and Belgium work jointly on training and qualifications programmes in the use of information technologies for economic promotion activities on the part of local governments. Taken as a whole, such experiences show that municipal initiatives in telematics systems are more profitable when, instead of running ahead of telecommunications operator equipment investments, they concentrate upon their own services and systems for cooperation between cities, services which would not exist if not promoted by local and regional governments. The creation of an intermunicipal telematics structure is a factor indispensable for the implementation of a cooperation strategy which fulfils the competitiveness strategy.

Source: Graham (forthcoming)

some marginal activity in alternative forums. This 'capitis diminutio' status characterizes the position of local authorities in international bodies and conferences, even ones dealing with themes of local competence. Secondly, the practice of three-way concerted agreement between international and local organizations in the drawing up and/or execution of programmes is very scant, as too is the contractualization of relations between central and local government for the execution of projects or the provision of services. Recent European experience is particularly useful in this field, and may be of interest to other regions of the world. Thirdly, recognition of the local dimension of economic, social, demographic, cultural and environmental problems comes into contradiction with the administrative inertia of national governments, which act along sectoral vertical lines of reasoning, and the fragmentation of local powers. The built up zones are often nowadays urbanregional areas acted upon by a range of local bodies with their own (even exclusive) competence, but without the legal, territorial and financial instruments to exercise them properly. In this case the most interesting experience is that of those cities (American and European, but also Pacific Rim) which have drawn up strategic plans or concerted global city projects or undertaken a set of integral or multipurpose large-scale projects connected with ambitious promotion policies (sometimes backed by the staging of an exceptional event). The fourth paradox is that local governments often suffer from a political weakness which does not help either the construction of promotional leadership in the city or relations of cooperation with civil society. In this case, too, the European experience could be of interest, due both to a long tradition of local autonomy and to more recent experiences of ambitious and successful promotional measures (although outside Europe, experiences as interesting or more interesting are also to be found in America, Asia and Australia). And finally, the emphasis placed on social cooperation and citizen participation often comes into contradiction with a distancing of political institutions from the citizenry and the bureaucratic practices of governments. There are nevertheless positive phenomena such as the increasing prestige of local authorities with respect to other powers further removed from civil society, the collective initiative of the people (often the ones who build the real city, rather than the government or the market, especially in the developing countries), or the multiplication of diverse forms of cooperation owing to the complexity and interdependence of local problems (eg citizen security, town planning and employment).

In short, glocalization is today a scantly institutionalized reality, though one which is none the less strong for that. It can only be regulated, however, through the action of the only mediators which have the means and the formal legitimacy to do so: the national governments.

The Right to Housing and Right to the City: International Recognition
Habitat I, Vancouver 1976, proclaimed the right to housing or, more precisely, the right of all to have access to a socially fit and legally recognized dwelling. It would seem important to maintain this principle or consideration of housing as a human right, in the same terms as education, health, employment, women's equality and personal security (against violence and arbitrary action). Here, however, we should look more fully into at least three aspects of this right.

Box 9.5 On Relations Between the United Nations and International Cities Organizations

In August 1994 the United Nations Headquarters in New York was host to a meeting of the main world and regional cities organizations. At the meeting it was agreed that a cities coordinating committee be created (the G4+), made up of four world organizations (IULA, FMCU-UTO, Metropolis and Summit) and six regional organizations (Citynet of Asia, Eurocities, Union of Arab Cities, Latin American Mayors and Municipal Associations Coordinator and Cities of North America). The World Assembly of Cities and Local Authorities (AMCAL) was also called for 1996, on the occasion of the Habitat Conference and with the aim of serving as the basis of a joint action and representation unitary organization for addressing international organizations. At the New York meeting a document (presented by J. Borja in the name of four world organizations) was debated and approved; this document analysed the current role of the cities in international life, outlined the present degree of world and regional organization of the local bodies, and made proposals for the relationship of United Cities with the United Nations.

We provide below a summary of these proposals.

- There is considerable diversity of status in the United Nations. The easiest to achieve, though the least advantageous, is consultative status as an NGO. The organization which represents cities and local authorities cannot be considered to be an NGO, especially if a unifying or world coordination structure is built up. There are at present various cities organizations such as IULA and FMCU which are so recognized, so it would be no progress if the AMCAL were to obtain it.
- The General Assembly can authorize the Social Economic Council to grant permanent or special observer status for a unitary cities organization – World Assembly of Cities and Local Authorities or its Standing Council. There are collaboration agreements with Islamic Conference, Red Cross, etc. This would also be the formula for the European Union. If there were such a cooperation agreement, AMCAL could take part on United Nations bodies, run programmes, etc. Observer status is in principle reserved for intergovernmental bodies or those placed on the same level through international regulations.
- Holding of collaboration agreements and memorandums with United Nations organizations and centres reporting to the General Secretariat. Some cities organizations, and some cities on their own account, have already done so with Habitat, Population Fund, UNESCO, ILO, UNICEF, WHO, etc.
- Another option would be for the AMCAL to become a subsidiary body of consultative nature on the Human Settlements Commission

of the Social and Economic Council, made up of local level representatives. The technical, economic and administrative infrastructure would be to the account of the United Nations Centre for Human Settlements, while relations with the states would be implemented through the Human Settlements Commission. This option could be generalized by means of derogation of the provisions of the organic Commissions Regulations of the Social and Economic Council in order to allow some non-governmental organizations, especially those which ensure joint representation of all or the most important in certain subject areas, to participate more fully in the activities of certain United Nations bodies.

- Establishment of general guidelines for the participation of NGOs on the preparatory committees of international conferences held on questions of local scope, such as those relating to population, housing, social development and so forth. This would be a matter of generalizing recent practice, though the organizations would have to be accorded a particular position with consultative status, as is the case with the cities organizations.

- Review of the arrangements for the holding of consultations with NGOs, in the direction of establishing a new category which encompasses city organizations and accords them a specific juridical system. The United Nations is currently reviewing the framework of regulation of relations with NGOs and negotiating with the latter on a mixed commission. A specific ad hoc group could be set up to review relations with cities and local authorities organizations and the future AMCAL.

- Attribution of intergovernmental nature or the equivalent to AMCAL or the organization coordinating and representing cities and local authorities. In this case it would not be an organization created by the governments of the states, but rather an organization of cities and local authorities which the states would recognize by signing a treaty. Various organizations – originally non-governmental or promoted by NGOs – have taken on this character, such as Interpol, International Tourism Organization, Flacso, Latin American Parliamentary Union, etc. This is from the outset a difficult and risky solution, since it could in certain cases give rise to the governments of states appointing their civil servants. It is nevertheless a solution that could be arrived at as the culmination of a process.

- Agreement for the composition of the state delegations before UN bodies and conferences called under its auspices be also made up of representatives of the local powers. The agreement could be of general character or limited to certain bodies or conferences. In addition to intergovernmental decision, it would require the setting out of internal legal mechanisms. Each state could even provide accordingly.

- Proposition to the UN General Secretariat that Habitat be made into a body which includes the representatives of cities organizations.

Some governments (eg France) and cities organizations and conferences have subsequently developed this proposal in the sense of making Habitat into an agency decentralized by regions or continents and directed by a mixed composition body – like the ILO – with the participation of national governments, cities associations and local authorities, and also having NGO representation (social, economic and professional organizations working on territorial, city and housing problems).

- Attribution to AMCAL of rights and obligations of an international character, or equivalent. This attribution could start with a UN declaration which would have political value due to being subscribed by the States, even though it had no binding juridical force. This declaration could contain much of the content of the proposals mentioned under previous points, and their application would generate a dynamic of reinforcement of the AMCAL, its finding a place in the UN system and greater recognition by the states. On this basis the intergovernmental (or equivalent) nature of AMCAL could be formalized by the States signing or joining an international treaty.

The urbanization process does not necessarily lead to the creation of a city, in the sense of a concentration of people with heterogeneity (social, cultural, economic, professional), with equality (formal rights, mobility, access to employment and to culture, etc). Urbanization without city also means the existence of spaces defined by flows, of territories with imprecise or superimposed boundaries and of places lacking in attributes and therefore lacking symbolic integration capacity. These are zones in which the presence of the state is almost always weak, legally based regulation scant and access to justice and to urban public services deficient and unequal. The right to housing must therefore today be linked with the right to the city. Boutros-Ghali's call (Geneva 1994) to a 'Cities Summit' was therefore prophetic in nature.

In the urban areas, where 90 per cent of the population will be living at the beginning of the twenty-first century, a valid dwelling is only such if it forms part of a whole comprising basic services (water, sanitation, power supplies, etc), access to the means of transport which ensure mobility throughout the area, training which confers the 'skills' to obtain employment and social acceptance and, of course, legal occupation of the land and juridical and cultural recognition of the zone or district as an integral part of the city. An urban dwelling is the sum of all these elements, not an element in isolation. A dwelling and its setting must ensure peaceful coexistence and security. In urban societies this guarantee is provided by the rule of law. If the presence of the state (including the police) is weak, if justice is practically inaccessible for the population of the urban outskirts, and social provision (especially that termed positive discrimination) does not reach everyone, then the urban habitat does not comply with the minimum prerequisites for providing security and facilitating peaceful coexistence. Therefore:

Box 9.6 On International Cities Organizations

The international movement of cities has undergone major development in recent years. Both world and regional cities organizations, and sectoral or thematic ones, practically unknown a decade ago, have burst onto the international scene. Three factors have contributed to this:

1. International conferences (especially UN ones) and the space won in them by NGOs, firstly, and then by representatives of the cities and local authorities. The Rio Conference (1992) saw the start of joint action of some 20 international cities organizations and the creation of a coordinating group (G4), later extended (New York 1994 – G4+) to call a World Assembly of Cities and Local Authorities (Istanbul 1996). 'Glocalization' enforces city participation in world regulation processes, while the end of the cold war and the rigid political military blocks facilitate it.
2. The creation and institutional consolidation of inter-State political and economic unions (the European Union, NAFTA in North America, Mercosur, etc) has created an international intervention opportunity for local and regional powers. On the one hand as a reaction in defence of and updating of their self-regulating capacity (self government, local autonomy), and on the other the will to have an influence on the supranational policies which have a major effect on local territories and populations (communication infrastructures, definition of priority action areas, social programmes, etc).
3. The political importance acquired by the leaders of the large cities and most important regions, due both to enhancement of these spheres of proximity and cohesion and the national and international political initiative of these leaders. One of the effects of glocalization has been the incorporation of mayors and other major local authorities into international associations and also the proliferation of organizations, networks and conferences promoted by the most dynamic cities.

The international cities movement nevertheless still suffers from some major weaknesses, such as:

- A lack of objectives and initiatives to meet the new challenges of globalization. The cities organizations are absent from negotiations on the regulation of international trade, migratory movements, international crime, and so forth.
- Little recognition by international organizations and conferences, almost always of exclusively intergovernmental character. We are still far from the United Cities in United Nations.
- The organizational weakness of the world associations and their division (which is not in accordance with the presence of the same cities on most of them and the similarity of objectives).

Despite this, we should stress that significant progress has been made on:

- Coordination of the great diversity and heterogeneousness of organizations.
- Bringing the objectives and lines of action of these organizations closer to each other.
- Greater recognition or acceptance by state governments and inter-governmental international organizations.

We present below the city organizations which are coordinated at world level under the name G4+. Four are organizations of world character, two of them of universal vocation (UTO-FMCU and IULA) and the other two large city organizations (Metropolis and Summit). The other six organizations are regional (continental) in sphere. At the meetings held on the occasion of the United Nations conferences or during preparatory processes for same, several dozen organizations, both regional and issue based, have taken part. The organizations of regional character may or may not have links with a world organization. The Council of Municipalities and Regions of Europe (CMRE), for example, is the European section of IULA, but it has its own history and a specific mission which goes beyond strict municipalism: to take part in the building of a united and democratic Europe. By means of national associations, the CMRE brings together over 100,000 local entities. There are other organizations which reach beyond the regional sphere because they take broader political-cultural areas as their terms of reference, such as Latin American or francophone or Commonwealth cities. The large cities have greater potential for intentionally promoting themselves and creating their own organizations, as is the case with Eurocities and Citynet (forming part of G4+), for example. But there are others, too, such as UCCI (Latin American cities) or Ciudades Mediterráneas (Group created on the occasion of the Intergovernmental Conference on the Mediterranean, Barcelona 1995).

The issue oriented organizations are generally created out of the suitability of promoting exchange of experiences in order to develop cooperation between cities, sometimes managing to set down common objectives and turn these into demands in some cases or joint projects or actions in others. Examples of world issue oriented associations are the Citizen Security Forum, Healthy Cities, Educational Cities, etc. Recent years have seen a tendency to form into networks directed at undertaking work of a very different kind, from data bases (for example, European Urban Observatory) to campaigns for reduced use of cars in cities (Car-Free Cities). See the chart on networks in Box 9.3.

The creation of supra-state political–economic unions, such as the European Union or Mercosur, has favoured the creation of regional issue-based associations or networks to promote certain policies. Eurocities and Eurometropolis (cities with universities and chambers of commerce) arose with this objective. More directly issue based associations have also been created (such as textile or car cities, districts in crisis, Elaine social integration network for migrant populations), or territorial based ones (Atlantic front, C6 for the cities of southern France and north east Spain, etc). In Latin America, on the occasion of the creation of Mercosur, a major group of cities formed Mercocuidades (Asunción, Rio, Porto Alegre, Montevideo, Córdoba, Rosario, etc).

Organizations Forming Part of G4+

* World Cities Coordinator created in New York (August 1994) within the framework of preparation for the UN Social Summit (Copenhagen 1995) and the Cities Summit or Habitat II (Istanbul 1996).
* IULA, founded in 1913, is the oldest and largest international organisation of local authorities in the world. It has a direct membership of over 250 organisations covering more than ninety countries, most of which are national or regional associations of local authorities, which in turn represent the majority if not all of local authorities within their respective countries. The indirect membership of IULA is therefore very significant and covers local authorities of all levels and sizes, urban and rural, around the world. IULA is a decentralized organisation, coordinating most of its activities and programmes via its six regional sections, which enable more region specific and direct support to and representation of the members. The regional sections are: IULA-Africa; IULA-ASPAC (Asia and Pacific); IULA-EMME (East Mediterranean and Middle East); IULA-CEMR (Council of European Municipalities and Regions); IULA-Latin America and IULA-North America. IULA also has a number of affiliated organisations, which deal in very specific areas of municipal concern. They operate as autonomous membership bodies, but with a close and regular exchange of information and whenever possible, joint activities. They are:
  - The International Council for Local Environmental Initiatives (ICLEI)
  - The International Daughter Companies Network (IDCN)
  - The Municipal Insurance Group (MI)
  - Towns and Development (T & D)
  - The World Academy for Local Government and Democracy (WALD) and
  - The World Union of Wholesale Markets (WUWM).
* UTO, founded in 1957, is a worldwide organisation of local and regional authorities active in over 100 countries. Its activities are based on building lasting peace, which it strives to achieve by promoting local autonomy and democracy as well as economic, social, technical and cultural development through international town-to-town cooperation activities. In 1989, UTO created a specialized decentralized cooperation agency, The United Towns Development Agency (UTDA) to facilitate new forms of local and international decentralized cooperation projects. The UTDA is also active and represents local authority interests in a number of thematic and regional networks.

- METROPOLIS, World Association of the Major Metropolises, was created in Montreal in 1985. It has an active membership of some 55 major cities and metropolitan regions (each with a population of over one million) from 39 countries around the world and a large number of associated members within its network, representing specific sectors of local authority responsibility, academic and research institutions and special interest groups. It aims to bring together the leaders, practitioners and citizens of the world's majors metropolises to share and discuss experiences and urban strategies, encourage social and technical innovation and implement programmes of cooperation.
- SUMMIT Conference of Major Cities of the World, a network of Major Cities of the World has a membership of 27 cities, which are all metropolises of one million or more people. There is a limit of one member city per country and the network actively pursues a balance between the difference regions of the world so that the various races and cultures of the globe are represented. The purpose of SUMMIT is to bring together key policy-makers in the administration of major cities, ie the mayors and governors, to exchange views and experiences on issues concerned with the management of major cities. At present these major meetings take place once every three years.

The Regional Representatives
- AFRICA
  The Union of African Towns (UAT)
  UAT, based in Rabat, Kingdom of Morocco since 1989, was first established in Cairo in 1975. It is a non-governmental organisation whose activities on the level of the continent cover all aspects of local government. UAT has a membership of almost 200 local authorities ranging from small villages to capital cities and megacities such as Cairo. There are two categories of membership – active members, namely local authorities from 36 African countries and associate members, which are associations, foundations and any institutions of a local, national or international character acting for the promotion and development of local authorities. UAT's activities in the field of international cooperation aim to complement the work being done by governments and intergovernmental organizations in fields which directly concern the population and local resources. They include the development of exchange of experience projects, urban planning strategies and the examination and comparison of different systems of municipal organisation within African towns.
- ARAB STATES
  The Arab Towns Organization (ATO)
  The Arab Towns Organization was established in 1967 with its headquarters in Kuwait City. Its membership, which is made up of Arab town local authorities is now around 400. The ATO aims to encourage cooperation and exchange of expertise among Arab

towns, to raise the standard of municipal services and utilities, assist with planning and cultural preservation programmes and develop and modernize municipal and local government institutions and legislation. The ATO also has two associated institutions, The Arab Towns Development Fund (ATDF), which specializes in financing the municipal projects of member towns through medium term soft loans, and the Arab Urban Development Institute (AUDI), which is the scientific and documentation body of the ATO, also engaging in training and colsuntancy work.

- ASIA AND PACIFIC
  Citynet
  Citynet is a multi-actor network of urban local governments, development authorities and non-governmental organizations in the Asia-Pacific region. It was officially established in 1987 with the assistance of ESCAP (UN Economic and Social Commission for Asia and the Pacific), with an initial membership of 12 and has now grown to an international organization consisting of 85 members. The 39 full members are local authorities in the Asia-Pacific region and the 46 associate members are relevant NGOs, development authorities and cities outside the region. The objectives of Citynet are to strengthen the capacities of local governments to effectively manage the urban development process and to develop partnerships between various actors at the local level, specifically between local authorities and NGOs.

- EUROPE
  Eurocities
  Eurocities is an association of European cities with a minimum population of 250,000, which have an international dimension and are important regional centres. It has 55 members within the European Union and 11 associate members in other European countries. It lobbies to ensure that the views of major cities are taken into account in policy development in Europe, encourages the transfer of knowledge, experience and best practice between city governments across Europe and facilitates practical cooperation projects in areas such as telematics, sustainable transport policies and the environment.

- LATIN AMERICA
  Network of Local Government Associations of Latin America
  The Latin American network (Red Latinoamericana) meets and liaises with a view to strengthening local self government and to promoting and encouraging the formation of national association of local authorities in the Latin American region. It is relatively new network and has so far had five meetings in Quito, Temuco, Cordoba, Bogota, Rio de Janeiro, and Santiago, on 13 and 14 November 1995, on the occasion of the Regional Habitat II PrepCom. The membership of the network is made up of the 17 national associations of 16 Latin American States, but meetings are also open to and have been attended by members of UCCI – the Iberoamerican Mayors of Capital Cities network (membership of 26).

- NORTH AMERICA
  Major Local Government Associations of North America
  The North America representation covers the four major local government associations of North America, namely the Federation of Canadian Municipalities (FCM), the National League of Cities (NLC), the National Association of Counties and the US Conference of Mayors. Their combined membership includes the vast majority of local authorities in North America and they also have close links with state associations of local authorities, other specialised networks and local authority-linked enterprises such as Public Technology Inc. (PTI). An informal network, the coordination role is currently carried out by the Federation of Canadian Municipalities.

  Source: Borja and IULA Secretary, working document, 1996

- the right to the city and the consequent obligation of urban policies to 'make city', that is, to generate centralities, to link the parts of the city into the whole and promote the multi-use nature and cohesion of each zone;
- the right to a setting which is legalized, socially valued, equipped with facilities, accessible and educational;
- the right to security and suitable treatment so that the rule of law is really accessible;

are rights of the people of the city and of each and every urban area.

Europe and America, in their joint status as cradles of human rights and city continents, can make a major contribution to Istanbul 1996. To make such a contribution understood, we believe that relativist proposals have to be combined with an affirmation of universalist principles.

- The conference documents and agreements must acknowledge the specific nature of the processes and forms of human settlement in each region of the world.
- The urbanization process is nonetheless an irreversible process, and in all cultures the city is the most complex and most satisfactory form of social organization. The city, not urbanization; the city, large or small, but dense, cohesive, multi-purpose and with good communications.
- The city is not exactly the product of historical fatalism, nor a result of an abstract market, or an expression of the political will of the sovereign. It is only partly those things. But (an often large) part of cities is the work of their people, of their work and of their hopes. In some cases, like America, because the cities have largely been constructed, almost on the fringes of the law and the market, by their inhabitants. In other cases, such as in Europe, because urban social life, probably the greatest wealth of our cities, is the result of the day-to-day joint action of the citizens.
- This recognition, however, does not justify omitting international organizations and national governments from the construction of the city.

Quite the contrary. Cities are today plurimunicipal places, region–cities, whose future is linked to the potential of the urban axes or systems of which they are or may be members and to their exterior promotion, which call for ambitious policies. Making the city the main form of regulation of urbanization processes is making a deliberate option which affects all dimensions and all levels of policy.

• Each country's forms of political organization have their own specific features. But just as democracy is in our times a universal value, the decentralization of national political systems strikes us as an indispensable corollary of economic globalization, of the creation of supra-state structures, of economic-social complexity and of the need to increase the mechanisms of public–private cooperation.

• In consequence, the call for democracy and local autonomies, permanent innovation for developing citizen participation, the political and juridical equality of all inhabitants and the concerted drawing up of city projects, seem to us to be basic conditions for good running of human settlements.

International conferences like Habitat should serve to take a major step forward in the participation of local governments and citizen organizations in international life, and this for three reasons.

1. Because it is advisable for the implementation of Conference accords and proposals. It is for this reason important to support and apply the United Nations recommendation that there be a significant presence of local government representatives on national committees and in delegations, and that a special delegation of representatives of international city organizations be included.

2. And there is a more general reason. Globalization calls for the creation of new regulatory mechanisms. The processes of global character, such as migratory movements and the contradictions between defence of the environment and economic growth, require policies based on local commitments and agreements. Now, such policies will only move forward if local governments and citizen organizations multiply exchanges and cooperation with each other and are present in international forums. That is, if they reinforce each other mutually.

3. Finally, there is the dialectic between universality and specificity. In the previous points we have referred to the need for universalist objectives and values to be infused into the situations inherent to each region of the world. If the local representatives fail to achieve an ongoing presence in international life, if their organizations do not have their rights and obligations in this sphere recognized, if they do not feel jointly responsible for the agreements and initiatives of the supra-state (or rather intergovernmental, like the United Nations itself) accords and initiatives, then it will be difficult to avoid phenomena of inward looking identity in some cases and action lacking in solidarity in others 'Cities of the Future', 1996; Wilheim, 1996; Cohen, 1996b; UTO, 1994; IULA, 1995).

Box 9.7 The Rio–Barcelona '92 Declaration

We feel that the text which we reproduce below suitably reflects the 'political culture' of the mayors and local organizations in respect of their will to be present on the world stage. This text is based on a document drawn up by one of the authors (J Borja) and made public in a teleconference between the mayors of Rio and Barcelona at the end of 1992.

On 22nd December, 1992, the mayors of Rio de Janeiro and Barcelona, Marcelo Alencar and Pasqual Maragall, signed the 'Rio-Barcelona '92 Declaration'. During 1992 these two cities were centres of attention for the whole world on the occasion of the holding of the United Nations Environment and Development Conference in Rio, and the Olympic Games in Barcelona. For this reason, the mayors of the two cities signed a declaration containing seven points, in which they undertake to use the prominent image obtained by both cities, putting it to the service of a world which increasingly aspires to be a united world. Through an agreement signed on 15th May, 1993, between the Prefecture of Rio de Janeiro and the Office of the Mayor of Barcelona, Mayor César Maia and Mayor Pasqual Maragall 'agree to ratify the Rio-Barcelona '92 Declaration and to spread its spirit throughout the world by means of various actions'. The Declaration obtained the adherence of almost all the big cities of the world, in addition to the world federations (UTO, CMRE, IULA etc), and in December, 1993, was delivered to the Secretary General of the United Nations, Boutros Boutros-Ghali. Given the magnitude of the declaration and the bilateral technical agreement which it involved, we shall reproduce the original text below.

In the year 1992, the cities of Rio and Barcelona have been capitals of the world, due to the United Nations Conference on the Environment and Development and the Olympic Games. Such a privilege implies we have the duty to use the power of our image to help a world which every day becomes a single world (Rio) and a humanity that wants to achieve peace and friendship (Barcelona). But this world, in spite of being only one, is deeply different and in danger, and the humanitarian desire for brotherhood is violated every day by war, violence, xenophobia, poverty, triviality and distance. The two cities, one in the northern hemisphere and the other in the southern, proclaim their certainty that the role cities can play in the world will increase and be positive.

Point 1

As witnesses of the end of a world divided into political-military blocks, in which a new freedom appears for international actions by cities and other public and private agents, besides states.

Having the possibility to build a better communicated and more helpful world, but also under the risk of multiplying conflicts, local wars, exclusive nationalisms, and the selfishness of the privileged; we are, and will be, undertaking all the actions we consider necessary to bring peace to violent areas, to help victims, and to rebuild what has been destroyed. We, cities, ratify our commitment to peace and offer our active solidarity with the peoples and the cities suffering war and other kinds of internal divisions which could eventually lead to war. We acknowledge the legitimacy of agreements made by international organizations, the United Nations Organization in the first place and, taking into account our governments' policies, we also declare that we are willing to develop our own actions in the international sphere.

As opposed to a border and exclusive policy, we look forward to a policy of global agreements, so that the development costs and benefits can be evenly distributed, as well as the world population, of its own free will. For us, the distinction between national and foreign is much less important than speaking of citizens of a same world. We know that cities, even though we were of one mind, would not be able to solve the conflicts and problems arising from inequalities and imbalances by themselves. But these problems revert back to our cities and our conscience, and we want the world society to be open and generous. This opening up, together with a spirit of tolerance have been, and are, the best virtues of the best cities.

Point 2

There does not exist a world for development and another one for the environment. The only world today is an urban one. Only one world: development for some may mean poverty for others; growth may mean destruction. But without growth, poverty will befall more than half of humanity.

The commitment to the environment and to development must take place at world level, although cities should put it into practice themselves. We must commit ourself to fight wastefulness in developed cities, and to build cities in agglomerations within the less developed world.

This commitment should be defined by means of regional agreements, aimed at:

- reducing pollution by means of a progressive decrease of carbon dioxide emissions (eg by the gradual use of non-contaminating vehicles and energy sources in cities).
- implementing resources generated by taxes applied to the use of non-renewable fuels in the development of countries and areas to be preserved, and to finance the costly adjustments of transport industry and the infrastructures in large cities;
- establishing programmes to guarantee, within a certain period, drinking water for all citizens, sewage and refuse dumping systems and, on the other hand, encouraging citizens to save water and energy;
- giving priority to the use of renewable resources and supporting self-sustained development strategies;
- elaborating mixed urban–regional development programmes, to ensure balance between the growth and renewal of natural resources, to become part of global compensating systems, in order to eliminate large poor areas.

Only by means of a joint effort against wastefulness and poverty, as a common responsibility, shall we be able to save our cities and the Earth.

Moreover, cities are designed to develop their roles of exchanges and centrality and, particularly in southern countries, they will continue to grow: therefore, a big effort should be made to build new infrastructures for urban services, both with regards communications as well as water and energy.

Point 3

Today's challenge is to turn increasingly larger and more heterogeneous cities into places for diversity and integration, tolerance and exchange. Should we fail, our civilization would take a terrible step backwards. Cities are the people that inhabit them. Places of freedom and progress, but also of exclusion and violence.

The people who live in our cities are not nationals or foreigners. They are citizens. Diversity is our wealth and tolerance our virtue. Only by this way, do cities make us free and progress is made possible. Cities are deeply responsible for active policies aimed at analysing, preventing and fighting off the reasons for racism and xenophobia.

For this reason, every city should know the limits of its power to absorb diversity and guarantee that, within these limits, the stand made in favour of tolerance and solidarity not only ratifies itself but also is practised without exception.

In an increasingly interdependent world, in which, at the same time, divisions are emphasized and group identities confronted, cities are privileged places of interculture, without which peaceful living together and freedom for each of us is impossible.

Urban policies (architecture and city planning, cultural and social action, education and employment) should enable the maintenance of group identities, but they should particulary stimulate integration in multicultural urban societies.

Point 4

According to its own national and regional traditions, every city should be acknowledged within its real geographical boundaries, including the leisure and working places of most of its inhabitants.

It is not positive that resources generated in a rich business centre or a high-income suburb should not go back to the neighbourhoods where most people live and work.

This would be the greatest lack of solidarity of all.

By having recourse to the inter-municipal collaboration or community procedures at the disposal of each nation or region, but without leaving local identities aside, which are extremely useful in order to generate citizen adherence to society and the common interest, the problems of autonomous spatial specialization should be resolved by means of a common management of the metropolitan area.

Granting this territory new centralities is a complex process that requires planning but which can not be clinically created as in a laboratory; on the contrary, they will probably be born out of the interaction of inhabitants' associations, urban promoters, and the city's government. We are aware of the fact that nowadays, in large cities, in the centre or in the outskirts, marginal areas, non-urbanised survival territories, the 'non-city', exists and develops. To build the city is a commitment that should be jointly undertaken by the local governments in the metropolitan city, together with economic and social protagonists.

Large cities tend to articulate increasingly larger metropolitan regions. We are not in favour of indefinite growth in the conurbation, but of urbanised regional systems in which a basic balance is maintained between concentrated areas and free, agricultural and natural areas, and which small and middle-sized cities can be real alternatives to large ones.

We also favour cultural differences, every city's own identity, and we believe that city planning and architecture should emphasize these proper symbols. Likewise, we must accept the new scale of urban life and find a new balance between the right to privacy and the possibility of taking part in collective urban life. The policy of public space, as opposed to trends to privatise them, as an attempt to respond to demands for security, differentiation, and privacy, is one of our most important challenges.

Point 5

Before the alarming divorce which seems to be occurring between society and politics, and between citizens and their parliamentary representatives in many countries in the world, Rio de Janeiro and Barcelona want to offer the role of cities as political and social mediators.

Our strategic plans include more and more social, political and academic sectors. Thus they are becoming fundamental factors for global development in our territories. People want clear and specific objectives, and cities can state them by means of collaboration between the closest general interest, which is the local one, and private initiative.

Cities will not solve their problems without close collaboration with federal, central or national powers, and regional or state powers, if appropriate.

The latter should express their territorial strategic options in such a way that cities knew what lies ahead.

Now, more than ever, progress requires working ahead of time and with a considerable margin of certainty. Otherwise, it is impossible to start large investments in urbanization and new centralities, communications and transport, and environmental improvement.

Similarly, cities must internally decentralize, in an effective manner. We do not want to make people believe that a large city, such as Rio or Barcelona, could look after each one of its inhabitants from their central agencies.

On the contrary, municipal services should be as respectful of their clients as are the best private and public companies, with well-known products and services.

The use of new technologies, such as cable TV, would indeed facilitate, at the beginning of the twenty-first century, the multiplication of information from the city to the citizen and vice versa.

New technologies will get the best results out of a city–citizen communication, if they are placed within a framework of participative management, public–private cooperation, progress in associative life, and defining public projects that interest the majority.

It is along these lines that democracy will advance.

Point 6

In southern cities, most inhabitants are less than 25 years old. But most young people do not find ways to become citizens. In northern cities, ageing is added to increasing loneliness, and the growth of the tertiary industry which empties whole areas of the city after business hours. There are no young people.

The city should offer life to young people. It should offer new external and internal boundaries, international cooperation and humanitarian action, solidarity and togetherness. But for this offer to be real, the city should provide education, housing and employment for young people. And, above all, means of social participation, cultural integration, and public acknowledgement.

Although our competences may be limited, from city governments we must contribute to create favourable conditions for a multifaceted education and for economic initiatives for young people.

Our cities should offer available housing, and therefore, those sectors that benefit from urban development should contribute to it. It is possible, for instance, to reach agreements with private sectors so that they give up their promotion, which will then be devoted to the young market, at cost price.

Point 7

Cities in the world: taking up a world role.

At present, the planet is an addition of interdependencies, economy has become universal, the elimination of blocks has pulled down political-military walls, and the new communication technologies make us accomplices in all the injustices and all the catastrophies. Being realities open to all exchanges, cities cannot isolate ourselves within a rigid geographical framework, however wide it may be. We must accept our share of world responsibility; we must take up certain cooperation duties with less fortunate countries and cities, sometimes because we are the cause of their misfortunes.

We want to be valid and acknowledged points of reference for large international organizations, in the first place for the United Nations, its organs, such as UNESCO, UNFPA, HABITAT, etc, and its programmes, such as the UNDP. The Rio 1992 conference for the first time enabled international associations of cities and local entities, led by IULA (International Union of Local Authorities) and UTO (United Towns Organisation), to appear together and to win a place of our own at the conference, and in the management of its programmes. Some cooperation experiences were also started between northern and southern cities, by means of programmes financed by the World Bank. This international presence requires of us a close collaboration, a permanent coordination and, if possible, some form of union among continental and world city associations. Our priority must be to promote the closest relationship between IULA and UTO, by far the two most important world organizations, in order to achieve unification within two to three years. At present, this objective is possible as the historical differences both organizations are no longer valid. We call upon the IULA and UTO presidents, our friends Triglia and Sampaio (who has just substituted P. Mauroy) to lead this project. We, the cities, cannot spread ourselves in various organizations with a similar nature and similar objectives, but we must speak with one voice before the major intenational organizations.

Final Point

Humanity has moved forward by means of cooperation, by creating increasingly broader, more complex and more diversified structures. Progress is related to association and exchange, to integrating existing units into larger units. This has occurred from families to clans; then towns and cities were created, and later countries and nations. Now we are realizing this major project: the European Union, and the American integration is also under way. By no means does the creation of a large association mean that its constituent units disappear. In the world there are families, towns, cities, regions, countries and nations. We believe the best guarantee for the progress of all of them and for their common existence is the government of the United Nations Organization. On the contrary, if higher associative links break, and are not substituted by others, this is dangerous for each of them, a risk for everyone.

Cities are the closest links, and the most open ones at their base; they generate a civic culture, made up of what is most characteristic, and which identifies each one with what is freer and universal. Therefore, nowadays community spirit and universality are the two sides of the same reality. One single world, united by the links established amongst the cities themselves. The world of the citizen.

Source: Ajuntament de Barcelona, 1993

Chapter 10
Conclusion

NEW CHALLENGES, NEW OBJECTIVES

The world is moving towards generalized urbanization. This forms part of the same process as economic globalization and the information revolution. This urbanization is at once creative and destructive for the city. The population is concentrated and new centralities are generated. But the space is fragmented, territories vanish and places are weakened. Urbanization is not city. Or, rather, is not city for all. In many countries the urban majorities are not citizen majorities: marginalized from the rule of law and from civic culture, underemployed or surviving in informality, located in areas with poor facilities and scarcely seen from the formal and legal city. This phenomenon which characterizes urbanization in the less developed world has not only become more acute but has become increasingly present in the metropolises of what used to be called the first world.

It is now commonplace to talk of a crisis of the city. But it is not the same crisis as those of the past, even the recent past. The problem to be resolved is not only that of providing housing and basic services for the urban and peri-urban population groups. The problem is on another scale, that of making city in the new urban–regional spaces. By making city we mean providing effective responses to at least five relatively novel challenges.

1. *Work, employment.* Competitiveness, and therefore productivity, is one part of this challenge. But the competitive urban–regional space by no means guarantees the socio-economic integration of the entire active population. The retention of some of each zone's productive activities, proximity of jobs (providing services for people or urban ecology) or intercitizen cooperation are also necessary responses.
2. *Security.* Here we refer not only to citizen security, to the reduction of urban violence. Security takes in a much broader field. It includes peaceful coexistence, feeling oneself accepted by the social setting, knowledge of the city and accessibility of its main points, whether facilities or government departments. The right to mobility and to safe roads. Access to welcoming and meaningful streets and public spaces. Also the security of having the right to social protection of education and health. Economic initiative also calls for a secure framework: the city, its government, public policies and social conventions must reduce the margins of uncertainty provoked by globalization – economic

uncertainty but also uncertainty of identity. And, clearly, security with respect to housing, shelter and land, and the basic services (water, sanitation, waste disposal, protection against the aggressions of the physical medium, etc). This security involves an obligation on the part of government bodies to cooperate with the citizens to promote legalization, the improvement and fitting out of houses and districts which have become urban areas because people have made a piece of city with their work and daily lives (Declaration of Caracas, 1991, and of El Salvador, 1993 (Box 10.1)).

3. *Sense.* The universalist ideologies have become weakened precisely in (or due to?) the age of information. Ghetto cultures, group cultures, 'community withdrawal', ethnic territories have been reinforced, on the other hand. This is the great failure of globalization. And the city which accumulates zoning segmentation, tailoring of competitiveness, privatization of territories, the marginality of some and the fear of others, contributes to this failure. But it can help to rebuild the meaning of life for individuals and groups. The city as producer of sense shows itself in urban projects which stimulate support, which reinforce citizen patriotism. New value is attached to aesthetics, monuments, the quality of public spaces, their symbolic value and their integrating function. It involves conceiving of housing and facilities as 'places', as constructions which help to lend daily life social and cultural meaning.

4. *Sustainability.* This is not a fashion, but rather a requirement of the times, of globalization, but not only of globalization. It is true that each territory must accept a commitment to its requirements for competitiveness and quality of life and the repercussions on the world ecological system (consumption of non-renewable energy sources, greenhouse effect, ozone layer, etc). It is also true that equilibriums in the sphere of the macroregions – which can even be subcontinents, such as the Mediterranean region – must be accepted. But sustainability is also a local challenge for preservation and improvement of the environment and its resources for the future generations. And in many cases for survival of present generations. This implies major changes in the running of economic activity and in consumer social behaviour patterns (in relation to water, for example).

5. *Governability.* This is not solely a political-administrative question. The new urban–regional territories are supra-municipal, sometimes even supra-departmental, or else they go beyond administrative regions and national frontiers. Furthermore, running the territory depends in turn upon a large number of public departments directed at the public, the undertaking and managing of large projects and facilities, relations which are more contractual than hierarchical and compartmentalized between these government bodies, and public–private concerted action for the execution and management of urban works and services. It is a new political, juridicial and administrative culture which must be constructed, made up of rules, habits and style. But governability of the territory has other dimensions of a socio-political and cultural character or, to put it another way, of means of relationship between the institutions/public agents and the population.

Box 10.1 Declaration of Salvador

Germany, Bangladesh, Belgium, Brazil, Chile, Colombia, Ecuador, El Salvador, Spain, France, Greece, Indonesia, Italy, Kenya, Nicaragua, The Netherlands, Senegal, South Africa, Tunisia, Venezuela, Vietnam, Inter-American Development Bank, World Bank, Health Pan-American Organization, are the country and organization signatories of the 'Declaration of Salvador de Bahia', reproduced below due to the importance of the knowledge, discussion and opinions presented.

3 December 1993

Preamble

In 1993, the living conditions of children, women and men across the world are precarious or unworthy of the level of development of the countries in which they live.

It is the duty of states to remedy such situations.

The rehabilitation of districts where poverty is increasing ranks among the top priorities.

It is a right for the inhabitants concerned to be consulted as to the planning, implementation, follow up and assessment of rehabilitation policies.

As national and local representatives, as officials in government offices, as representatives of district inhabitants, as experts convinced of these duties and rights, we came from seventeen countries and four continents to Salvador de Bahia in Brazil, where we held a meeting from November 29th to December 3rd, 1993.

Exactly two years ago, political representatives and government officials in charge of rehabilitation policies in various regions of the globe gathered in Caracas, Venezuela, to compare their experiences. They concluded that to be efficient public policies should rest on basic principles that are the same everywhere although situations differ widely from one country to the next. These principles were set forth in the Declaration of Caracas.

Since we share their conclusions and are convinced that the statement of these principles should be followed by a strong determination to enforce them, we have decided in Salvador to lay the grounds of a strategy designed to implement them. As signatories of the Declaration we pledge to contribute to the application of these principles.

In all our countries, whether rich or poor, we have noticed the deterioration of some urban areas: makeshift districts, older districts in city centers, districts consisting of depreciated welfare housing.

For a long time people thought that this situation was temporary and that economic development in itself would suffice to solve any problems. Such is not the case. Social exclusion tends to concentrate in certain districts because our current patterns of development generate or tolerate permanent exclusion. At the same time monetarist principles governing international policies reinforce this trend.

These districts, these breeding grounds of poverty will go on existing for years. It will therefore take ambitious long term policies to integrate these people into social life, to alter their living conditions while safeguarding their rights, their dignity and their abilities.

Such rehabilitation policies should be in keeping with a more global strategy that provides for the development of the rural world and smaller towns, in order to avoid a concentration of population in big cities, and fit into urban policies aimed at improving the reception of newcomers in urban areas. It should be financed and enforced in such a way as to build a fairer world, more aware of its responsabilities.

It is the duty of the international community, states and local administration to design and carry out rehabilitation policies. We claim that in the various stages of their design and implementation, policies should meet the six principles set forth in the Declaration of Caracas.

1. To acknowledge the dynamic currents existing in underpriviliged districts, to support them and foster them.
2. To afford the inhabitants of these districts a feeling of greater safety, to pledge not to drive them out from their dwelling place.
3. To admit that representative democracy alone cannot deal with the aspirations of certain categories of citizens – children, women, foreigners, refugees, elderly people, and to find the means by which these aspirations can be made known and taken into account.
4. To improve the enforcement of public policies at every level so as to devise together with the inhabitants concerned case by case solutions. Also, to implement comprehensive policies that take into account various aspects of their individual and community life.
5. To subordinate the policies implemented to the actual social tempo of the districts concerned as well as their inhabitants, which goes from finding the right solutions to urgent problems to monitoring long term strategies.
6. To set up funding means that match the goals being sought. Every district, every town, every country is unique. There are common principles that apply to the rehabilitation of each one. However there is no uniform solution; each one must fit the case under consideration. Hence, it is essential, at state, regional and basic community levels,
   – to specify and use the means designed to meet the six principles set forth in the Declaration;
   – to organize an exchange of experiences between district inhabitants and professionals, so that each one may learn from other's experience;
   – that the official means to follow up and conflictingly assess the policies that are being implemented be set up.

Any rehabilitation policy should, at every stage of the planning process, of the decision making, of the implementation and the assessment work, rely on the active participation of its own organizations and of that of the district's inhabitants.

It is a good thing that authorities admit thay cannot substitute themselves for the inhabitants, they can in no way hand over their responsibilities to the inhabitants of already underpriviliged district. We clearly claim that the state and local administrations are fully responsible for solidarity, social cohesion, consistent urban planning and for the availability of social services. They may subcontract some of their responsibilities, but they cannot by any means pass them off to others.

Equity and solidarity imply that at every level the authorities concerned, whether federation, state, region or town, a clear assessment of the amount of financial means required be made in order that rehabilitation policies actually match the existing needs. They also require clear commitments to ensure the availability of such financial means.

Implementing rehabilitation policies implies a sound structuring of the various levels of decision-making. Steps meant to enforce the six principles set forth in the Declaration of Caracas should be planned and carried out according to the real needs of the population in the districts concerned. By so doing their involvement in the decision-making process is guaranteed and specific features of each district are taken into consideration.

It is the duty of the superior decision-making levels:

- to raise and allocate the funds required;
- to provide an adequate legal and institutional framework for those who do the field work;
- to ensure that the six principles mentioned earlier serve as a guideline;
- to act in the place of basic local communities if the latter do not wish to implement rehabilitation policies;
- to ensure a continuous assessment of the results obtained.

Federal authorities or the state must have a determining action. They should

- set up required funds;
- set up clear and stable rules that are made known to the public, and according to which funds are allocated;
- devise adequate legal and institutional implements that will not take the shape of restrictive technical standards;
- suggest approaches that rest on the experience of the community;
- publicize the most promising innovations, support professional networks;
- assist district representatives in exchanging experiences;
- support exchanges with other countries and continents.

We consider that the declarations of Caracas and Salvador can be used as an efficient tool to implement the principles in which we believe. Hence, we suggest that:

- states, local communities and international organizations formally support these declarations, thus committing themselves to choosing and using the proper means to implement the principles set forth; we suggest that they involve themselves actively in domestic and international networks of exchange of experiences and accept being submitted to an assessment of the results obtained at fixed periods of time;
- these two declarations be widely circulated and discussed among local communities, district inhabitants and professionals adapting the discussion to each specific case;
- these declarations be used as common reference for training sessions;
- these declarations be used at a local level as a reference for rehabilitation charters that clearly specify procedures adopted for partnership;
- they be used as basic criteria for public assessment of policies enforced at various levels;
- to support the establishment of regional, national and international networks in charge of exchanging experiences between representatives of deteriorated districts, who are the first concerned and therefore the most aware of adequate solutions.

The meeting at Salvador de Bahia was an opportunity to confront the experience acquired in various countries with regard to the implementation of the six principles set forth in the Declaration of Caracas. The text that follows has no ambition of being a universal proposal, it is a mere collection of ideas, leads for thought, experiences that supplement the work started in Caracas two years ago, and which is to be continuously enriched from now on by the network of exchange of experiences.

First principle: Learning to Identify, Intensify and Stimulate Dynamic Currents in Districts

1. Do not mistake knowledge of problems for acknowledgement of inhabitants.
   Technical studies and diagnoses are useful if they are also specified, carried out and shared by the inhabitants themselves. Otherwise, instead of serving as grounds for the dialogue between authorities and inhabitants, they turn into means to devise solutions in the inhabitants' place.
2. Identifying inhabitants means identifying their background and their culture, it means acknowledging the value of the district, its shape in terms of space and the fact that it is made to withstand the long term.
3. Inhabitant dynamics often take informal patterns or appear beyond normal legal boundaries. The form under which they appear (such as for instance, various types of mutual aid, of exchanges of services) should be recognized even if it means altering existing legislation.

4. Recognizing inhabitants means firstly acknowledging their work, that is, recognizing and utilizing the results of the work done on constructions, furthermore, it means recognizing the professional value of efforts made to organize the social structure of districts and to provide for the representation of inhabitants.

5. Living in the same neighbourhood doesn't mean necessarily sharing the same fate; acknowledging inhabitants also means identifying their differences.

6. In certain cases district inhabitants have lost their self-confidence, their confidence in their ability to act, in their creativeness. Training to recover self-confidence is thus compulsory. If the districts start to recognize themselves, acknowledgement by others will follow. The first stage of that process is very simply the construction of speech and the organization of the means to be heard.

7. The special recognition of the aspirations and dynamics of women and the youth is crucial. Young people particularly wish feeling useful. This may be the starting point of some social qualification, of some training to citizenship.

8. The characteristics of the district appear in the organizational patterns developed by its inhabitants. These patterns do not spring up by themselves, they are the result of a cultural apprenticeship inherited from history or which inhabitants should acquire now, and in this last case time has to be considered.

Second Principle: Reinforcing the Status of Inhabitants

1. The status of inhabitants is essentially reinforced by the claim, at a national level, to recognize makeshift districts and by the pledge to implement rehabilitation policies which do not evict their inhabitants.

2. The reinforcement of the inhabitants's status or, in the case of makeshift or illegal districts, the sorting out of their position with regard to law does not necessarily mean granting them plots under full ownership. Although granting is often useful because of its symbolic meaning and the opportunities it provides to merge the district with the town, it may in some cases have a negative effect, for instance:
   - donating land unfit for development conflicts with long term urban planning;
   - as in the case of farmland distribution, there is a risk of more or less rapid private land concentration, the most underpriviliged selling their piece of land;
   - the selling or the granting of land may encourage local communities to transfer responsibility for the district to its own inhabitants;
   - land granting may reinforce vote-catching tendencies within the relationships between local representatives and inhabitants;
   - public ownership of a share of the land is in fact essential for

the urban planification policies;

- the reception of newcomers is a source in a district of which available land has already been distributed.

This only shows that in this field too there are no miracle solutions that are applicable anywhere, anytime. Besides, the aspiration to individual ownership of land is not that strong in every country. In certain cases it makes up the chief claim because the legislation that governs the ownership of land is a prerequisite to be allowed access to public utilities – water and power supply, mail, etc – or is considered as the surest protection against eviction.

3. Many other interesting methods are used to consolidate the inhabitants' position:
   - joint ownership of the land by man and woman, which consolidates the family's nucleus;
   - collective transfer of plots to a neighbourhood unit; creation of a special ownership status;
   - extra long term rental.
4. Discussing with inhabitants the methods to be used to reinforce their occupancy rights is as important as the choice of these methods.

Third Principle: The Aspirations and Interests of Inhabitants

1. Political commitments to solve problems of urban precariousness, ensure economic, social and human promotion, and alter living conditions in underpriviliged districts by long term action, can never be taken for granted. Because such policies are far from meeting the wishes and matching the interests of many voters. That is why a great many generous policies on integrated development only exist in writing or under the form of experiments.
2. The inhabitants of precarious districts in general give little credit to the interplay of political forces and to politicians themselves. Being used to being the usual targets of vote-catching campaigns, they have grown tired of promises that never materialize. Confidence in authorities cannot build up without a deep change in the attitude of political decision-makers themselves, that is, open funds management, meeting promises, sustained action, providing for the means to assess a policy's efficiency. Confidence is also here the result of apprenticeship.
3. Many representatives believe that they are qualified to interpret people's aspirations simply because they were elected by some people. It is an illusion, and it is even more so when the aspirations of women and children living in precarious conditions are concerned.
4. To stimulate political action, the best solution is to use various means to reinforce the inhabitants' ability to be heard and to have their say in the decisions that are of their concern, and of which consequences they should be aware. The circulation of knowledge

originating from succesful undertakings and from innovative approaches, proves there are feasible methods that channel aspirations and the will to take action. This is an effective means to encourage authorities to monitor rehabilitation policies.

5. Political practices, the ties between the governing and the governed, the extent of the bonds between the governing and prevailing economic interests or mafia interests, traditions of political ethics differ considerably from one country to the next.

   Steps such as assisting and financially supporting the development of inhabitant social organisations, finding new ways by which social groups may express themselves when traditional people's organizations decline, are crucial everywhere.

6. The commencement of a group's voice, the appearance of social organizations and among inhabitants the appearance of an ability to make proposals often need the support of professional organizations and universities who ease the process. It is essential that this support is provided on clear grounds, within the framework of specified responsabilities, otherwise those providing support end up wrongfully assuming the authority to speak, taking over the inhabitants' project as well as speaking and acting in their names.

   To avoid this, priority should be given to helping inhabitants of precarious or deteriorated districts to inform themselves, to train (they are often unaware of their rights and of the possibilities that law provides), to make themselves available (they seldom receive compensation for the time spent on meetings); to helping their leaders rise, to helping them confront their experiences with others at a town, region, country and world level. It is undoubtedly between inhabitants themselves, between districts, that exchanges of experiences are mostly required and urgent. The most explicit test of the authorities' will to act lies in the support they provide to the training of inhabitants and to the exchange of experiences, to organizations that are set up by inhabitants, and to the quest for adequate ways of guiding public debate towards choices and action.

7. Marginalization is a vicious circle. Social, economic and urban marginality mutually reinforce. Inhabitants of precarious or deteriorated districts feel a social barrier between themselves and other inhabitants and the result is they are not encouraged to consider themselves as full citizens. A rehabilitation policy that contributes to restore pride may on the contrary generate a positive spiral that encourages citizens to build their speech and formulate their own projects. It may also encourage citizens to use their voting power to better defend their interests.

8. The inhabitants' ability to voice their interests directly and the rise of leaders among them should not be idealized. The pitfall lying ahead is that these leaders who are asked to negotiate with new partners, may gradually part from the rank and the file and be dragged in the traditional political game, in that case everything has to start over again. Is this inevitable?

9. The dialogue between district inhabitants and authorities is often eased if it can rest on some neutral grounds, beyond a setting in which negotiating and power relations prevail.
10. The building of speech lies on that of memory. This is a priviliged sphere of action for the organizations that are dedicated to supporting inhabitants, it allows people's organizations to capitalize and make their own experience known to others.
11. There are various interesting methods to call the participation of inhabitants to decisions they are concerned with: setting up local economic and social committees in which women and young people may be better represented compared to elected assemblies, organizing public debates, taking decisions that directly concern inhabitants. This new form of democracy upsets habits and makes the decision process more 'complicated'. In this field also training sessions should be organized. However one should be aware of dissillusions caused by an open debate that offers prospects which never materialize.
12. The existence of organized local authorities and services, of whose line of work is sustained during a certain period of time, and who have the ability to make long term contractual committments, allow for the learning to be confident and opportunities to negotiate long term rehabilitation policies. Such is not the case everywhere.

Fourth Principle: Improving Public Action

1. Public action is compulsary at any level. Private initiatives (NGOs, associations) are very useful, however they cannot substitute for authorities. It is only the involvement of national or federal states that can offer financial, jurisdictional and institutional responses that match global stakes. Local authorities are responsible for the conception of the methods and the details of implementation adapted to the given social and physical realities of the districts.
2. Public action should be improved to:
   • establish a relationship between steps that are taken along the lines that were set out, public utilities, and the support to economic and social promotion of inhabitants;
   • build up partnership and contractual relations with the inhabitants;
   • monitor lasting action;
   • improve the efficiency of decision-making processes and methods for allocating money (many people point out the very low productivity of the allocation of money originating from the state or from international cooperation; the bulk of it is consumed by bureaucracy and by the diversion from initially planned targets or destination, or it isn't even spent because of serious dysfunction of procedures).
3. Mechanisms should be simple. Intricate procedures for interservice or interdepartment coordination are perfect in written form, however they are often counterproductive: they are often confined to a mere ritual, they dissuade initiatives, they impose useless prescriptive

restrictions on users and sometimes simply jam the mechanism. Attention should be given to:
- contractual targets that encourage the authors of undertakings to explain how they intend to reach the targets that have been set forth, instead of imposing in advance prescriptive procedures on them as to the way to proceed;
- the implements for open public management and assessment;
- the grounds of dialogue and initiation to negotiation;
- the circulation and the discussion of experiences and methods that may serve as a reference and not as models or compulsory procedures; this is how people may gradually learn methods of doing.

4. The major stake is in the end to obtain that qualified professionals, who are dedicated to reach the goals that are pursued and who can be at ease in particularly demanding jobs, are working in the field of urban planning, housing, education, health and urban services. Experience proves that activism, an essential feature, cannot suffice and that it wears out as the years go. It is therefore essential to set up mechanisms that afford support to professionals, to create places where knowledge can be acquired, where ideas can be debated, where methods can be confronted, where people can train and where experience can be capitalized. The support of research and of the universities should allow matters to be viewed in another perspective. It is necessary to help a speech be heard and to encourage the appearance of technical expertise. This is how institutional, financial and technical engineering capable of devising solutions adapted to each situation, will gradually develop.

Fifth Principle: Linking Administrative and Political Working Tempo to Social Working Tempo

1. Districts and cities are just like human beings, living organisms and intricate bio-socio-technical systems. The human being is regulated by a series of cyclical rhythms that range from a few seconds to a minute, a day, a month or a year. These rhythms may be adapted to external events, however they must globally be respected. Many social rhythms correspond to these biological rhythms.

   Similarly, a district has its own rhythm, rites and beats that make up its richness and originality. This rhythm must be respected, however it can usefully be taken into account to allow the district to adapt itself to environment changes and to the policies that are implemented with the regard to it.

2. In practice experience proves how difficult it is to reorientate administrative and political systems and change their rhythm. It is especially at local level that different administrative and political rhythm can be usefully summarized, within the framework of a project's implementation.

   The clear statement of local responsibilites in the elaboration and implementation of projects should allow to link administrative rhythms to social rhythms, even when there is substantial national funding.

3. The integration of district life rhythms into administrative rhythms can be eased once the criteria and simple as well as open methods for the financing of policies and projects are specified.

Sixth Principle: Setting up Financing Mechanisms in Keeping with the Goals Pursued

1. A significant share of the financing should proceed from the national level and show:
   - the required national solidarity in the face of exclusion phenomena;
   - financial means involved must be in keeping with the size of the challenge.

   The recommendation is that this takes the form of a firm and long term commitment of the government on the share of national income that is spent on the rehabilitation of the precarious and deteriorated districts.

2. The size of the stakes, the impact of international ouverture on the development of countries call for international solidarity to take a share in the financing of policies and projects. The contribution of governmental and non-governmental organizations play their role in guaranteeing that policies and projects are sustained in time.

3. In each district, the financial means allocated by the national or the local community to rehabilitation should necessarily be in the form of a global amount that allows much flexibility in its allocation to such or such field of action.

4. It should be possible to convert this global amount into different investment income to:
   - be able to finance by using various methods, land acquisitions, infrastructures, urban services, the improvement of housing, the monitoring of the process, the organization of inhabitants and the exchange of experiences as well as economic action;
   - combine public investment and private investment of households or of economic agents, according to the field of action;
   - create different products according to short-term priorities or long-term action.

   There are so many methods available that the international exhange of experiences between professionals should chiefly rest on this financial engineering.

5. The criteria for allocating public financing must absolutely be:
   - simple;
   - easily checked;
   - submitted to an assessment at fixed periods of time.

   They must be in keeping with the general philosophy and rest chiefly on:
   - the demonstration that a mechanism and a project allowing for

> the respect of the six principles set forth in the Declaration of Caracas were set up at a local level;
> - the principles of a sustainable development that integrates the relationship between people, the relations between people and their environment and the safeguard of the interests of future generations;
> - the encouragement to self-organization.
> 6. Experience proves that money lent in the framework of human promotion, rehabilitation and local development policies is even better repaid since people know where the sums repaid are going to be used. This casts special light on working capital that is reinvested similarly.
> 7. Mechanisms designed for a social control of the sums allocated to rehabilitation under whatever form should be set up.
> 8. The economic calculations and the financing of programmes dealing with the improvement of housing, the creation of community services and the monitoring of rehabilitation processes, must clearly integrate the work contribution of inhabitants.
> 9. The right to be granted loans, in other words reliability, is a basic right that is used against exclusion. Conventional commercial banks are generally too poorly tooled to grant loans to people who provide little security. This points to the importance of establishing interdependent banks of which operating rules and requested guarantees match the characteristics of the people concerned. International experience shows that this is possible and that it works.

We would especially like to emphasize the following:
- The lack of definition of a concept of citizenship as a set of rights and duties, of shared civic culture and compatible life styles which are applied to the new urban–regional realities (see Charte de la citoyenneté, 1996).
- The bureaucratic anachronism of government department organization and operation. We have already referred to this in discussing the decentralization of large cities and of citizen participation. Another relevant aspect is the contradiction between social life rhythms (organization and management of their demands and projects by citizen bodies) and political-administrative work rates (electoral, budgetary) and the absurd nature of subordinating the first to the second.

As a result of all this, we make so bold as to propose three principles or broad objectives for the city:

1. *The right to the city.* Recognition of this right for all population groups experiencing urbanization processes. The exercise of this right includes fit and non-precarious housing, socially valued districts provided with basic services, communication with the city as a whole and mobility to make central provision accessible, job possibilities and suitable training for the social membership and political and legal equality of all inhabitants (residents–users).

2. *National and international legitimacy of governments of proximity.* This means recognition of local and regional governments as necessary partners of states and of international organizations (UN, GATT, World Bank/IMF, etc) for taking part in the drawing up and application of agreements and programmes directed at regulating globalization of economic, social and cultural processes, and political, military and security processes.

3. *Universal declaration of the rights of citizens.* The steadily increasing participation of city organizations and local authorities in international forums, and the increasing initiative and innovation capacity of non-governmental organizations in these same forums creates favourable conditions for the drawing up and approval of a Citizenship Declaration which legitimates the rights and duties of urban populations. The multiplication of information networks between cities, local authorities and NGOs creates the material foundations for the dissemination of a political culture with common values (see Ministerio de Obras Publicas, 1995 (Box 10.2)).

CITIES IN GLOBALIZATION

By way of summary, we put forward three sets of conclusions on local democracy, urban policies and cities in the sphere of international relations.

Local Democracy in Globalization

Just One World, an Urbanized World: the Value of the Local Setting
The global economy, the information era, the breaking down of the politico-military blocks and the reinforcement of international institutions have shaped a new political space world-wide. This new situation is neither more just nor more regulated than in the past. On the contrary: the large multinational economic groups act in brutal, distorted markets. Aggressive, desperate nationalisms and fundamentalisms are breaking out, and the weakest fail to find the backing they need in international organizations. Yet in parallel with this, local and regional spheres are being reinforced as economic configurations, spaces of collective identity and political participation, and also as a concentrated expression of the problems and challenges facing humanity: growth and the environment, waste and poverty, possible liberties and real exclusions. Cities are nowadays the symbolic manifestation for the majority of our way of life, its contradictions and potential. Yet although it is true that urban populations tend to be the majority, it needs to be borne in mind that some of that population, though urban, does not have the rights that are inherent to citizenship, and that the aggravation of imbalances between urban and rural zones sparks off migrations that cities find difficult to endure, and that make the rural areas even poorer.

The City as a Space for Democracy
A city is a chance to build a democracy of proximity, of participation by all in the management of public affairs, reinforcing integrating collective identities. The principle of subsidiarity, which should be understood as the

BOX 10.2 CONCLUSIONS OF THE EUROPEAN REGIONAL MEETING OF NATIONAL COMMITTEES, HABITAT II (MADRID, 27–28 NOVEMBER 1995)

A Presentation by Jordi Borja and Félix Arias

Foreword

In the framework of the preparatory activities for the Habitat II Conference, and following the recommendations of the United Nations in resolution 47/180 of the General Assembly, of December 1992, the Spanish Presidency of the European Union convened the European Regional Meeting of National Committees HABITAT II, which was held in Madrid on 27 and 28 November 1995.

Present were delegations from the following National Committees of European Union member States: Belgium, Denmark, Finland, France, Germany, Greece, Italy, Portugal, Spain, Sweden and the United Kingdom. Also attending were delegations from the following bodies: the European Commission, the Secretary of Habitat (UNCHS), The Economic Commission for Europe (ECE) and the G4+ city networks and the Union of American Capital Cities (UCCI).

The aim of the meeting was to examine and assess the characteristics of the urbanization process and the cities in the Union, and experiences in action and government in connection with cities and the territory. Reflection on the problems themselves and necessary reforms in policies concerning cities should serve to spur on application of the Habitat Agenda in our countries, and to explain to the Conference and other world regions the concerns of the States of the European Union regarding the situation of urbanization and territorial and urban policies in our countries.

Conclusions

The National Committees of the European Union wish to contribute to the Habitat II Conference the experience of a continent of cities. We are aware of the differences between the various regions of the world, and we are not seeking to put forward a model. Nevertheless, in a world experiencing a strong urbanization process – which in many cases does not mean the development of cities – we believe that it is useful to reflect on the experience of the problems and advantages of European cities.

The European city is a complex organization characterized by density of population and social relations, by the heterogeneous nature of functions and activities, by the diversity of their inhabitants, by the existence of a civic culture and by the tradition of self-government. Each city does not develop these potentials to the full, and furthermore the cities are currently suffering major critical processes, yet the general balance for this city model is regarded as positive and adequate for the purpose of overcoming internal problems and the problems of relating to other territories and cities.

1. Globalization sharpens the demand that territories be competitive and efficient. We take the view that this competitiveness must be based on the urban system of large and medium sized cities, articulating the territory as a whole and the rural spheres. Cities conceived as centralities must be nodes in the communications network that are to integrate the diffuse urbanization spaces and rural areas.

2. Sustainability is a fundamental problem in the European urban system, and one that needs to be approached at various levels:
   - the natural medium and specific culture of cities, their neighbourhoods and districts, and of their hinterlands (metropolitan regions, ecosystems that support the city, etc);
   - the country or nation, and the countries of the European Union (transborder matters), for subjects needing more global treatment, such as the management of certain natural resources (such as water, forestation, desertification, etc);
   - the global repercussions at planet level (the greenhouse effect, the ozone layer, consumption of non-renewable energy resources, etc).

3. It is necessary to reconstruct and develop a city model taking in formal continuity, functional proximity and social diversity. The design of large cities, in particular, and of urban systems in general, must foster the creation of a set of centralities, and the organization of their infrastructures, bestowing accessibility and attractiveness on each of their parts, including relations with rural spheres on the basis of their specific values.

4. The right to the city for all population groups experiencing urbanization processes, fostering real access for them to the city and to citizenship, must be a basic principle for public action. The right to the city includes housing, neighbourhoods that are equipped in material terms and esteemed in social terms, articulation with the city as a whole, with easy access to its centralities, possibilities for employment and suitable training, and political and legal equality for all inhabitants. Exercising this right may require positive discrimination policies, and cultural upgrading, for neighbourhoods or groups that are in situations of marginalization for economic, social or cultural reasons, both in cities as such and in the peripheries and rural areas.

5. The right to housing is an objective for public policies as a whole. Progressive fulfilment of this objective requires the use of a set of diversified instruments to take account of the variety of problems and demands. From among these instruments could be cited support measures for property and building land markets that are effective and diversified, a building land policy that combats social segregation and segregation of urban functions, programmes

agreed between administrations and with private agents, facilitating access to housing and credit for low income sectors, economic aid to families, and specific attention for excluded groups. The range of urban housing on offer can only be regarded as housing when it has a well equipped and well communicated setting.

6. The objectives of social cohesion and cultural integration must be incorporated into all policies on the city, as opposed to the fragmenting dynamics that often stem from economic globalization and from responses made through one off or sector based initiatives. Urban development and modernization programmes must also express the same will to achieve functional and social versatility, and the capacity to integrate the population in material and symbolic terms. Stimulating citizen initiatives and cooperation with the social groups concerned are indispensable instruments for the success of these policies.

7. Experience of inter-administration negotiations for the design and implementation of integrated policies on the city, tackling the main problems of competitiveness, social cohesion and sustainability, are regarded as positive and should come into general use. These actions normally require ambitious drive from the public sector, incorporating the administrations in their design and development in order to achieve social consensus and to foster a global project for the city. For this purpose, it is also necessary to develop ways to incorporate the local communities and the private sector, in accordance with the features of each programme.

8. National governments, and regional ones where applicable, in their functions as definers of European Community policies, as those responsible for drawing up the regulatory and financial frameworks, and as promoters of action in cities, must accept and ensure the implementation of these objectives through their support, and participation in any appropriate way, in developing policies for cities.

9. Progress must be made in developing the concept of local democracy and autonomy, in recognition of the principle of subsidiarity or proximity, and of the promotional leadership territorial governments are to pursue. We regard as positive European experience in the constitutional and international protection of these principles through the Council of Europe. On this basis it is more feasible to develop state decentralization processes and to improve the government of our regions and cities, through a more balanced distribution of competencies among administrations along with financing mechanisms that are appropriate for exercising them.

10. Viewed as fundamental is promoting civic participation and constant innovation in the procedures and techniques for administration/civil society relations, communication and cooperation. City policies need backing from the citizens.

11. The political will to make cities privileged places for the construction of European citizenship should be reasserted, enhancing their role in exchanges between and the integration of all Europeans.

12. Cities can play an important part at a world level in economic, social and cultural exchanges, in executing cooperation programmes and in making progress in the universalist values of solidarity and tolerance. We therefore defend the advisability of international bodies and national governments giving their support to networks of cities, to their local authorities and to civil society for the development of cooperation programmes, particularly when they refer to the specific issues facing cities or to human settlements.

These conclusions can by synthesized in two points that we regard as essential:

1. The city is a form of living together that has become consolidated over history, that is basic for the sustainable development of our societies, and that is currently demanding policies that take in competitiveness, social cohesion and sustainability in an integrated way.
2. Efficacy in the governability of territories must be based on public–authority cooperation, taking on leadership of the city's policies and basic projects, facilitating the participation of all its agents and developing the spirit of citizenship based on active participation in urban life.

decentralization of power and areas of competence along with the availability of financial resources to make it practicable. Politics, in the sense of public management, should not be pursued at higher levels when it can be pursued at the local level. A worldwide policy is needed in order to lay down regulatory systems that ensure broad balances and fair exchanges. And the importance of states must be stressed as guarantors of policies aimed at social cohesion and the protection of the rights and liberties of all citizens. Yet emphasis must also be laid on the significance of this third dimension of politics: the local, the government of cities and civic participation. As essential and legitimate as the other two.

Local Democracy is Citizenship

All men and women living in cities are and must be equals in political and social rights. There is no citizenship if there is no legal equality regardless of national or ethnic origin. For that reason all the inhabitants and all the families have a legitimate right to take part in local political life. Yet neither is their citizenship if there is social exclusion, if ghettos are formed for the immigrant population, if the differences and identities of each group are not tolerated, and if intolerance is tolerated. There is no citizenship if the city as a set of basic services does not reach all its inhabitants, and if it does not hold out the hope of work, progress and participation to all. The city must be a space of fraternity.

Democratic Innovation

Cities today are privileged places for democratic innovation. What is called the crisis of representative institutions and bureaucratic organizations can be overcome through the many possibilities for direct elector–elected relationships, for easy access to public administrations, for immediate consultation, for public–private cooperation and for social self-management that can arise in cities. For that purpose cities must be able to innovate in three fields:

1. the structuring of spheres of metropolitan management, representation and participation;
2. the internal decentralization of large cities;
3. establishing new modes of participation and shaping new social rights.

Communication – a Prerequisite for Citizens' Democracy

There can be no active, responsible citizens if they are not well informed and if they lack any real opportunity to receive and respond to messages from the public and private agents who take decisions concerning the city. Provision must be stimulated in all forms of communication within cities, ranging from the most traditional forms such as district civic cultural centres to the most modern forms such as local radio and television stations and the cabling of the city. Nobody, no public or private agent, is entitled to monopolize communication. The socialization of new communication technologies in the service of civic participation is a historical opportunity.

City Management and Public–Private Cooperation

Local government, duly elected and representative, should go for leading the collective management of the city, yet without monopolizing it. All spheres of city life can be opportunities for public–private cooperation and the involvement of society. No economic promotion, environmental protection, public safety, social solidarity or cultural tolerance exist without public–private cooperation. Neither political monopoly by the administration nor the market exclusively and excludingly can meet the challenges of the city today. Public–private cooperation can be formalized in an all-embracing city project going beyond the limitations of the traditional plans or neoliberal deregulations.

The New Local Autonomy

Though it is an important dimension which is not always instituted, local autonomy is not just a matter of political-legal recognition and legal protection of an inherent and specific sphere of competence for urban planning and management of services. Nor can it rest on the existence of clearly separate functions of the various government levels. Local autonomy today, on the basis of the democratic origin of local governments, must take in new realms of content, such as:

- the right to political innovation over and above the strictly uniform approach of state legislation (electoral systems, organization, decentralization, metropolitan coordination, civic participation);

- recognizing the coordinating capacity of the various public authorities and companies in order that integral policies rather than sectorial ones may be applied in cities;
- the possibility of taking on competencies and functions in spheres that are not traditionally regarded as local but which are nonetheless fundamental, such as economic promotion and employment, justice and security, international presence, management of the new systems of communication, etc.
- the right to demand of the state that all necessary legal competencies and financial resources be transferred down in order to be able to exercise the social functions expected of local governments in areas such as health, education, the environment, the struggle against poverty, housing and public transport;
- recognizing the principle of financial autonomy as an essential part of local autonomy.

Urban Policies: New Objectives and New Instruments

The City: Balancing Economic Development and Quality of Life
The economy of cities as a whole must be competitive on an international scale. To that end, they must have powerful communication infrastructures (particularly logistics zones based on telecommunications) and develop areas of centrality that are articulated with other cities, though also integrated in the city in general. There is no insuperable contradiction between competitiveness and social integration, between growth and quality of living. In the long run, the most competitive cities in international terms are those offering the best quality of life to their inhabitants.

Rich Cities, Poor Cities
While it is true that there are areas of great poverty in the richest cities, and opulent sectors in the poorest, we cannot overlook the enormous differences there are between the cities of the more highly developed world, in which we find scandalous waste and ostentation, and those of the less developed areas, where most of the population lack even the most indispensable goods and services. It is therefore necessary to draw up and put forward models for growth that ensure rational, austere use of resources in rich cities and that foster solidarity exchanges with poorer cities.

The City for Everybody: Centralities and Mobility
We cannot accept the dual city, the city that consolidates centres and peripheries that are mutually exclusive, or the city that segregates population groups and activities in social and functional terms. Cities must be polycentric, neighbourhoods must be plural, and activity zones multifunctional. Each part of the city must have its own buildings of interest, symbology and identity. Yet a democratic city is also one that maximizes mobility possibilities for all its inhabitants. Accessible mass public transport systems are often a precondition for access to employment and housing and are also a prerequisite for building a sense and a collective project for the city.

Employment and Housing, Requisites for Citizenship
Unemployment, or surviving in the informal economy, hinders the exercise of citizenship. City governments must foster economic growth, lay bridges between the formal and the informal economy, and innovate in the formulation of jobs too. Proximity services, urban ecology and the maintenance of infrastructures and facilities can become major generators of employment alongside the more traditional public works and facilities policies. Housing is a fundamental right of citizens. Public authorities cannot always offer immediate up to standard housing for all the inhabitants, but they can recognize human settlements, establish cooperation mechanisms with their occupants to improve their dwellings, and arrange for basic urban services to reach them.

Education and Training, Health and Collective Services as Citizens' Rights
Basic education and basic health services should be accessible and free to the entire population. There is no citizenship without access to the education and culture of the city, without continuous training, without accessible health services or without collective services such as water and the treating and ecological conditioning of waste. This is so because exercising these rights underpins the quality of housing, access to employment and the dignity of family life. There is no economic argument that can justify the absence of these services for part of the urban population.

Public Safety as a Precondition for Liberty
Fear generates intolerance, and insecurity runs counter to the exercise of citizenship. The criminal economy and poverty are factors behind insecurity. The marginalization and exclusion of some generates intolerance in others. A safe city is one that combats poverty and intolerance, one that continually launches solidarity projects and fosters communication between all its inhabitants. To counter insecurity, it is necessary to have a social and cultural integration policy and to recognize the right to be different, as well as to have integral prevention programmes. But also effective justice close to the citizens, civic police and administration which is honest and accessible with participation possible for all. Preventive policy is, however, the best security policy, yet its effectiveness depends not only on public management but also on the individual and collective responsibility of all the citizens.

The New Urban contract
An integral city policy requires an urban contract between the government and the citizens, between the administration and companies, between public bodies and citizen associations. Yet it also demands fresh consideration of the relations between the state and local authorities. Hierarchical relations, when not justified on the basis of functionality and equality, should be gradually replaced by contractual relations that ensure efficient coordination between public agents and that enable the local authority, in accordance with its capacities, to exercise a function in coordinating the public sector and arranging for civil society's participation.

Cities – a Force in International Relations

At present, exchange and cooperation relations between cities are on the increase, and numerous regional and issue specific networks and regional associations involving cities are being created, both with local authorities and with civil society institutions. There is gradual acceptance of the legitimacy, appropriateness and right of cites, and particularly their democratic governments, to play a part in international political, economic and cultural life. Recognizing this right is today a key factor in democratizing international relations and essential for making the agreements and programmes of international conferences and bodies efficient.

Local Association Forming, an Objective of Global Importance

The democratization of international relations also involves the development of international associations of cities and local authorities and their unity. The existence of strong, united associations is the best basis for getting states to recognize the right of local governments to participate in international life, with greater autonomy as well, to more effective urban power and to greater competencies and resources in the national framework. Thus approval for the Court for European Local Autonomy was achieved. The unity of city and local authority associations is currently an objective that is shared by the main world organizations.

Municipalism at World Level

The existence of a number of issue specific and regional organizations expresses the diversity and richness of the municipal movement. Yet it also seems necessary to be able to act in a united way at world-wide level, and with respect to the large international organizations that are exclusively inter-governmental at present. Significant progress in this direction is the convening of the World Assembly of Cities and Local Authorities held in parallel to the Habitat conference and the United Nations' City Summit. This Assembly can become a permanent structure for coordinating and representing city organizations, and it will thus encourage the gradual unification of the main world-wide and regional city organizations since they now share their main objectives and bring together largely the same cities.

United Nations with United Cities

The Habitat conference and the forming of the World Assembly of Cities may mark the beginning of a new period in international life involving recognition by local governments and the participation of cities united through their permanent assembly in the United Nations system. To this end national governments must foster this process both within central bodies of the United Nations and in the specialized ones (UNESCO, Habitat, WHO, UNICEF, etc) and in the economic bodies (OECD, World Bank, etc). But a good point of departure is the participation of mayors and international organizations of cities in conferences arranged by the United Nations and other international bodies. The participation of city organizations should take account those of a specialized nature (such as Public Safety Forums, Mayors for Children, Educator Cities, etc) and regional or continental ones, in the conferences and bodies they direct and in their objectives.

Decentralized Cooperation

Participation in international bodies can back up international cooperation and solidarity activities pursued by cities. For that purpose cities and their organizations must be able to:

- take a share in the resources and management of international cooperation programmes;
- manage a significant proportion of national public funds devoted to cooperation in each developed country;
- arrange in some cases cooperation programmes with local authorities and non-governmental organizations in less developed countries without depending on national governments;
- articulate the cooperation of local authorities with social and cultural organizations, companies in general and with civil society;
- view cooperation in addition to exchange, as mutual benefit, and combat any obstacles hindering it.

Cities and Regulating Globalization

The major challenges facing humanity today have a global dimension, such as:

- Demands for a new economy, one compatible with environmental sustainability and the progressive reduction of poverty.
- Regulating population shifts, recognizing universal mobility and equality of rights and duties for populations living in one territory.
- Attacking and penalizing the various forms of criminal activity, yet formalizing those activities which are more harmful when kept illegal.
- Democratic control of the new technologies of communication, and the socialization of their use.
- Reforming states and international political organizations that are relatively inoperative on account of their financial deficit, their organizational bureaucracy and their distance from the citizens.

These challenges, however, need local responses. Only at that level can regulatory agreements and action programmes be adapted to each specific situation, and the essential cooperation between public institutions and civil society be established. In view of the above, recognition must be accorded to the right and duty of cities, alongside nations and their states and international political, economic, social and cultural organizations, to participate with equal legitimacy in the forums in which regulations and programmes are drawn up, and in the bodies charged with implementing them.

References

Acebillo, J A (1995) 'La intervención sobre los sistemas generales', *Barcelona, un modelo de transformación urbana* World Bank, Quito

Advisory Commission on Intergovernmental Relations (1993) *Metropolitan Organization: Comparison of the Allegheny and St Louis Case Studies* ACIR, Washington DC

Aguiar, N (1994) *Rio de Janeiro Plural: Um Guia para Politicas Socisia por Genero e Raca* IUPERJ, Rio de Janeiro

Ahlbrandt, R (1990) 'The Revival of Pittsburgh – A Partnership Between Business and Government' *Long Range Planning* vol 23, no 5

Ajuntament de Barcelona (1990) *The Educating City* City of Barcelona, Barcelona

Ajuntament de Barcelona (1991) *Réegimen Especial para las Grandes Ciudades* City of Barcelona, Barcelona

Ajuntament de Barcelona (1995) *Plan Integral de Desarrollo de los Servicios Sociales*, City of Barcelona, Barcelona

Alape, A (1995) *Ciudad Bolivar: La Hoguera de las Ilsiones* Planeta Colombiana Editorial, Santafe de Bogota

Alberti, M, G Solera and V Tsetsi (1994) *La Città Sostenibile* Franco Angeli, Milan

Alemany, J and J Borja (1986) *Formas de Organización Institucional y Sistemas de Competencias de las Areas Metropolitanas* Insituto del Territorio y Urbanismo, Madrid

Alguacil, J, C Denche and A Hernández (1994) 'La eclosión de la sociedad urbana: desorden o medio ambiente urbano' *Ciudad Y Territorio Estudios Territoriales* nos 100–101

Aliyar, V and S Shetty (1992) 'Shelter Policy: Implications for Women in Development' in Dandekar, M (1992) op cit

Alonso Zaldívar, C and M Castells (1992) *España: Fin de Siglo* Alianza Editorial, Madrid

Alund, A and CU Schierup (1991) *Paradoxes of Multiculturalism* Avebury, Aldershot

Amin, A and K Robins (1991) 'These are not Marshallian times' in R Camagni (ed) (1991) op cit

Angeli, F (ed) (1993) *Planning Theory* no 9, spring

Aoyama, Y (1996) *Locational Strategies of Japanese Multinational Corporations in Electronics* Department of City and Regional Planning, University of California, Berkeley

Araneta, F (1995) *Mexico City in the Global Economy* Department of City and Regional Planning, University of California, Berkeley

Arias, F and V Gago (1989) 'Las Estrategias Territoriales de Ambito Sub-Regional' *Revista Urbanismo* Coam no 8, September

Arquitectura de la Ciudad (1992) *Transportes e Medio Ambiente* Ministerio de Obras Públicas, Madrid

Ascher, F (1995) *Metapolis* Editions Odile Jacob, Paris

∎

Ascher, F, J Borja, M de Forn and M Parkison (1992) 'Una politica para les ciudades en Europa' *Revista Estudios Territoriales* no 39

Ascher, F (1995) *Le Logement en Questions* Editions de l'Aube, Paris

Avendaño, ME (1994) *Bogotá Strategic Plan Presentation* Bogotá

'Barcelona' *Rassegna* no 147 (anon) (1989)

'Barcelona '92' *Arredo Urbano* Rome (anon) (1991)

Barcelona Metrópolis Meditteránea (1990) *La Ciudad ante al 2000* City of Barcelona, Barcelona

Barrig, M (1991) 'Women and development in Peru: old models, new actors' *Environment and Urbanization* vol 3, no 2, October

Belil, M (1991) *Informe Sobre Organización de las Areas Metropolitanas* Metropolis, Melbourne

Belil, M and J Borja (1988) *Cities of the World: Urban Survey* Institut d'Estudis Metropolitans Barcelona/United Nations Population Fund, Barcelona

Belil, M, J Borja and M de Forn (1992) *Development Strategies and Internationalization of European Cities: City Networks* Consultores Europeos Asociados/DG16/European Commission, Barcelona/Brussels

Benveniste, G (1989) *Mastering the Politics of Planning: Crafting Credible Plans and Policies that Make a Difference* Jossey-Bass, San Francisco

Beneria, L and M Roldan (1987) *The Crossroads of Class and Gender: Industrial Homework, Subcontracting and Household Dynamics in Mexico City* University of Chicago Press, Chicago

Berry, BJL (1976) *Urbanization and Counter-Urbanization* Sage, Los Angeles

Bhatnagar, KK (1992) 'Women's role in shelter planning', in Dandekar, M (1992) op cit

Bilbao, A, E Barco, R Fernández Duran, M Kabunda, P Franke, A Estevan, M Roitman and C Vaquero (1994) *Desarrollo, Pobreza y Medio Ambiente: FMI, Banco Mundial, Gatt, al Final del Siglio* Talasa Ediciones, Madrid

Billiard, I (1988) *Espaces Publics* Plain Urbain/La Documentation Français, Paris

Blakely, E and W Goldsmith (1992) *Separate Societies* Temple University Press, Philadelphia

Blanc, CS (1994) *Urban Children in Distress: Global Predicaments and Innovative Strategies* Gordon and Breach, Reading

Bohigas, O (1985) *Reconstrucció de Barcelona* Editions 62, Barcelona

Bohigas, O (1994) *La Ville: Six Interviews d'Architectes* Pompidou Centre, Paris

Borja, J (1987) *Descentralización y Participación Ciudadana* Instituto Nacional de la Administración Pública, Madrid

Borja, J (1988) *Estado y Ciudad* PPU, Barcelona

Borja, J (1991) *Barcelona Draft Municipal Charter* City of Barcelona, Barcelona

Borja, J (1995) *Nota Para Global Plan of Action* Ministerio de Obras Publicás, Madrid

Borja, J (1996a) *Cities: New Roles and Forms of Governing* Wilson Center/Smithsonian Institute, Washington, DC

Borja, J (1996b) *Le Monde des Villes ou les Villes Hors du Monde* Transversales, Paris

Borja, J (1996c) 'The city, democracy and governability: the case of Barcelona' *International Social Science Journal* no 147

Borja, J et al (1995) *Barcelona, un Modelo de Transformación Urbana* Programa de Gestión Urbana/World Bank, Quito

Borja, J, M Castells, R Dorado and I Quintana (1990) *Las Grandes Ciudades en la Década de los Noventa* Editorial Sistema, Madrid

Borja, J and M De Forn (1994–96) (working document) Bogotá 2000 Strategic Plan Consultants

Bosch, G, P Dawkins and F Michon (eds) (1994) *Times are Changing: Working Times in 14 Industrial Countries* International Labour Organization, Geneva

Bouinot, J and B Demils (1993) *Projets de Ville et Projets d'Enterprise* Paris

Brotchie, J (1995) *Cities in Competition: Productive and Sustainable Cities for the twenty-first Century* Longman Australia, Sydney

Bullard, R, E Grigsby and C Lee (1994) *Residential Apartheid: The American Legacy* University of California, California

Burgel, G (1993) *La Ville Aujourd'hui* Hachette, Paris

Busquets, J (1988) 'Les differents escales de la projectació urbanística' *Urbanisme a Barcelona*, Ajuntament de Barcelona, Barcelona

Busquets, J (1989) 'La calle en el proyecto de ciudad' *Casabella* no 553–554

Busquets, J (1991) *Arees de Nova Centralitat* Ajuntament de Barcelona, Barcelona

Busquets, J (1992) *Barcelona* MAPFRE, Barcelona

Busquets, J (1995) 'Sobre la coherencia urbanística del programa '92' *Barcelona, un Modelo de Transformación Urbana* Programa de Gastión Urbana/World Bank, Quito

Busquets, J et al (1990) *Puerto Madero Strategic Plan* Consultores Europeos Asociados, Barcelona

Caldeira, T (1996) 'Building up walls: the new pattern of spatial segregation in São Paulo' *International Social Science Journal* no 147

Calhoun, C (ed) *Social Theory and the Politics of Identity* Blackwell, Oxford

Camagni, R (1993) 'Organisation économique et réseaux de ville' in Sallez, A (ed) *Les Villes Lieux d'Europe* Editions l'Aube, La Tour d'Aigues

Camagni, R (1991) *Innovation Networks: Spatial Perspectives* Belhaven Press, London

Camagni, R and MC Gibelli (1994) 'Réseaux de villes et politiques urbaines' *Flux* no 16, April–June

Campbell, D (1994) 'Foreign investment, labour immobility and the quality of employment' *International Labour Review*, no 2

Caplow, T (1991) *Recent Social Trends in the US* McGill University Press, Montreal

Cappelin, R (1991) 'International networks of cities' in R Camagni (ed) (1991) op cit

Carnoy, M and M Castells (1996) *Sustainable Flexibility: Work, Family and Community in the Information Age* OECD, Paris

Carrión, F (1994) *En Busca de la Ciudad Perdida* Codel, Quito

Castaño, C (1994) *Tecnologia, Empleo y Trabajo en España* Alianza Editorial, Madrid

Castells, M (1983) *The City and the Grassroots: a Cross-Cultural Theory of Urban Social Movements* University of California, Berkeley

Castells, M (1989) *The Informational City: Information Technology, Economic Restructuring and the Urban Regional Process* Blackwell, Oxford

Castells, M (1995) 'La democracia electrónica', paper presented to the International Symposium on Post-Liberal Democracy, 14–15 December, Madrid

Castells, M (1996a) *The Information Age: Economy, Society and Culture: Volume 1 – The Rise of the Network Society* Blackwell, Oxford

Castells, M (1996b) 'The space of flows: elements for an urban theory of the information age' *New Media: Technology, Science and Culture* no 2

Castells, M et al (1986) *Nuevas Tecnologías, Economía y Sociedad en España* Alianza Editorial, Madrid

Castells, M, L Goh and RYW Kwok (1990) *The Shek Kip Mei Syndrome: Public Housing and Economic Development in Hong Kong and Singapore* Pion, London

Castells, M and P Hall (1994) *Las Tecnópolis del Mundo* Alianza Editorial, Madrid

Castells, M and M Kiselyova (1995) *The Missing Link: Siberia and the Russian Far East in the Pacific Rim Economy* University of California, Berkeley

Castells, M, S Yazawa and M Kiselyova (1996) 'Insurgents against the new global order: a comparative analysis of Zapatistas in Mexico, the American militia and Japan's Aum Shinrikyo' *Berkeley Journal of Sociology*, Spring

Castillo, H, B Navarro, M Perló, I Plaza, D Wilk and A Ziccardi (1996) *Ciudad de Mexico: Retos y Propuestas para la Coordinación Metropolitana* Autonomous Metropolitan University, Mexico

Castro, R (1994) *Civilisation Urbaine ou Barbarie* PLON, Paris

CEC (Commission of the European Communities) (1992) *Europa 2000: Perspectivas de Desarrollo del Territorio de la Comunidad* European Commission, Brussels

CEC (1994) *Competitividad y Cohesion: las Tendencias de las Regiones. Quinto Informe Periódico Sobre la Situación y Evolución Socioeconómica de las Regiones de la Comunidad* European Commission, Brussels

Chapman, G P and K M Baker (eds) (1992) *The Changing Geography of Asia* Routledge, London

Charte de la Citoyenneté Maison Grenelle, Paris (1996)

Charte Européenne des Femmes dans la Cité Eurocultures, Brussels (1994)

Cheshire, P *Europe's Urban System, 1981–1991: A New Phase in its Development* Colloque Ville, Lille

Chesnais, F (1994) *La Mondialisation du Capital* Syros, Paris

Chion, M (1995) *Globalization and Urban Restructuring in Lima*, Peru University of California, Berkeley

Choay, F (1994) *La Ville: Art et Architecture* Pompidou Centre, Paris

'Cities of the future: managing social transformations' *International Social Science Journal* no 147 (anon) (1996)

Coase, R (1988) The Firm, the Market and the Law University of Chicago Press. Chicago

Cohen, MA (1991) *Política Urbana y Desarrollo Económico: Un Programa para ed Decenio de 1990* World Bank, Washington, DC

Cohen, MA (1996a) 'The hypothesis of urban convergence: are cities in the North and South becoming more alike in an age of globalizations?' in Cohen, MA et al (1996) op cit

Cohen, MA (1996b) 'Habitat II and the challenge of the urban environment: bringing together the two definitions of habitat' *International Social Science Journal* no 147

Cohen, MA, BA Ruble, JS Tulchin and AM Garland (1996) *Preparing for the Urban Future* Smithsonian Institute, Washington, DC

Cohen, S and J Zysman (1987) *Manufacturing Matters* Basic Books, New York

Cole, J and F Cole (1993) *The Geography of the European Community* Routledge, London

Concha, A, F Carrión, G Cobo (1994) *Ciudad y Violencias en América* Latina World Bank, Quito

Conseil Communes et Régions Europe (CCRE) (1994) *Guide pour la Réalisation des Plans Stratégiques de Développement des Villes Moyennes* CCRE, Lisbon

Consejo Territorial de Planeación Santafé de Bogotá (1995) *Transformar la Ciudad con la Ciudadanía* Consejo Territorial, Santafé de Bogotá

Consoni, G, A Becchi, J Benni and G Bettin (1991) 'La città la sua gestione' *La Terra* no 1, Rome

Council of Europe (1993) 'Europe 1990–2000: Multiculturalism in the City; the Integration of Immigrants' *Studies and Texts* no 25, Strasbourg

Cuadrado Roura, JM (1994) *Nuevas Divisiones Territoriales* Madrid

Cupertino, MAM (1990) 'The employment of minors in Brazil' *Environment and Urbanization* vol 2, no 2, October

Curti, F and L Diappi (1992) *Gerarchie e Reti di Città: Tendenze e Politiche* Franco Angeli, Milan

Dandekar, M (ed) (1992) *Shelter, Women and Development: First and Third World Perspectives* George Wahr, Ann Arbor

Daniels, PW (1993) *Service Industries in the World Economy* Blackwell, Oxford

Datta, S (ed) (1990) *Third World Urbanization: Reappraisals and New Perspectives* Swedish Council for Humanities and Social Sciences, Estocolmo

Davies, RJ (1981) 'The spatial formation of the South African city' *Geo* supplementary issue 2, pp59–72

Day, L and Ma Xia (eds) (1994) *Migration and Urbanization in China* ME Sharpe, New York

De Cáceres, R (1992) *Barcelona, Espacio Público* Ajuntament de Barcelona, Barcelona

De Forn, M and JM Pascual (1995) *La Planificació Estratègica Territorial* Diputació de Barcelona, Barcelona

Dear, M (1992) 'Comprendre et surmonter le syndrome NIMBY' *Journal of the American Planning Association* vol 58, no 3

Declaration of Caracas Fondation Progrés de l'Homme, Paris (anon) (1991)

Declaration of El Salvador Fondation Progrés de l'Homme, Paris (anon) (1993)

Delarue, JM (1991) *Banlieues en Difficulté: La Relégation* Editions Syros Alternatives, Paris

Délégation interministérielle à la ville (1995) *Zones Urbaines et Cohesion Sociale en Europe: Quelle Action Publique pour les Villes?* Délégation interministérielle à la ville, Paris

Delfau, G (1994) *Le Retour de Citoyen: Démocratie et Territoire* Editions de l'Aube, Datar

de Queiroz, LC (1994) *Globalizaçao, Fragmentaçao e Reforma Urbana: O Futuro das Cidades Brasileiras na Crise* Editora Civilizaçao Brasileira, Rio de Janeiro

Dethier, G and A Guiheux (1993) *La Ville: Art et Architecture* Pompidou Centre, Paris

Dosi, G (1988) *Technical Change and Economic Theory* Frances Pinter, London

Doyle, M (1992) *The Future of Television: A Global Overview of Programming, Advertising, Technology and Growth* NTC Business Books, Illinois

Ducci, ME (1996) 'The politics of urban sustainability' in *Preparing for the Urban Future* Washington

Dumont, GF (1993) *Economie Urbane: Villes et Territoires en Compétition* Editions Litec, Paris

Dunford, M and G Kafkalas (eds) (1992) *Cities and Regions in the New Europe: The Global–Local Interplay and Spatial Development Strategies* Belhaven Press, London

Dupuy, G (1991) *L'Urbanisme des Réseaux* Editions Armand Colin, Paris

Dupuy, G, F Godard and M Roncayolo (1994) *La Ville* PIR Villes, Paris

Dupuy, JP and O Eymard-Duvernay (1989) 'L'économie des conventions' *Revue Economique* vol 40, no 2, March

Enderwick, P (ed) (1989) *Multinational Service Firms* Routledge, London

Esteban, J and A Ferrer (1995) 'La transformación urbanística de la ciudad' Barcelona, *Un Modelo de Transformación Urbana* Programa Gestión Urbana/World Bank, Quito

Eurocities (1994) *European Urban Management* PGI, London

European Commission (1993) 'Europe 1990–2000: Multiculturalism in the city: the integration of immigrants' *Studies and Texts* no 25

Fernández De Luco, M (1995) 'La arquitectura en el plan' *ARQUIS* no 6

Fernández, R (1995) 'Mar del Plata; arquitectura sí, urbanismo no' *ARQUIS* no 6

Fernandez-Kelly, MP (1981) *For We Are Sold, Me and My People* State University of New York Press, New York

Figueroa, A, Altamirano, T and D Sulmont (1996) *Social Exclusion and Inequality in Peru* International Institute of Labour Studies, Geneva

Figueroa, O (1995) *El Rol de las Municipalidades en la Gestión del Transporte y del Desarrollo Metropolitano* World Bank/Cepal/Unión de Ciudades Capitales Iberoamericanas, Santiago

Findley, S (1993) 'The Third World city: development policy and issues' in Kasarda and Parnell (1993) op cit

Fiola, J (1990) *Race Relations in Brazil: A Reassessment of the 'Racial Democracy' Thesis* University of Massachusetts, Amherst

Fitzgerald, J and Simmons, L (1991) 'From Consumption to Production: Labor Participation in Grass-Roots Movements in Pittsburgh and Hartford' *Urban Affairs Quarterly* vol 26, no 4, June, pp212–227

Fonseka, L and DD Malhotra (1994) 'India: urban poverty, children and participation' in Blanc (1994) op cit

Foray, D and C Freeman (eds) (1992) *Technologie et Richesse des Nations* Economica, Paris

Fortier, B (1995) *L'amour des Villes* Editions Mardaga, Liège

Franck, K and S Ahrentzen (eds) (1989) *New Households, New Housing* Van Nostrand, New York

Freeman, C and L Soete (1994) *Mass Unemployment or Work for All?* Pinter, London

Gamboa de Buen, J (1994) *Cuidad de México: Una Visión* Fondo De Cultura Económica, Mexico City

García, A (1994) 'Condicionantes ambientales al desarrollo local' *Ciudad y Territorio Estudios Territoriales* no 102

García, J and M Villalante (1995) 'Movilidad: circulación y transporte' Barcelona, Un Modelo de Transformación Urbana Programa Gestión Urbana/World Bank, Quito

Garreau, J (1991) *Edge City: Life on the New Frontier* Doubleday, New York

Ghorra-Gobin, C (1994) *Penser la Ville Plurielle: Qu'est-ce Qui Institue la Ville?* Editions l'Harmattan, Paris

Gelb, J and M Lief Pillay (eds) *Women of Japan and Korea: Continuity and Change* Temple University Press, Philadelphia

Giarratani, F and Houston, D (1989) 'Structural Change and Economic Policy in a Declining Metropolitan Region: Implication of the Pittsburgh Experience' *Urban Studies* vol 26, pp549–558

Gibelli, MC (1992) 'La crisi del piano fra logica sinottica e logica incrementalista: il contributo dello strategic planning' in Lomberdo, S and G Preto (1992) *Innovazione e Transformazione della Città* Franco Angeli, Milan

Godet, M (1991) *De l'Anticipation à l'Action* Dunod, Paris

Goldstein, S (1993) 'The impact of temporary migration on urban places: Thailand and China as case studies' in Kasarda, J and A Pernell (eds) *Third World Cities: Policies and Prospects* Sage Publications, London

Gordon, R (1994) *Internationalization, Multinationalization, Globalization: Contradictory World Economies and New Spatial Divisions of Labor* (working document) University of California, Santa Cruz

Graham, S (1994) 'Networking cities: telematics in urban policy – a critical view' *International Journal of Urban and Regional Research* vol 18, no 3, pp416–431

Graham, S (forthcoming) 'From urban competition to urban collaboration? The development of inter-urban telematics networks' *Environment and Planning, Government and Policy*

Graham, S and S Marvin (1996) *Telecommunications and the City* Routledge, London

Green, D (1987) 'Long-run vehicle travel prediction from demographic trends' in anon, *Working Women and the Ageing: Impact on Travel Patterns and Transportation Systems* Transportation Research Record no 1135, Transportation Research Board, Washington

Grieco, M, L Pickup and R Whipp (eds) (1989) *Gender Transport and Employment: The Impact of Travel Constraints* Avebury, Aldershot

Grimberg, E (1994) 'O futuro das ciudades' *Pólis* no 16

Grootaert, C and R Kanbur (1995) 'Child labor: a review' Policy Research Working Paper 1454, World Bank, Washington, DC

Hall, P (1989) 'La planificación de una Europa de regiones' *Urbanismo Coam* no 8, September

Hall, P (1993) 'Forces shaping urban Europe' Urban Studies vol 30, no 6, pp883–898

Hall, P (1995) 'Towards a general urban theory' in J Brotchie (ed) Cities in Competition: Productive and Sustainable Cities for the 21st Century Longman Australia, Sydney, pp3–32

Hall, P (1996) 'The global city' International Social Science Journal no 147

Hamilton, K and L Jenkins (1989) 'Why women and travel?' in Grieco et al (1989) op cit

Harasim, L (1993) Global Networks MIT Press, Massachusetts

Hardoy, JE (1992) The Urban Child in the Third World UNICEF, Florence

Hardoy, JE, S Cairncross and D Satterthwaite (1990) The Poor Die Young: Housing and Health in Third World Cities Earthscan, London

Hardoy, JE, D Mitlin and D Satterthwaite (1992) Environmental Problems in Third World Cities Earthscan, London

Harris, R (1991) 'The geography of employment and residence in New York since 1950' in Mollenkopf and Castells (1991) op cit, pp 129–154

Harrison, B (1994) Lean and Mean: The Changing Landscape of Corporate Power in the Age of Flexibility Basic Books, New York

Hathaway, D (1993) Can Workers Have a Voice? The Politics of Deindustrialization in Pittsburgh Pennsylvania State University Press, University Park

Hayden, D (1981) The Grand Domestic Revolution MIT Press, Massachusetts

'Health and wellbeing in cities' Environment and Urbanization (anon) (1993)

Heinz, W and G Jeannot (1993) Le Partenariat Public/Privé: Une Voie Nouvelle pour les Politiques Urbaines? Difu, Stuttgart

Henry, G (1992) Barcelona: Dix Annés d'Urbanisme: La Renaissance d'Une Ville Editions du Moniteur, Paris

Herce, M (1983) 'Los indicadores topológicos y la red viaria de Cataluña' Documents d'Anàlisi Geogràfic, Autonomous University of Barcelona, Barcelona

Herce, M (1993) 'El impacto de los Juegos Olímpicos: sistemas de transporte y transformación metropolitana' in Ciudad y Territorio, Madrid

Herce, M (1995a) 'Una década de renovación urbana' in Barcelona, Un Modelo de Transformación Urbana Programa Gestión Urbana/World Bank, Quito

Herce, M (1995b) 'Variantes de carretera y forma urbana' (doctoral thesis) Universitat Politècnica de Catalunya, Barcelona

Hsing, Y (1995) New Patterns of Property Development in Chinese Cities working document, University of British Columbia, Vancouver

Hsing, Y (1996) Making Capitalism in China: The Taiwan Connection Oxford University Press

Imai, K (1990) Joho Netto Waku Shakai No Tenbo Chikuma Shobo, Tokyo

'Innovazioni nella città' Inchieste no 106 (anon) (1994)

International Labour Office (ILO) (1991) Child Labour, Law and Practice ILO, Geneva

International Union of Local Authorities (IULA) (1995) Local Challenges to Global Change Sdu Publishers, The Hague

Jacquier, C Dix Quartiers Européens en Crise Editions l'Harmattan, Paris

Jarreau, P (1988) L'Image de Marque des Villes et le Marketing Territorial Cristal-Plan Contruction et Architecture

Jezierski, L (1990) 'Neighborhoods and Public–Private Partnerships in Pittsburgh' Urban Affairs Quarterly vol 26, no 2, December

Jones, T (1993) Britain's Ethnic Minorities Policy Studies Institute, London

Kanji, N (1995) 'Gender, poverty and economic adjustment in Harare, Zimbabwe' Environment and Urbanization vol 1, April

Kasarda, J and A Parnell (eds) (1993) Third World Cities: Problems, Policies and Prospects Sage Publications, London

Kirkby, R (1985) Urbanization in China Oxford University Press, Oxford

Kiselyova, E, M Castells and A Granberg (1996) *The Missing Link: Siberian Oil and Gas in the Pacific* Economy research monograph, University of California, Berkeley

Koolhass, R (1995) 'Más que nunca la ciudad es todo lo que tenemos' *Arquis* no 6

Kresl, PK and G Gappert (eds) (1995) *North American Cities and the Global Economy* Sage Publications, California

Kunstler, JH (1993) *The Geography of Nowhere* Simon and Schuster, New York

Kusow, A (1992) 'The role of shelter in generating income opportunities for poor women in the Third World' in Dandekar (1992) op cit

Kwok, RYW y So and Y Alvin (eds) *The Hong Kong–Guangdong Link: Partnership in Flux* ME Sharpe, New York

Lachaud, JP (1994) *Pauvrete et Marche du Travail Urbain en Afrique Subsaharienne: Analyse Comparative* ILO/Institut International d'Etudes Sociales, Geneva

Landaburu, Eneko (1993) 'La Communauté européenne et son territoire' in *L'Evénement Européen* (1993) op cit

La Terra no 1 (anon) (1995)

La Terra no 9, including articles by B Bogdanovic, J Borja and F Borella (anon) (1995)

Lawton, R (ed) (1989) *The Rise and Fall of Great Cities* Belhaven Press, London and New York

Leal, J (1994) 'Cambio social y desigualdad espacial en el área metropolitana de Madrid (1986–1991)' *Economía y Sociedad* no 10, June, p77

Leal, J and L Cortés (1993) *La Desigualdad Social en España* Autonomous University of Madrid, Madrid

Leal, J and L Cortés (1995) *La Dimensión de la Ciudad* Centro de Investigaciones Sociológicas, Madrid

Lee-Smith, D and CH Trujillo (1992) 'The struggle to legitimize subsistence: women and sustainable development' *Environment and Urbanization* vol 4, no 1, April

Leira, E (1987) 'Expo-Sevilla–92: ande o no ande... caballo grande' *Geometria* no 3

Leira, E (1990) 'The Bilbao river basin' *Rassegna* no 42

Leira, E (1991) *Consultation Internationale sur l'Axe Historique a l'Ouest de la Grand Arche de la Defense* Mission Grand Axe, Paris

Leira, E (1992) 'Operazione Siviglia: primo bilancio. Più di una esposizione universale' *Casabella* no 593, September

Leira, E (1995) 'Per Bilbao: una nuova città lineare lungo la Ría' *Casabella* no 622

Leira, E (1995) 'Alto do lumiar: la extensión y ensanche de Lisboa: un atractivo proyecto urbano que cambiará la fisonomía de la capital' *Urbanismo Coam* no 26

Leira, E (1996) 'Una apuesta por Bilbao: proyecto estratégico de transformación del entorno urbano de la Ría' *Urbanismo Coam* no 27

Lenoir, R (1992) *Ou Va l'Etat? La Souveraineté Economique et Politique en Question* Editions le Monde, Paris

L'Evénement Européen (1993) 'Europe: espace ou territoire?' Edition de la SACP Initiatives, Paris

Leung, CK (1993) 'Personal contracts, subcontracting linkages, and development in the Hong Kong–Zhujiang Delta region' *Annals of the Association of American Geographers* vol 83, no 2, pp272–302

LGMB (Local Government Management Board) (1995) *Local Agenda 21: United Kingdom* Sustainability Indicators Research Project, London

Ling, KK (unpublished) 'A case for regional planning: the Greater Pearl River Delta – a Hong Kong perspective' seminary investigation work CP229, University of California, California

Lo, CP (1994) 'Economic reforms and socialist city structure: a case study of Guangzhou, China' *Urban Geography* vol 15, no 2, pp128–149

Lusk, MW (unpublished) 'Street children of Rio de Janeiro: preliminary issues and findings' mimeo, Rio de Janeiro: cited in Rizzini et al (1994) op cit

Machimura, T (1994) *Sekai Toshi Tokyo no Kozo Tenkan [Tokyo: The Structural Transformation of a Global City]* University of Tokyo Press, Tokyo

Machimura, T (unpublished) 'Symbolic use of globalization in urban politics in Tokyo' investigation work, Hitotsubashi University

Mahajan, S (1992) 'Shelter and income opportunities for women in India' in Dandekar (1992) op cit

Maragall, P (1995) *El Tema es Barcelona* Ediciones la Campana, Barcelona

Mare, G (1993) *Ethnicity and Politics in South Africa* Zed Books, London

Marianacci, G (1995) 'El programa de desconcentración y decentralización de Córdoba: los centros de participación comunal' *Arquis* no 6

Martín, EF (1995a) 'Redes transeuropeas de transportes: caminos sin fronteras' *MOPTMA (Ministerio de Obras Públicas, Transportes y Medio Ambiente) Journal* no 430, April

Martín, EF (1995b) 'Conferencia internacional sobre reservas de la biosfera: préstamo y custodia' *MOPTMA Journal* no 431, May

Martinotti, G (1993) *Metropoli: La Nuova Morfologia Sociale Della Città* Il Mulino, Bologna

Massey, D (1995) 'Getting away with murder: segregation and violent crime in urban America' *University of Pennsylvania Law Review* vol 143, no 4, May, pp1203–1232

Massey, D (1995) 'The new immigration and ethnicity in the United States' *Population and Development Review* vol 21, no 3

Massey, D and N Denton (1993) *American Apartheid: Segregation and the Making of the Underclass* Harvard University Press, Cambridge, Massachusetts

Massolo, A (1992) *Por Amor y Coraje: Las Mujeres en los Movimientos Urbanos* El Colegio de México, Mexico City

McKnight, C (1994) 'Transportation with women in mind' *Journal of Urban Technology* vol 2, no 1, autumn

Messmacher, M (1987) *Mexico, Megalopolis* DF, Mexico City

'Metrópolis, territorio y crisis' *Alfoz*, Madrid (anon) (1985)

Meyer, R et al (1995) *Centro XXI Viva O Centro*, Sao Paulo

Michelson, RL and JO Wheeler (1994) 'The flow of information in a global economy: the role of the American urban system in 1990' *Annals of the Association of American Geographers* vol 84, no 1, pp87–107

Mignaqui, I (1995) 'Buenos Aires, ciudad metropolitana: intervenciones urbanas y políticas de ajuste ¿Modernismos sim modernizacíon?' *Arquis* no 6

Minakir, P (ed) (1994) *Ekonomika Dal'nego Vostoka: Reforma I Krisis* Dalnauka, Khabarovsk-Vladivostok

Ministère de l'Equipement (1994) *Architecture des Espaces publics modernes* Editions du Plan Constructions et Architecture, Paris

Ministerio de Obras Públicas (1995) *Declaration of the Meeting of European National Committees* Transporte e Medio Ambiente, Madrid

Miraftab, F (1992) 'Shelter as sustenance: exclusionary mechanisms limiting women's access to housing' in Dandekar (1992) op cit

Mitlin, D and D Satterthwaite (1994) 'Cities and Sustainable Development' *Global Forum 1994* IIED, London

Mollenkopf, J (ed) (1989) *Power, Culture and Place: Essays on New York City* Russell Sage Foundation, New York

Mollenkopf, J and M Castells (eds) (1991) *Dual City: Restructuring New York* Russell Sage Foundation, New York

Morandi, C (1994) *I vantaggi competitivi della città: un confronto in ambito europeo* Franco Angeli, Milan

Moser, C (1987) 'Mobilization is women's work: struggles for infrastructure in Guayaquil, Ecuador' in Moser and Peake (1987) op cit

Moser, C (1993) *Gender, Planning and Development* Routledge, London

Moser, C and L Peake (1987) *Women, Human Settlements and Housing* Tavistock, London

Moss, M (1987) 'Telecommunications, world cities and urban policy' *Urban Studies* no 24, pp 534–546

Municipality of Seattle (1993) *Indicators of a Sustainable Community* Municipality of Seattle, Seattle

Navarro, V (1994) *La Politica del Estado del Bienestar* Critica, Barcelona

Negroponte, N (1995) *Being Digital* Alfred A Knopf, New York

Nello, O (1995) 'El territorio metropolitano de Barcelona' *Barcelona, un Modelo de Transformación Urbana* Programa de Gestión Urbana/World Bank, Quito

Nelson, B and N Chowdhury (1994) *Women and Politics Worldwide* Yale University Press, New Haven

Nelson, K (1984) *Back Office and Female Labour Markets* (unpublished doctoral thesis) University of California, California

Neuschwander, C 'Réseaux d'acteurs et réseaux de villes' in *L'Evénement Européen, Europe: Espace ou Territoire?* Edition de la SACP Initiatives, Paris

Nimpuno-Parente, P (1987) 'The struggle for shelter: women in a site and service project in Nairobi, Kenya' in Moser and Peake (1987) op cit

Norman, AL (1993) *Informational Society: An Economic Theory of Discovery, Invention and Innovation* Kluwer Academic Publishers, Boston

OECD (1992) *Urba 2000: Délégation interministérielle à la Ville* Villes et Technologies nouvelles, Paris

OECD (1994) *OECD Jobs Study* OECD, Paris

Omer, MIA (1990) 'Child health in the spontaneous settlements around Khartoum' *Environment and Organization* vol 2, no 2, October

Omvedt, G (1986) *Women in Popular Movements: India and Thailand During the Decade of Women* UNRISD, Geneva

Ordóñez, JL (1993) 'Planes intermodales de transportes en Madrid y Barcelona: una buena trama' *Moptma* no 415, December

Papademetriou, G and P Martin (eds) (1991) *The Unsettled Relationship: Labor Migration and Economic Development* Greenwood Press, Westport

Paquot, TH (1994) *Vive la Ville* Editions Arléa-Corlet, Paris

Percq, P *Les Habitants aménageurs* Editions de l'Aube, Paris

Peterson, R and L Krivo (1993) 'Racial segregation and black urban homicide' *Social Forces* no 71

Piore, M and C Sabel (1984) *The Second Industrial Divide* Basic Books, New York

Polèse, M and JM Wolfe (eds) (1995) *L'Urbanisation des Pays en Développement* Economica, Paris

Portas, N (1985) 'Políticas metropolitanas y transformaciones territoriales en Europa' *Alfoz*, Madrid

Porter, M (1992) *La Ventaja Competitiva de las Naciones* Plaza y Janés, Barcelona

Portes, A, M Castells and L Benton (eds) (1989) *The Informal Economy* Johns Hopkins University Press, Baltimore

Prud'Homme, R (1994) 'Villes: l'intervention modeste' *Observateur de l'OCDE* no 18, April/May

Pumain, D et al (1991) *Le Concept statistique de Ville* Eurostat, Luxembourg

Reese, E (1995) 'Córdoba: de la recuperación de la ciudad a la articulación del epacio metropolitano' *Arquis* no 6

Reich, RB (1991) *The Work of Nations* Vintage, London

Rizzini, Irene, Irma Rizzini, M Muñoz-Vargas and L Galeano (1994) 'Brazil: a new concept of childhood' in Blanc (1994) op cit

Robson, B (1992) 'Competing and collaborating through urban networks' *Town and Country Planning* September, pp236–8

Rodríguez, A and L Winchester (1996) 'Cities, democracy and governance in Latin America' *International Social Science Journal* no 147

Rolnik, R (1994) 'Planejamento urbanao nos anos 90: novas perspectivas para velhos temas' in de Queiroz (1994) op cit

Roncayolo, M (1990) *La Ville et ses Territoires* Editions Gallimard, Paris

Roncayolo, M et al (1993) 'Métropoles hier et aujourd'hui' *Métropoles en Déséquilibre* Editions Economica, Paris

Rosa, K (1994) 'The conditions and organizational activities of women in Free Trade Zones' in Rowbotham and Mitter (1994) op cit

Rosenbloom, Sandra (1987) 'The impact of growing children on their parents' travel behavior: a comparative analysis' *Working Women and the Ageing: The Impact on Travel Patterns and Transportation Systems* Transportation Research Board, Washington

Rowbotham, S and S Mitter (eds) (1994) *Dignity and Daily Bread: New Forms of Economic Organising Among Poor Women in the Third World and the First* Routledge, London

Rubert de Ventós, X (1994) *Nacionalismos: El Laberinto de la Identidad* Espasa Calpe, Madrid

Rusell, SS et al (1990) *International Migration and Development in Subsaharan Africa* World Bank Discussion Papers 101–102, World Bank, Washington, DC

Rutelli, F (1996) 'Interview: Rome, sustainable city' *International Social Science Journal* no 147

Sachs, C (1990) *São Paulo: Politiques publiques et Habitat populaire* Maison Sciences de l'Homme, Paris

Sachs, C (1996) 'Humanizing the City' *International Social Science Journal* no 147

Sachs, I (1993) *L'Ecodeveloppement: Stratégies de Transition Vers le XXI Siècle* Syros, Paris

Sachs, I (1995) 'A la recherche de nouvelles stratégies de developpement' *Enjeux des Sommet Social*, UNESCO, Paris

Saff, G (1994) 'The changing face of the South African city: from urban apartheid to the deracialization of space' *Urban Affairs Review* vol 30, no 6

Sallez, A (1993) *Les Villes lieux d'Europe* Editions l'Aube, Paris

Sánchez, AL (1995) *Procesos Urbanos Contemporáneos* Fundación Alejandro Angel Escobar, Colombia

Sassen, S (1988) *The Mobility of Labor and Capital* Cambridge University Press, New York

Sassen, S (1991a) *The Global City: New York, London, Tokyo* Princeton University Press, New Jersey

Sassen, S (1991b) 'The informal economy' in Mollenkopf and Castells (1991) op cit, pp 79–102

Sassen, S (1994) *Cities in a World Economy* Pine Forge Press, California

Satterthwaite, D (1995) *Global Report on Human Settlements* UNCHS, Nairobi

'Sauver la ville' *Monde des Debats* no 25 (anon) (1994)

Savitch, HV (1996) 'Cities in a global era: a new paradigm for the next millennium' *Preparing for the Urban Future* Washington

Saxenian, AL (1994) *Regional Advantage* Harvard University Press, Massachusetts

Sbragia, A (1990) 'Pittsburgh's "Third Way": The Nonprofit Sector as a Key to Urban Regeneration' in D Judd and M Parkinson (eds) *Leadership and Urban Regeneration: Cities in North America and Europe – Urban Affairs Annual Review Volume 37* Sage Publications, Newbury Park

Schmink, M (1982) 'Women in the urban economy in Latin America' in various authors, *Women in Low-Income Households and Urban Services* University of Florida, Florida

Schneider, C (1995) 'Pittsburgh Prospers' *Computerworld* vol 29, no 34, 21 August

SEADE (1994) *Survey of Living Conditions in the Metropolitan Area of São Paulo* International Labour Office, Geneva

Secchi, B *Un Progetto per l'Urbanistica* Picola Biblioteca Einaudi, Torino

Sennett, R (1994) *Flesh and Stone* New York

Serageldin, I and MA Cohen *Enabling Sustainable Community Development* World Bank, Washington, DC

Serageldin, I, R Barrett and J Martin-Brown (eds) (1994) *The Business of Sustainable Cities* World Bank, Washington, DC

Serageldin, I, MA Cohen and KC Sivaramakrishnan (1994) *The Human Face of the Urban Environment* World Bank, Washington, DC

Servon, L (1995) *Alleviating Urban Poverty* University of California, California

Shegal, N (1995) *Women, Housing and Human Settlements* Ess Ess Publications, New Delhi

Siimo, C (1994) 'La ville et le chomage' *Revue d'Economie regionale et urbaine* no 3, pp324–352

Singer, P, R Rolnik, L Kowarik and N Somekh (1993) 'São Paulo: crisis y transformación' *Medio Ambiente y Urbanización* no 43–44

Singh, A (1980) *Women in Cities: An Invisible Factor in Urban Planning in India* Population Council, New York

Singh, V and Borzutsky, S (1988) 'The State of the Mature Industrial Regions in Western Europe and North America' *Urban Studies* vol 25

Sit, VFS (1991) 'Transnational capital flows and urbanization in the Pearl River Delta, China' *Southeast Asian Journal of Social Science* vol 19, nos 1 and 2, pp154–179

Sivaramakrishnan, KC (1996) 'Urban governance: changing realities' *Preparing for the Urban Future* Washington

Skezely, G (1993) 'Mexico's international strategy: looking east and north' in B Stallings and G Skezely *Japan, The United States and Latin America* Johns Hopkins University Press, Baltimore

Solà Morales, M (1988) 'El proyecto urbano' *UR* no 6

Solà Morales, M (1993) *Les Formes del Creixement Urbà* Edicions Universitat Politècnica de Catalunya, Barcelona

Soldatos, P (1995) *Les nouvelles Villes internationales: Profils et Planification stratégique* Sederco, Aix-en-Provence

Sorkin, DL et al (1987) *Strategies for Cities and Countries* Public Technology Inc, Washington, DC

Sprague, JF (1991) *More than Housing: Lifeboats for Women and Children* Butterworth, Boston

Stalker, P (1994) *The Work of Strangers: A Survey of International Labour Migration* International Labour Office, Geneva

Storper, M (1994) 'Desenvolvimiento territorial na economía global do aprendizado: o desafio dos paises em desenvolupamento' *Globaliçao Fragmentaçao e Reforma Urbana* Editora Civilizaçao Brasileira, Rio de Janeiro

Strategic Plan Technical Unit (1995) *Bogotá 2000: Síntesis de Diagnóstico, Temas Críticos, Líneas Estratégicas, Objetivos y Subobjetivos* United Nations Development Programme (UNDP), Bogotá

Sullivan-Trainor, M (1996) *La Autopista de la Información: Realidad y Perspectivas* Alianza Editorial, Madrid

Surjadi, C (1993) 'Respiratory diseases of mothers and children and environmental factors among households in Jakarta' *Environment and Urbanization* vol 5, no 2, October

Tarr, J and Dupuy, G (eds) (1988) *Technology and the Rise of the Networked City in Europe and America* Temple University Press, Philadelphia

Tate, J (1994) 'The Netherlands' in M Martens and S Mitter (eds) *Women in Trade Unions: Organizing the Unorganized* International Labour Office, Geneva

Telles, E (1992) 'Residential segregation by skin color in Brazil' *American Sociological Review* vol 57, April

Telles, E (1995) 'Race, class and space in Brazilian cities' *International Journal of Urban and Regional Research* vol 19, no 3

Thomas, M (1990) 'The planning project' in *Planning Theory: Prospects for the 1990s* Oxford Polytechnic, Oxford

Thrift, NJ (1986) *The Fixers: The Urban Geography of International Financial Capital* University of Wales, Lampeter

Thrift, NJ and A Leyshon (1991) 'In the wake of money: the City of London and the accumulation of value' in Budd, L and Whimster, S (eds) *Global Finance and Urban Living: A Study in Metropolitan Change* Routledge, London

Tinker, I (1992) 'Global policies regarding shelter for women' in Dandekar, op cit

Todes, A and ? Walker (1992) 'Women and housing policy in South Africa: a discussion of Durban case studies' in Dandekar, op cit

Topalov, C (1987) *Le Logemont, Une Marchandise impossible* Presses de la Fondation nationale des Sciences politiques, Paris

Tulchin, JS (1995) *Global Forces and the Future of the Latin American City* Woodrow Wilson Center, Washington, DC

United Nations (1994) *Trends in Total Migrant Stock* Department of Economic Information and Policy Analysis, United Nations, New York

United Nations Centre for Human Rights (1991) *Study on the Rights of Persons Belonging to Ethnic Religious and Linguistic Minorities* United Nations, New York

United Nations Children's Fund (UNICEF) (1995) *Progress of Nations* UNICEF, New York

United Nations Department for International Economic and Social Affairs (1991) *World Urbanization Prospects: Estimates and Projections of Urban and Rural Populations and of Urban Agglomerations* United Nations, New York

United Nations Development Programme (UNDP) (1995) *Human Development Report 1995* Oxford University Press, New York

Urbanisme no 280 'Quelle politique pour quelles villes?' (anon) (1995)

Veltz, P (1995) *Mondialisation, Villes et Territoires: L'Economie d'Archipel* PUF

Ventura, Z (1995) *Cidade Partida* Companhia das Letras, São Paulo

Virilio, P (1994) *Villes et Transports* Ministère de l'Equipement, Paris

Vourg'h, C and M Marcus (1993) *Securité et Démocratie* Forum Européen pour la Sécurité urbaine, Paris

Wachs, M and M Crawford (eds) (1992) *The Car and the City: The Automobile, the Built Environment and Daily Urban Life* University of Michigan Press, Ann Arbor

Wieczorek, J (1995) 'Sectoral trends in world employment' working paper no 82, International Labour Organization, Geneva

Wilheim, J (1983) *Proyecto São Paulo* Paz e Terra, São Paulo

Wilheim, J (1996) 'Urban challenges of a transitional period' *International Social Science Journal* no 147

Wilmsen, E, S Duhow and J Sharp (1994) 'Ethnicity, identity and nationalism in Southern Africa' *Journal of Southern African Studies*

Wong, L (1994) 'China's urban migrants – the public policy challenge' *Pacific Affairs* vol 67, no 3

Woo, ESW (1994) 'Urban development' in YM Yeung and DKY Chu, *Guangdong: Survey of a Province Undergoing Rapid Change* Chinese University Press, Hong Kong

World Federation of United and Twinned Towns/UTO (1994) *International Cooperation of Local Authorities* UTO, Paris

Ziccardi, A (1995) 'De la reforma urbana a la democratización de los gobiernos locales' *Procesos Urbanos Contemporáneos* Fundación Alejandro Angel Escobar, Colombia

Zukin, S (1992) *Landscapes of Power* University of California Press, Berkeley

Index

Page references in **bold** refer to Boxes and in *italics* to Tables. A lower case 'f' after the page reference refers to Figures.

Seaside

by Annabelle Lynch

W

First published in Great Britain in 2015 by The Watts Publishing Group

Series editor: Julia Bird
Series consultant: Catherine Glavina
Series designer: Peter Scoulding

Every attempt has been made to clear copyright. Should there be any inadvertent omission please apply to the publisher for rectification.

Picture acknowledgements: Peter Chadwick/Gallo Images/Alamy: 13, 22cl. Melissa Anne Colors/Shutterstock: 8-9, 22bl. James Forte/National Geographic/Alamy: 1, 12, 22tl. Gledriiis/Shutterstock: 14-15. GoBob   Shutterstock: 6-7, 22cr. ksl/Shutterstock: 18-19, 22cla. MartiniDry/Shutterstock: 4-5, 22br. Rolf Schlegel/Alamy: front cover. Vilaincrevette/Shutterstock: 16-17, 22tr. Yobro10/Dreamstime: 20-21. Feng Yu/Shutterstock: 10-11.

HB ISBN: 978 1 4451 3853 4
PB ISBN: 978 1 4451 3855 8
Library ebook ISBN: 978 1 4451 3854 1

Dewey number: 570

Printed in China

MIX
Paper from
responsible sources
FSC® C104740

FSC
www.fsc.org

Franklin Watts
An imprint of
Hachette Children's Group
Part of The Watts Publishing Group
Carmelite House
50 Victoria Embankment
London EC4Y 0DZ

An Hachette UK Company
www.hachette.co.uk

www.franklinwatts.co.uk

Contents

The
seaside!

The seaside is where land and sea meet.

Sand or pebbles?

The seaside can have sand, rocks or pebbles.

Shells

You can find shells
at the seaside.

Tides

At the seaside, the
tide comes in and goes
out every day.

Rock
pools

When the tide
is out, you can
see rock pools.
Animals live
in them.

Crab

Sea birds

Birds live at the seaside. They catch crabs and fish to eat.

Fish in
the sea

All sorts of fish live in the sea. Many live near coral reefs.

Boats

Boats carry people on the sea. Ferries carry lots of people.

Seaside fun

Splash!

Have fun at the seaside.
Splash in the sea or
build a sandcastle!

Word bank

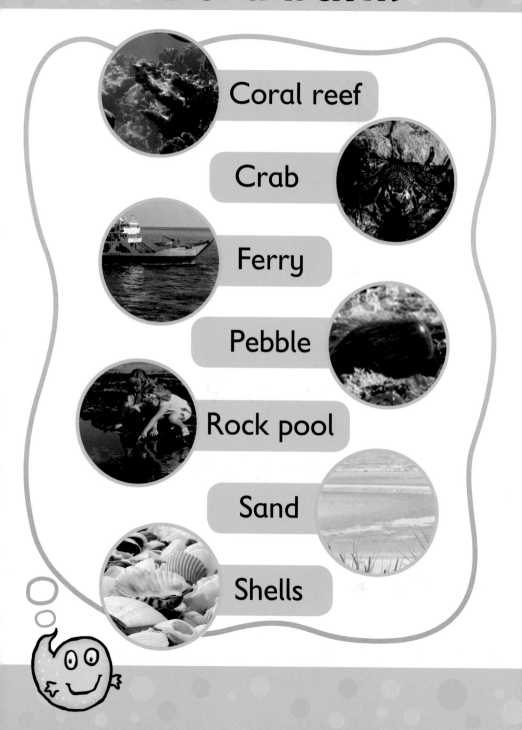

Coral reef

Crab

Ferry

Pebble

Rock pool

Sand

Shells

Quiz

1. At the seaside, you can find

a) shells
b) sausages
c) socks.

2. The tide goes

a) up and down
b) in and out
c) round and round.

3. Ferries carry lots of

a) fish
b) frogs
c) people.

Turn over for answers!

Notes for adults

TADPOLES are structured to provide support for newly independent readers. The books may also be used by adults for sharing with young children.

Starting to read alone can be daunting. **TADPOLES** help by providing visual support and repeating words and phrases. These books will both develop confidence and encourage reading and rereading for pleasure.

If you are reading this book with a child, here are a few suggestions:

1. Make reading fun! Choose a time to read when you and the child are relaxed and have time to share the book.

2. Talk about the content of the book before you start reading. Look at the front cover and blurb. What expectations are raised about the content? Why might the child enjoy it? What connections can the child make with their own experience of the world?

3. If a word is phonically decodable, encourage the child to use a 'phonics first' approach to tackling new words by sounding the words out.

4. Invite the child to talk about the content after reading, returning to favourite pages and pictures. Extend vocabulary by examining the Word Bank and by discussing new concepts.

5. Give praise! Remember that small mistakes need not always be corrected.

Answers

Here are the answers:

1.a 2.b 3.c

Index